Monte Carlo Methods in Finance

Wiley Finance Series

Modeling, Measuring and Hedging Operational Risk
  Marcelo Cruz

Securities Operations: A guide to Trade and Position Management
  Michael Simmons

Building and Using Dynamic Interest Rate Models
  Ken Kortanek and Vladimir Medvedev

Structured Equity Derivatives: The Definitive Guide to Exotic Options and Structured Notes
  Harry Kat

Advanced Modelling in Finance Using Excel and VBA
  Mary Jackson and Mike Staunton

Operational Risk: Measurement and Modelling
  Jack King

Advance Credit Risk Analysis: Financial Approaches and Mathematical Models to Assess, Price and Manage Credit Risk
  Didier Cossin and Hugues Pirotte

Dictionary of Financial Engineering
  John F. Marshall

Pricing Financial Derivatives: The Finite Difference Method
  Domingo A Tavella and Curt Randall

Interest Rate Modelling
  Jessica James and Nick Webber

Handbook of Hybrid Instruments: Convertible Bonds, Preferred Shares, Lyons, ELKS, DECS and Other Mandatory Convertible Notes
  Izzy Nelken (ed)

Options on Foreign Exchange, Revised Edition
  David F DeRosa

The Handbook of Equity Derivatives, Revised Edition
  Jack Francis, William Toy and J Gregg Whittaker

Volatility and Correlation in the Pricing of Equity, FX and Interest-Rate Options
  Riccardo Rebonato

Risk Management and Analysis vol. 1: Measuring and Modelling Financial Risk
  Carol Alexander (ed)

Risk Management and Analysis vol. 2: New Markets and Products
  Carol Alexander (ed)

Implementing Value at Risk
  Philip Best

Credit Derivatives: A Guide to Instruments and Applications
  Janet Tavakoli

Implementing Derivatives Models
  Les Clewlow and Chris Strickland

Interest-Rate Option Models: Understanding, Analysing and Using Models for Exotic Interest-Rate Options (second edition)
  Riccardo Rebonato

Monte Carlo Methods in Finance

Peter Jäckel

JOHN WILEY & SONS, LTD

Other Wiley Editorial Offices

John Wiley & Sons Inc., 111 River Street, Hoboken, NJ 07030, USA

Jossey-Bass, 989 Market Street, San Francisco, CA 94103-1741, USA

Wiley-VCH Verlag GmbH, Boschstr. 12, D-69469 Weinheim, Germany

John Wiley & Sons Australia Ltd, 33 Park Road, Milton, Queensland 4064, Australia

John Wiley & Sons (Asia) Pte Ltd, 2 Clementi Loop #02-01, Jin Xing Distripark, Singapore 129809

John Wiley & Sons Canada Ltd, 22 Worcester Road, Etobicoke, Ontario, Canada M9W 1L1

Wiley also publishes its books in a variety of electronic formats. Some content that appears
in print may not be available in electronic books.

Library of Congress Cataloging-in-Publication Data

Jäckel, Peter
    Monte Carlo methods in finance / Peter Jäckel.
        p. cm.—(Wiley finance series)
    Includes bibliographical references and index.
    ISBN 0-471-49741-X (alk. paper)
    1. Monte Carlo method. 2. Business mathematics. I. Title. II. Series.

QA298 .J33 2002
519.2'82—dc21

                                        2001046997

British Library Cataloguing in Publication Data

A catalogue record for this book is available from the British Library

ISBN 0-471-49741-X

Typeset in 10/12pt Times by Laserwords Private Limited, Chennai, India
Printed and bound in Great Britain by The Cromwell Ltd, Trowbridge, Wiltshire
This book is printed on acid-free paper responsibly manufactured from sustainable forestry
in which at least two trees are planted for each one used for paper production.

Disclaimer

In this book, I have tried to give an introductory overview of Monte Carlo methods in finance known to expert practitioners and, in places, I may not always have given due credit to all the pioneers who contributed to this borderline area of mathematics and finance. Wherever I fail to give explicit reference to the original inventor of any given method, this is not to mean I wish to pretend that it is my own development, it is merely my own laxness about the whole issue of referencing and citations. In fact, I may use phrases like 'I present below', etc. repeatedly, but they just stand for their literal meaning, namely that I present, not that I claim to have invented the particular method. I did consider it much more important to focus on an as-good-as-possible explanation of the techniques and mathematics, rather than spending time on exhaustive research through a whole string of references to establish who actually was the originator of the subject at hand. I include a rather-too-long bibliography at the end of the book, and I did try to reference and cite wherever I could see a direct link, but I may have failed many great researchers in the field of Monte Carlo methods by not referencing them in the right places, or not referencing them at all. *Mea culpa, mea maxima culpa.*

Contents

Preface   xi

Acknowledgements   xiii

Mathematical Notation   xv

1   Introduction   1

2   The Mathematics Behind Monte Carlo Methods   5
    2.1   A Few Basic Terms in Probability and Statistics   5
    2.2   Monte Carlo Simulations   7
          2.2.1   Monte Carlo Supremacy   8
          2.2.2   Multi-dimensional Integration   8
    2.3   Some Common Distributions   9
    2.4   Kolmogorov's Strong Law   18
    2.5   The Central Limit Theorem   18
    2.6   The Continuous Mapping Theorem   19
    2.7   Error Estimation for Monte Carlo Methods   20
    2.8   The Feynman–Kac Theorem   21
    2.9   The Moore–Penrose Pseudo-inverse   21

3   Stochastic Dynamics   23
    3.1   Brownian Motion   23
    3.2   Itô's Lemma   24
    3.3   Normal Processes   25
    3.4   Lognormal Processes   26
    3.5   The Markovian Wiener Process Embedding Dimension   26
    3.6   Bessel Processes   27
    3.7   Constant Elasticity Of Variance Processes   28
    3.8   Displaced Diffusion   29

4   Process-driven Sampling   31
    4.1   Strong versus Weak Convergence   31
    4.2   Numerical Solutions   32

	4.2.1	The Euler Scheme	32
	4.2.2	The Milstein Scheme	33
	4.2.3	Transformations	33
	4.2.4	Predictor–Corrector	35
4.3	Spurious Paths		36
4.4	Strong Convergence for Euler and Milstein		37

5 Correlation and Co-movement   **41**
5.1	Measures for Co-dependence		42
5.2	Copulæ		45
	5.2.1	The Gaussian Copula	46
	5.2.2	The t-Copula	49
	5.2.3	Archimedean Copulae	51

6 Salvaging a Linear Correlation Matrix   **59**
6.1	Hypersphere Decomposition		60
6.2	Spectral Decomposition		61
6.3	Angular Decomposition of Lower Triangular Form		62
6.4	Examples		63
6.5	Angular Coordinates on a Hypersphere of Unit Radius		65

7 Pseudo-random Numbers   **67**
7.1	Chaos		68
7.2	The Mid-square Method		72
7.3	Congruential Generation		72
7.4	Ran0 To Ran3		74
7.5	The Mersenne Twister		74
7.6	Which One to Use?		75

8 Low-discrepancy Numbers   **77**
8.1	Discrepancy		78
8.2	Halton Numbers		79
8.3	Sobol' Numbers		80
	8.3.1	Primitive Polynomials Modulo Two	81
	8.3.2	The Construction of Sobol' Numbers	82
	8.3.3	The Gray Code	83
	8.3.4	The Initialisation of Sobol' Numbers	85
8.4	Niederreiter (1988) Numbers		88
8.5	Pairwise Projections		88
8.6	Empirical Discrepancies		91
8.7	The Number of Iterations		96
8.8	Appendix		96
	8.8.1	Explicit Formula for the L_2-norm Discrepancy on the Unit Hypercube	96
	8.8.2	Expected L_2-norm Discrepancy of Truly Random Numbers	97

9 Non-uniform Variates   **99**
| 9.1 | Inversion of the Cumulative Probability Function | | 99 |
| 9.2 | Using a Sampler Density | | 101 |

	9.2.1	Importance Sampling	103
	9.2.2	Rejection Sampling	104
9.3	Normal Variates		105
	9.3.1	The Box–Muller Method	105
	9.3.2	The Neave Effect	106
9.4	Simulating Multivariate Copula Draws		109

10 Variance Reduction Techniques   **111**
    10.1   Antithetic Sampling   111
    10.2   Variate Recycling   112
    10.3   Control Variates   113
    10.4   Stratified Sampling   114
    10.5   Importance Sampling   115
    10.6   Moment Matching   116
    10.7   Latin Hypercube Sampling   119
    10.8   Path Construction   120
            10.8.1 Incremental   120
            10.8.2 Spectral   122
            10.8.3 The Brownian Bridge   124
            10.8.4 A Comparison of Path Construction Methods   128
            10.8.5 Multivariate Path Construction   131
    10.9   Appendix   134
            10.9.1 Eigenvalues and Eigenvectors
                   of a Discrete-time Covariance Matrix   134
            10.9.2 The Conditional Distribution of the Brownian Bridge   137

11 Greeks   **139**
    11.1   Importance Of Greeks   139
    11.2   An Up-Out-Call Option   139
    11.3   Finite Differencing with Path Recycling   140
    11.4   Finite Differencing with Importance Sampling   143
    11.5   Pathwise Differentiation   144
    11.6   The Likelihood Ratio Method   145
    11.7   Comparative Figures   147
    11.8   Summary   153
    11.9   Appendix   153
            11.9.1 The Likelihood Ratio Formula for Vega   153
            11.9.2 The Likelihood Ratio Formula for Rho   156

12 Monte Carlo in the BGM/J Framework   **159**
    12.1   The Brace–Gatarek–Musiela/Jamshidian Market Model   159
    12.2   Factorisation   161
    12.3   Bermudan Swaptions   163
    12.4   Calibration to European Swaptions   163
    12.5   The Predictor–Corrector Scheme   169
    12.6   Heuristics of the Exercise Boundary   171
    12.7   Exercise Boundary Parametrisation   174
    12.8   The Algorithm   176

12.9   Numerical Results   177
12.10 Summary   182

13 Non-recombining Trees   **183**
13.1   Introduction   183
13.2   Evolving the Forward Rates   184
13.3   Optimal Simplex Alignment   187
13.4   Implementation   190
13.5   Convergence Performance   191
13.6   Variance Matching   192
13.7   Exact Martingale Conditioning   195
13.8   Clustering   196
13.9   A Simple Example   199
13.10 Summary   200

14 Miscellanea   **201**
14.1   Interpolation of the Term Structure of Implied Volatility   201
14.2   Watch Your CPU Usage   202
14.3   Numerical Overflow and Underflow   205
14.4   A Single Number or a Convergence Diagram?   205
14.5   Embedded Path Creation   206
14.6   How Slow is Exp()?   207
14.7   Parallel Computing And Multi-threading   209

Bibliography   **213**

Index   **219**

Preface

This book is about Monte Carlo methods and close relatives thereof. It is about the application of traditional and state-of-the-art sampling techniques to problems encountered in the world of modern finance. The approach I take is to explain methods alongside actual examples that I encountered in my professional working day. This is why there may be a bias towards applications to investment banking and derivatives pricing in particular. However, many of the methods presented here apply equally to similar mathematical problems that arise in market risk management, credit risk assessment, the insurance businesses, strategic management consultancy, and other areas where the effect of many unknown variables (in the sense that we can only make assumptions about their probability distributions) is to be evaluated.

The purpose of this book is to be an introduction to the basic Monte Carlo techniques used nowadays by expert practitioners in the field. There are so many areas of Monte Carlo methods in finance that any attempt to try and provide a book on the subject that is both introductory *and* comprehensive would have meant many years of (part-time) writing. Instead, in order to fill the need for an introductory text in a more timely manner, I decided rather to focus on the issues most pressing to any novice in financial Monte Carlo simulations and to omit many of the more advanced topics. The subjects not covered include the whole family of Markov chain techniques, and almost all of the recent advances in Monte Carlo methods tailored specifically to the pricing of American, Bermudan, or any other derivative contract whose ideal value is given by the maximal (discounted) expected payoff over all possible exercise strategies, i.e. by finding the truly optimal exercise strategy. An exception to this is perhaps the identification of a suitable exercise boundary optimisation for the purpose of Bermudan swaption pricing in the Brace–Gatarek–Musiela/Jamshidian framework presented in Chapter 12. At the same time, though, I have tried to include most of the presently used techniques that enable the practitioner to create rather powerful Monte Carlo simulation applications indeed.

Whilst I always endeavour to explain the basic principles of the particular problem to which a technique is applied, this book is not meant to be an introduction to financial mathematics. I assume that the reader either has background knowledge in the relevant areas, or could follow up the given references for a deeper understanding of the financial and/or economic reasoning behind specific mathematical assumptions. After all, this is not a book about the reasoning behind option pricing. This is a book about mathematical and numerical techniques that may be used for the solution of the mathematical equations that were derived by experts in financial theory and economics. I do not attempt to give a justification for the assumption of complete markets, market efficiency, specific stochastic differential equations, etc.; I leave this up to the authors of the excellent books on those subjects in the literature [Hul97, Mer90, Reb98, Wil98]. Instead I have focused on the implementational aspects of Monte Carlo methods. Any Monte Carlo method will invariably have to run on a computing device, and this means numerical issues can be of paramount importance. In order for this book to be of some practical value to the practitioner having to implement Monte Carlo methods, I made the attempt to link the fundamental concepts of any one technique directly to the algorithm that has to be programmed, and often explicitly in terms of the C++ language, often taking into account aspects of numerical analysis such as roundoff error propagation, etc.

The nature of the subject of this book is strongly entwined with the concept of *convergence*. In general, Monte Carlo methods give us at best a statistical error estimate. This is in contrast to various other numerical methods. A Monte Carlo calculation is typically of the following structure: carry out the same procedure many times, take into account all the individual results, and summarise them into an overall approximation to the problem in question. For most Monte Carlo methods (in particular those providing serial decorrelation of the individual results), we can choose any subset of the individual results and summarise them to obtain an estimate. The numerically exact solution will be approached by the method only as we iterate the procedure more and more times, eventually converging at infinity. Clearly, we are not just interested in a method to converge to the correct answer after an infinite amount of calculation time, but rather we wish to have a good approximation quickly. Therefore, once we are satisfied that a particular Monte Carlo method works *in the limit*, we are naturally interested in its *convergence behaviour* or, more specifically, its *convergence speed*. A good part of this book is dedicated to various techniques and tricks to improve the convergence speed of Monte Carlo methods and their relatives. In order not just to present the reader with a description of the algorithms, but also to foster an intuitive grasp of the potential benefits from the implementation of a specific technique, we have attempted to include many diagrams of typical convergence behaviour: frequently these are used to highlight the differences between the performances of different methods. In particular, where such comparisons are made, we often display the convergence behaviour as a function of CPU time used by the different methods, since the human user's utility is much more closely related to the time elapsed until a calculation of sufficient accuracy has been completed than to the number of actual iterations carried out.

You may wonder why there is no explicit chapter on option pricing, considering that's one of the most immediate applications of Monte Carlo methods in finance. As it happens, there isn't *one* chapter on option pricing, but *every* chapter is written with option pricing in mind. My foremost use of Monte Carlo methods has been in the area of derivatives pricing. Since a lot of the examples I give are directly with respect to option valuation, I considered it unnecessary to have a chapter on the subject itself, only to repeat what is written in other chapters already. I hope the reader will agree with me.

Acknowledgements

The first person the author wishes to thank is undoubtedly Dr. Henrik Neuhaus. It was his vision and inspiration that brought together the Group Risk Division of Nikko Securities Global Holdings in Victoria Street, London, opposite New Scotland Yard. During the little over a year of its existence, prior to the equity buy-in of Citigroup into Nikko (Japan) and the subsequent demise of the London operation of Nikko Europe, I had the pleasure to learn a great deal from Henrik and to be given guidance as I was finding my financial legs and beginning to employ Monte Carlo techniques for derivatives modelling and derivatives model validation. Equally, my thanks go to Yasuo Kusuda, who was always ready to share his business experience, financial expertise and mathematical knowledge with me. At the same time I met Professor Carol Alexander, whose ubiquitous enthusiasm to share with other people the results of her own research, and whose continuous encouragement for others to do the same, gave part of the motivation to start this project. I would like to thank her for repeated invitations to speak at her courses on market risk, which allowed me to gain a feeling for the extent to which there may actually be use for a book specifically on Monte Carlo techniques. And of course, I am deeply indebted to Dr. Dongning Qu and Dr. Russ Bubley whom I had the pleasure to work with in my days at Nikko. I had many interesting discussions with both of them on the subject of derivatives pricing and Monte Carlo methods.

Another person I thank is Dr. Riccardo Rebonato, from whom I learned about the BGM/J market model approach to interest rate derivatives. Dr. Rebonato founded what was first the NatWest Group Risk Quantitative Research Centre, then the Royal Bank of Scotland Group Risk Quantitative Research Centre, and appointed my former two colleagues Dr. Chris Hunter and Dr. Mark Joshi to whom I also express my thanks. Chapter 12 is largely based on my experience gained in our time of developing BGM/J models.

I would also like to thank my colleagues in the Financial Engineering team of Commerzbank Securities, London. It has been most enjoyable to work with them, and I had many ideas for this book as a result of discussions with my colleagues there. The following fellow financial engineers requested to be mentioned by name, and it is my pleasure to do so: 'CurryMan' Dr. Peter Robinson, Dr. Rhys Mainwaring and Dr. Carl Seymour.

Furthermore, I am indebted to Dr. Alexander McNeil for his advice on some of the finer details of copula theory. Also, my thanks go to Mike Curran for his invaluable patience in reading the first draft version of this book with such exhaustive attention to detail.

And finally, there are a number of people whom I would like to thank for their support of this project or the guidance they may have given me in the past. The complete list would be rather long so, for the sake of brevity, I name but a few: my D.Phil. supervisor Professor Tom Mullin, my friend Dr. Paul Wilmott, and my grandmother.

Mathematical Notation

int[x]	the largest integer that is equal to or less than x
$A \wedge B$	A or B is true, or both
$m \,\text{XOR}\, n$	bitwise exclusive OR operation on the binary representation of the two integers m and n, also known as binary addition without carry
$m \oplus_2 n$	the same as XOR
$\propto$	proportional to
$f^{-1}(x)$	the inverse of the function $f(x)$, i.e. the unique solution for y in $f(y) = x$, if it exists
$\sim$	has distribution, i.e. meets the right-hand-side probability density law
$\mathbb{Z}$	the set of integers including 0
$\mathbb{N}$	the set of natural numbers, i.e. the positive integers $1, 2, \dots$
$\mathbb{R}$	the set of real numbers
$:=$	defined as
$\equiv$	identically equal to
$\approx$	approximately
$x^{\top}$	transpose of the vector x
$\partial_x f$	$\dfrac{\partial f}{\partial x}$
$\partial_{xy}^2 f$	$\dfrac{\partial^2 f}{\partial x \partial y}$
$Pr[A]$	the probability of some event A occurring
$E_\psi[X]$	the expectation of the random variable X with distribution density ψ
$\langle X \rangle$	the same as $E[X]$
$V_\psi[X]$	the variance of the random variable X with distribution density ψ
$Cov_\psi[X, Y]$	the covariance of the random variables X and Y under the joint distribution density $\psi(X, Y)$
$Corr_\psi[X, Y]$	the correlation of the random variables X and Y under the joint distribution density $\psi(X, Y)$
$||X||_p$	the L_p-norm of X defined as $||X||_p := \sqrt[p]{E\big[|X|^p\big]}$
$\mathcal{U}(a, b)$	the uniform distribution with equal probability density $\dfrac{1}{b-a}$ everywhere on the open interval (a, b)

$\mathcal{N}(\mu, \sigma)$	the cumulative normal distribution with mean μ and standard deviation σ
$\varphi(z)$	the standard normal distribution density function, i.e. $$\varphi(z) = \frac{1}{\sqrt{2\pi}} e^{-\frac{1}{2}z^2}$$
$N(z)$	the standard cumulative normal distribution probability function, i.e. $N(z) = \int_{z'=-\infty}^{z} \varphi(z')\,dz'$
$N^{-1}(p)$	the inverse cumulative normal probability function, i.e. $N(z) = p \implies N^{-1}(p) = z$
δ_{ij}	the Kronecker symbol which is 1 if $i = j$, otherwise 0
$\delta(x - x_0)$	the Dirac density whose singularity is located at x_0
$h(x - x_0)$	the Heaviside function whose discontinuity is located at x_0. The connection to the Dirac density is $h(x - x_0) = \int_{x'=-\infty}^{x} \delta(x' - x_0)\,dx'$
$\mathbf{1}_{\{expression\}}$	1 if *expression* is true, otherwise 0
$B\left(S, K, \sigma\sqrt{T}\right)$	the Black call option formula, i.e. $$B\left(S, K, \sigma\sqrt{T}\right) = S \cdot N\left(\frac{\ln\left(\frac{S}{K}\right)}{\sigma\sqrt{T}} + \frac{1}{2}\sigma\sqrt{T}\right) - K \cdot N\left(\frac{\ln\left(\frac{S}{K}\right)}{\sigma\sqrt{T}} - \frac{1}{2}\sigma\sqrt{T}\right)$$
$\sigma_{Black}(v, S, K, T)$	the Black call option implied volatility, i.e. $$B\left(S, K, \sigma\sqrt{T}\right) = v \implies \sigma_{Black}(v, S, K, T) = \sigma$$
$\sigma(t)$	some kind of instantaneous volatility
$\hat{\sigma}(T)$	an implied volatility given by the root mean square of its instantaneous counterpart, i.e. $\hat{\sigma}(T) = \int_{u=0}^{1} \sigma^2(u \cdot T)\,du$
$B(p, q)$	the beta function, also known as Euler's integral of the first kind, defined as $B(p, q) := \int_0^1 t^{p-1}(1-t)^{q-1}\,dt$
$B_x(p, q)$	the incomplete beta function, defined as $B_x(p, q) := \int_0^x t^{p-1}(1-t)^{q-1}\,dt$
$\Gamma(x)$	the gamma function, also known as Euler's integral of the second kind, defined as $\Gamma(x) := \int_0^\infty e^{-t}t^{x-1}\,dt$. Its relation to the beta function is $B(p, q) = \dfrac{\Gamma(p)\Gamma(q)}{\Gamma(p+q)}$. Note that $\Gamma(n+1) = n!$ for $n \in \mathbb{N}$
$\Gamma(x, y)$	the incomplete gamma function, defined as $\Gamma(x, y) := \int_y^\infty e^{-t}t^{x-1}\,dt$
C_e	Euler's constant' defined as $C_e := \lim_{n\to\infty}\left[\left(\sum_{k=1}^{n}\frac{1}{k}\right) - \ln n\right]$. $C_e \approx 0.577215664901532$
$\zeta(s)$	Euler's zeta function, defined as $\zeta(s) := \lim_{n\to\infty}\sum_{k=1}^{n}\frac{1}{k^s}$. It can also be represented as the following infinite product: $\zeta(s) \equiv \prod \dfrac{1}{1 - p^{-s}}$ where p takes on the values of all prime numbers
$\dfrac{\partial(f(x))}{\partial(x)}$	the Jacobian matrix of the transformation $x \to f(x)$
$\lvert A \rvert$	the determinant of the matrix A

1

Introduction

We are on the verge of a new era of financial computing. With the arrival of ever faster desktop computers, clustering technology, and the tools to utilise spare cpu cycles from a variety of sources, computer processing power has expanded dramatically. This expansion, coupled with the development of new numerical methods, is making techniques which were previously considered to be prohibitively computationally expensive not only feasible, but the method of choice. There are countless examples of mathematical problems faced by the quantitative analyst which used to require employing either analytical approximations or numerical truncations. This usually meant that the mathematical model that was ideally desired could not be used given the constraints of having to integrate its implementation into existing systems which would not tolerate long calculation times for individual models. Even where integration into a corporate IT infrastructure was not required, the user of a model might have limited patience or business needs that necessitated a comparatively speedy response. Whilst a front-office trader in a securities and derivatives house would usually not be concerned if a model built for him by his quantitative support team were to take anything between a few seconds and possibly several minutes in order to price a complex structure with calibration to market data, having to wait several hours would make the model unviable.

This is the reason that to date, when the choice between a conceptually superior but numerically less tractable model and one that lends itself to easy analytical evaluation has to be made, very often the easier model is chosen even though everyone agrees that it oversimplifies the matter at hand. With the aid of ever faster computers and improved Monte Carlo techniques, however, we are nowadays more often than not in the position to use the conceptually superior and more realistic modelling approach.

Even where we appear to have analytical solutions it is often desirable to have an alternative implementation that is supposed to give the same answer. The reason for this is that very often the final formulae of the analytical solution, although mathematically of very elegant appeal, prove to be numerically difficult to evaluate since they still involve one or two one-dimensional integrations, contour integrals in the complex plane, back transformations from Laplace or Fourier space, or simply the evaluation of special functions that are numerically very difficult to produce, such as the confluent hypergeometric functions or the modified Bessel function of the second kind for large parameters. Examples of the above include option pricing for generic distributions [CM99], stochastic volatility models [Hes93], analytical approximations for Asian options [FMW98], Variance Gamma processes [MS90, MM91, MCC98], or the Constant Elasticity of Variance process.

Finally, there are myriads of situations when we are very satisfied with a certain approximation but would like to have a Monte Carlo simulation tool for comparison, just in case. A good example for this is the difference between *continuously monitored* and *discretely monitored* payoff functions such as barrier or American-style digital options. There is an excellent approximation by Broadie, Glassermann, and Kou [BGK99] that relates the price

V of all simple continuous barrier contracts in a Black–Scholes framework of constant volatility σ to their discretely monitored equivalent where the period of time between monitoring points is τ as follows. Say the barrier level as it is specified on a term sheet of a discretely monitored contract is H_d and we have an analytical formula[1] $V_c = F(H_c)$ for the continuously monitored equivalent contract in a Black–Scholes framework setting. Then, the value of the discretely monitored contract is approximately

$$V_d \approx F\left(e^{\pm\frac{\zeta\left(\frac{1}{2}\right)}{\sqrt{2\pi}}\sigma\sqrt{\tau}} \cdot H_d\right). \tag{1.1}$$

with

$$\frac{\zeta\left(\frac{1}{2}\right)}{\sqrt{2\pi}} = 0.5825971579390010670205177164187631154729093870198\text{7}\ldots. \tag{1.2}$$

In other words, the discretely monitored contract is approximated as a continuously monitored contract with a shifted barrier level given by

$$H_c \approx e^{\pm\frac{\zeta\left(\frac{1}{2}\right)}{\sqrt{2\pi}}\sigma\sqrt{\tau}} \cdot H_d. \tag{1.3}$$

The sign in the exponent in equations (1.1) and (1.3) is selected according to whether the initial spot level is above or below the threshold barrier. Barriers that are above the initial spot level need to be amended upwards when we go from discrete to continuous monitoring, and so the positive sign is used. For barriers that need to be crossed from above for an event to be triggered, the negative sign applies. This approximation works extremely well as long as τ is significantly smaller than the remaining time to maturity of the contract and as long as the current spot level is not too close to the barrier, and most exotic derivatives traders are happy to use it under those circumstances. When a given contract comes close to its expiry, though, or the spot level gets dangerously close to a barrier, traders frequently wish to know to what extent a different, not-so-approximate, valuation would differ. In a situation like this, a fast-convergence Monte Carlo simulation that also provides the hedge parameters can make all the difference for the exotic derivatives trader.

The concept of random sampling as a computational means has long been established. A well-known example is the idea to calculate the circle number π by randomly placing points in a unit square with an enclosed circle around the centre of that square. In the limit of many samples, the ratio of points that happen to be inside the circle to the total number of samples approaches $\frac{\pi}{4}$. A way to compute π is thus to carry out this experiment for an ever increasing number of samples, take the hit ratio, and multiply it by 4. An alternative method attributed to the French Naturalist Comte de Buffon [Hol59, CK85, Sch74, Ree01] is to draw parallel lines on a board at a distance l between each adjacent pair of them, and to throw pins of length l randomly onto this board. The ratio of all the

---

[1]There are many good sources for exotic option formulae. One of my favourites is [Hau97].

pins crossing a line to all those that were thrown should converge to

$$\frac{\displaystyle\int_0^{\frac{\pi}{2}} \cos\alpha \, d\alpha}{\displaystyle\int_0^{\frac{\pi}{2}} d\alpha} = \frac{2}{\pi} \tag{1.4}$$

for large numbers of pins. Before the invention of fast computing machines, however, these approaches were rather time-consuming and cumbersome.

The history of Monte Carlo methods as a computational method for the calculation of expectations on potentially high-dimensional domains starts in the mid-1940s with the arrival of the first programmable computers. The main originators are considered to be the American mathematicians John von Neumann, Stanislav Ulam and Nicholas Metropolis [UvN47, MU49, Sob94]. The first published mentioning of the name 'Monte Carlo Method' is an article by Metropolis and Ulam in 1949 [MU49]. In this article, the authors explain how they view the calculation of multi-dimensional integrals resulting from the analysis of the transport problem of radiation and energetic particles governed by the Fokker–Planck equation as a statistical problem. Instead of attempting to carry out directly high-dimensional integrations involving the transition probabilities of many possible intermediate events and states by the use of lattice methods, they sampled single chains of events. The name of the method is only mentioned casually:

> 'The idea of using a statistical approach at which we hinted in the preceding examples is sometimes referred to as the Monte Carlo method.'

In fact, the term had been used before amongst those scientists in allusion to the principality of Monaco that is so famous for its casinos and to the fact that the roulette wheel represented the archetypical random number generator. Another reason why this allusion is rather appropriate is that some of the early mathematicians who contributed greatly to the development of statistics and probability theory did so in the pursuit of gaining riches at the gambling tables. In the same paper, the authors also establish the result that the Monte Carlo method enables us to evaluate the expectations of functionals of certain variables without a knowledge of the distribution of the variables themselves: all that is needed is a description of the process that generates those variables, and off we go! What's more, *in 1949*, Metropolis and Ulam already point out that the Monte Carlo method is easily amenable to parallelised computing. The only problem was, as one of my colleagues once put it, that few people had more than one machine the size of a tennis court[2] called 'a computer' readily at their disposal at the time.

In 1947, a Monte Carlo simulation involved many problems, not only the sheer size of the machine. Apart from the fact that the mathematical relations between the partial differential equations describing the problems the scientists were investigating, the associated multi-dimensional integrals, and their formulation as a stochastic process that can readily be simulated were only just being established, the actual simulation was a rather formidable enterprise itself. In those days, a computer was a rather large machine indeed, and to operate it involved several *machine operators*. The most advanced input/output

---

[2] This is a joke, I don't actually know what size the computer(s) used by von Neumann, Metropolis and Ulam were. It is probably safe to assume, though, that they were substantially larger than today's desktop PCs, and they certainly were a lot harder to come by.

device available was a punch card reader and a card puncher. The generation of random numbers was a huge problem and many different ways were explored. It may seem somewhat unreal when we think about it now, but one of the approaches taken at the time was as follows. A special project codenamed RAND was set up [Bro48, Bro51] whose aim, amongst others, was to accumulate a set of numbers that were considered to be sufficiently random for Monte Carlo simulations. RAND devised an electronic roulette wheel by combining a random frequency pulse source with a constant frequency pulse ($\approx$1 Hz) which provided about 100,000 pulses per second. The regularised pulses were passed to a five-place binary counter which effectively resulted in the equivalent of a roulette wheel with 32 positions. After a binary to decimal conversion, these numbers were then fed to an IBM punch, thus generating cards of random digits. Exhaustive tests on the so-generated set of numbers revealed some slight bias and they were later modified by shuffling and other further processing until they finally met the applied statistical tests [Bro51]. However, let me just give you a feeling for how serious the whole business was with the following quote taken from George Brown's report [Bro51] on the RAND project published in the National Bureau of Standard's booklet [Mon51] on the Monte Carlo Method in 1951.

> 'Production of random numbers really began on April 29, 1947, and by May 21 there were half a million digits generated. [...] By July 7 there were a million digits available [...] At this point we had our original million digits, 20,000 IBM cards with 50 digits to a card [...].'

Fortunately, computers, Monte Carlo methods, and algorithms for number generation have come a long way since, and their application to the mathematical problems encountered in modern finance is what this book is about.

2

The Mathematics Behind
Monte Carlo Methods

The theoretical understanding of Monte Carlo methods draws on various branches of mathematics. In this chapter, a few useful facts and results from the areas of probability, statistics, calculus and linear algebra are summarised. Some of them are going to come in handy in the following chapters, and the remainder are presented here for reference. Most readers will already be familiar with the contents of this chapter, and may as well skip it.

2.1 A FEW BASIC TERMS IN PROBABILITY AND STATISTICS

A *random experiment* is a process or action subject to non-deterministic uncertainty. We call the outcome of a random experiment a *draw* or a *variate* from a distribution. An example for this would be the flipping of a coin, or to be precise the face shown once the coin has come to rest. A *distribution density* is a generalised function that assigns *likelihood* or *probability density* to all possible results of a random experiment. A synonym for *distribution density* is *probability density function*. For our purposes, a *generalised function* can be an ordinary function, or a linear combination of an ordinary function and any finite number of *Dirac densities* $\delta(x - x_0)$. The *Dirac density* is the equivalent of assigning a finite probability to a single number on a continuous interval. This means, the Dirac density $\delta(x - x_0)$ is zero everywhere where it is defined, and strictly speaking undefined at x_0. However, its integral is given by the Heaviside function, i.e. $h(x - x_0) = \int_{x'=-\infty}^{x} \delta(x' - x_0)\,dx'$, which is zero for $x < x_0$ and one for $x > x_0$.

The relationship between the probability that the outcome X of a random experiment is an element of some set $\mathcal{S}$ and the distribution density $\psi(x)$ of the random experiment is

$$Pr[x \in \mathcal{S}] = \int_{\mathcal{S}} \psi(x)\,dx. \tag{2.1}$$

We call the set of all attainable outcomes X of a random experiment the *domain* $\mathcal{D}(X)$ *of the random experiment*. Whenever $\mathcal{D}(X)$ is an ordered set, i.e. when we can decide whether any one element is less than any other element of $\mathcal{D}(X)$, we define the *cumulative probability function* or just *cumulative* for short as

$$\Psi(x) = \int_{x'=\inf(\mathcal{D})}^{x} \psi(x')\,dx' = Pr[X < x]. \tag{2.2}$$

All distribution densities are normalised, i.e.

$$\int_{\mathcal{D}} \psi(x)\,dx = 1. \tag{2.3}$$

Note that in the probability sciences the cumulative is also referred to plainly as the *distribution function* or simply the *distribution*. Since this can lead to situations of ambiguity, I always explicitly state whether I am talking about the distribution density or the cumulative.

The *expected value* of a quantity subject to uncertainty is the probability weighted average. Our notation for the expected value of a quantity f with respect to a probability density ψ is

$$E_\psi[f] : \text{expected value of } f \text{ with respect to } \psi. \qquad (2.4)$$

Very often, there is no ambiguity about the relevant distribution. In this case we may just write $E[f]$. Alternatively, there may be a parametric description of the distribution of f. This means that f is actually a function of some other uncertain variable x. Given the distribution density of x, say $\psi(x)$, we would denote the expectation of f as $E_{\psi(x)}[f(x)]$. This is just to say

$$E_{\psi(x)}[f(x)] = \int_{-\infty}^{\infty} f(x)\psi(x)\,\mathrm{d}x. \qquad (2.5)$$

Analogously, we will need to make statements about the variance of a given uncertain quantity f — intuitively this is the variability of a quantity from its expected value. The variance of f is denoted by $V[f]$. It is defined by

$$V[f] = E\left[(f - E[f])^2\right] = E\left[f^2\right] - (E[f])^2. \qquad (2.6)$$

The *standard deviation* of a random variate or distribution is defined as the square root of its variance.

The *covariance* of two quantities f and g is defined as

$$\mathrm{Cov}[f, g] = E[f \cdot g] - E[f] \cdot E[g] \qquad (2.7)$$

and based on covariance is the concept of linear correlation

$$\mathrm{Corr}[f, g] = \frac{\mathrm{Cov}[f, g]}{\sqrt{V[f]V[g]}}. \qquad (2.8)$$

The correlation coefficient is by construction always in the interval $[-1, 1]$.

The *nth moment of a distribution* is defined as

$$E_{\psi(x)}[x^n] = \int x^n \psi(x)\,\mathrm{d}x. \qquad (2.9)$$

Jensen's Inequality

For any convex function $g(x)$ and any distribution density $\psi(x)$ the following inequality holds:

$$E_\psi[g(X)] \geqslant g\left(E_\psi[X]\right). \qquad (2.10)$$

Hölder's Inequality

For any two random variates X and Y

$$E[XY] \leqslant \|X\|_p \cdot \|Y\|_{\frac{p}{p-1}} \tag{2.11}$$

for any $p > 1$.

Minkowski's Inequality

For any two random variates X and Y

$$\|X + Y\|_p \leqslant \|X\|_p + \|Y\|_p \tag{2.12}$$

for any $p \geqslant 1$.

2.2 MONTE CARLO SIMULATIONS

The most common use of Monte Carlo simulations in finance is when we need to calculate an expected value of a function $f(x)$ given a specified distribution density $\psi(x)$ over $x \in \mathbb{R}^n$:

$$v = E_{\psi(x)}[f(x)] = \int f(x)\psi(x)\,dx^n. \tag{2.13}$$

In a strictly mathematical sense, *Monte Carlo maximisation* (i.e. the search for the maximum value of $f(x)$ for x in a given domain D) can also be formulated as in equation (2.13). This can be seen as follows. Provided that f is non-negative everywhere in D, define

$$m_s = \sqrt[s]{\int_D [f(x)]^s \, \psi(x)\,dx^n}. \tag{2.14}$$

The maximum of f in D is then given by $\lim_{s\to\infty} m_s$. Whilst in practice one would not use this limit procedure[1] to determine the actual maximum of a function f in a domain D, it is a very useful formal trick when the objective is to derive a partial differential equation for the value of a derivative contract that depends on the maximum value of an underlying asset over a given time interval [Wil98].

The easiest form of *Monte Carlo integration* of integrals like equation (2.13) can be summarised as follows.

- Establish a procedure of drawing variates x from the target distribution density $\psi(x)$.
- Set up a running sum variable `double RunningSum=0;`, a running average variable `double RunningAverage;` and a counter variable `unsigned long i=0;`.
- Draw a variate vector x_i and evaluate $f_i := f(x_i)$.
- Add the computed function value to `RunningSum`.
- Increment i, i.e. `++i;`.

---

[1]One would, of course, simply keep track of the maximum value of f seen thus far as we iterate through more and more samples.

- Set the running average to `RunningAverage = RunningSum/i;`. This gives us the *Monte Carlo estimator*

$$\hat{v}_N := \frac{1}{N} \sum_{i=1}^{N} f(\boldsymbol{x}_i). \tag{2.15}$$

- Keep iterating until either the required number of iterations has been carried out, or a specific error estimate (see section 2.7) has decreased below a predetermined threshold.

For more sophisticated methods, when a procedure to draw variates exactly from the target distribution $\psi(\boldsymbol{x})$ is either not available or computationally too expensive, see Chapter 9.

2.2.1 Monte Carlo Supremacy

The concept of Monte Carlo integration becomes ever more appealing as the dimensionality of the domain increases. This becomes clear as we look at the convergence behaviour of lattice methods in comparison to Monte Carlo methods. For a given d-dimensional hypercube of volume λ^d the error $\varepsilon_{\text{lattice}}$ of approximating the integral of a given function over the hypercube's interior by linear approximation decreases as $\mathcal{O}(\lambda^2)$. In a regular grid over a d-dimensional domain D, the number of points N relates to the subdivision length λ as

$$N \propto \left(\frac{1}{\lambda}\right)^d \tag{2.16}$$

which implies

$$\lambda \propto N^{-\frac{1}{d}}. \tag{2.17}$$

Thus, for a fixed number N of evaluations of the function which is to be integrated on a d-dimensional domain, the relative error of a lattice method relates to N and d according to

$$\varepsilon_{\text{lattice}}(N, d) \propto N^{-\frac{2}{d}}. \tag{2.18}$$

Picking the sample points at random, however, the relative error relates to N and d according to

$$\varepsilon_{\text{MC}}(N, d) \propto N^{-\frac{1}{2}} \tag{2.19}$$

and is thus *independent of the dimensionality*. Note that equations (2.18) and (2.19) imply that in the limit of many sampling points, the Monte Carlo method breaks even with lattice techniques as of $d = 4$, and outperforms regular grid methods for $d > 4$. For much higher dimensionalities, lattice methods become utterly unusable, whence the term *curse of dimensionality*.

2.2.2 Multi-dimensional Integration

This brings us to the question: what *is* the total mathematical dimensionality of a Monte Carlo simulation? Well, for simple problems such as the expected return from a portfolio given a multi-dimensional joint distribution for the returns of all underlying assets out to a specific time horizon, it would just be the number of those underlying assets. However, if we are carrying out a Monte Carlo evaluation of an expectation of a function(al) of discretised paths of a set of financial assets over some monitoring dates, then the state vector x represents the realisations of all involved assets at all future times of relevance, and the density $\psi(x)$ is the *joint distribution density* of all those realisations. The dimensionality of the integration domain is then

$$d = k \cdot l \tag{2.20}$$

with k being the number of assets and l being the number of time horizons in the time discretisation of the evolution paths.

2.3 SOME COMMON DISTRIBUTIONS

In general, most of the problems that we deal with when we resort to Monte Carlo methods are based on a quantity whose distribution is more or less well known analytically from the mathematical formulation of the chosen model. In this section, some of the more frequently used distributions are listed.

Uniform

A random experiment that can have a continuum of outcomes X which are all equally likely or *equiprobable* is said to have a *uniform distribution*. Most uniform distributions that we encounter in finance are either on a single closed interval $[a, b]$ or a single open interval (a, b). In the former case, we say

$$X \sim \mathcal{U}[a, b] \quad \text{which means} \quad \mathcal{D}(X) = [a, b]$$

and in the latter

$$X \sim \mathcal{U}(a, b) \quad \text{which means} \quad \mathcal{D}(X) = [a, b].$$

In either case, the probability density is given by

$$\psi(x) = \left(\frac{1}{b - a}\right) \cdot \mathbf{1}_{\{x \in \mathcal{D}\}}.$$

Normal

Very often, the quantity of interest depends on underlying variates *that are normally distributed with mean μ and standard deviation σ*. In this case, we say that a variate X has the distribution $\mathcal{N}(\mu, \sigma)$, i.e. $X \sim \mathcal{N}(\mu, \sigma)$. The distribution density function is

$$\psi(x; \mu, \sigma) = \frac{1}{\sigma\sqrt{2\pi}} e^{-\frac{1}{2}\frac{(x-\mu)^2}{\sigma^2}}. \tag{2.21}$$

Of particular common usage are standard normal variates. A variate Z is said to be a *standard normal variate* if

$$Z \sim \mathcal{N}(0, 1). \tag{2.22}$$

I usually denote the standard normal distribution density function by

$$\varphi(x) = \frac{1}{\sqrt{2\pi}} e^{-\frac{1}{2}x^2}. \tag{2.23}$$

The standard normal distribution is symmetric around the origin and thus all odd moments vanish. For even moments, we have

$$E\left[X^{2k}\right] = \frac{2^k}{\sqrt{\pi}}\Gamma\left(k + \frac{1}{2}\right) = \prod_{m=1}^{k}(2m - 1) = \frac{(2k - 1)!}{2^{(k-1)}(k - 1)!} \quad \text{for } k > 0. \tag{2.24}$$

The standard *cumulative normal probability function* is

$$N(x) = \int_{-\infty}^{x} \varphi(x') \, dx'. \tag{2.25}$$

The function $N(x)$ relates to the *error function* via

$$N(z) = \frac{1}{2}\left[1 + \text{erf}\left(\frac{z}{\sqrt{2}}\right)\right] \tag{2.26}$$

and

$$\text{erf}(x) = 2N(\sqrt{2}x) - 1. \tag{2.27}$$

At the time of writing, most compiler systems provide a highly accurate and fast implementation of the error function. These implementations are usually based on rational Chebyshev interpolation schemes for the error function which have been around for a long time, are well understood, highly reliable and very accurate [Cod69]. One such implementation is included on the accompanying CD, just in case your compiler system and libraries lack it. Since the cumulative normal distribution function is very frequently used in financial calculations, it is advisable to implement it in terms of a highly accurate and efficient error function by virtue of equation (2.26).

Equally, for the inverse cumulative normal function $z = N^{-1}(p)$, there are several numerical implementations providing different degrees of accuracy and efficiency [MZM94]. A very fast and accurate approximation is the one given by Boris Moro in [Mor95]. The most accurate whilst still highly efficient implementation currently freely available, however, is probably the algorithm by Peter Acklam [Ack00]. When allowing for an additional evaluation of a machine-accurate cumulative normal distribution function, Acklam's procedure is able to produce the inverse cumulative normal function to full machine accuracy by applying a second stage refinement using Halley's method [ST95, Pic88]. A C++ implementation of Acklam's method is also included on the CD.

Bernoulli or Dichotomic

A variate X is said to be *dichotomic* or *Bernoulli* distributed if it can take on only two discrete values, say A and B. Since the associated probabilities must add up to 1, we have

$$p := Pr[A] = 1 - Pr[B].$$

Binomial

The *binomial* distribution is generated by repeating a Bernoulli experiment, say, n times. The Binomial variate is then the number of times that one of the two states was attained. The probability that A occurs k times in n repetitions of a Bernoulli experiment is

$$Pr[X = k] = \binom{n}{k} p^k (1 - p)^{n-k}. \tag{2.28}$$

Thus, the distribution density of the Binomial variate X is

$$\psi(x) = \sum_{k=0}^{n} \binom{n}{k} p^k (1 - p)^{n-k} \delta(x - k). \tag{2.29}$$

The cumulative probability function results by integration to the same sum as in (2.29), only with the Dirac densities replaced by Heaviside functions.

Geometric

The *geometric* distribution describes the number of times one has to repeat a Bernoulli experiment until state B occurs for the first time. Since

$$Pr[X = k] = p^{k-1}(1 - p) \tag{2.30}$$

we have

$$\psi(x) = \sum_{k=1}^{\infty} p^{k-1}(1 - p) \delta(x - k) \tag{2.31}$$

for the geometric distribution, and similarly with Heaviside functions instead of Dirac densities for the cumulative.

Poisson

This distribution is closely related to the concept of point processes. Assume there is a probability intensity λ that in any one time interval dt a certain event happens. In other words, the probability of the said event occurring in any time interval dt is $dp = \lambda dt$. The probability that this event has occurred k times over a time span $[0, T]$ is given by

$$Pr[X = k] = e^{-\lambda T} \frac{(\lambda T)^k}{k!}. \tag{2.32}$$

The density and cumulative result again by summing up probability-weighted Dirac densities and Heaviside functions, respectively.

Exponential

Assume again that there is a probability $dp = \lambda dt$ of an event occurring over any one time interval. The probability density of the time one has to wait until the next event happens is given by the *exponential* distribution density

$$\psi(t) = \lambda e^{-\lambda t}. \tag{2.33}$$

The cumulative probability is

$$\Psi(t) = 1 - e^{-\lambda t} \tag{2.34}$$

and the moments of the exponential distribution are

$$E\left[t^k\right] = \frac{k!}{\lambda^k}. \tag{2.35}$$

Beta

Beta variates are distributed according to

$$\psi(x) = \frac{\Gamma(\alpha + \beta)}{\Gamma(\alpha)\Gamma(\beta)} x^{\alpha-1}(1 - x)^{\beta-1} = \frac{x^{\alpha-1}(1 - x)^{\beta-1}}{\mathrm{B}(\alpha, \beta)} \tag{2.36}$$

for $x \in [0, 1]$ and some $\alpha, \beta > 0$. It can be seen as a generalisation of the uniform distribution in the sense that it is a smooth curve on the interval $[0, 1]$, identically 0 at either end, and by a suitable choice of the parameters α and β it can be made very similar to the uniform distribution. Expectation, variance and moments of the beta distribution are

$$E[X] = \frac{\alpha}{\alpha + \beta}, \quad V[X] = \frac{\alpha\beta}{(\alpha + \beta + 1)(\alpha + \beta)^2} \quad \text{and} \quad E\left[X^k\right] = \frac{\Gamma(\alpha + k)\Gamma(\alpha + \beta)}{\Gamma(\alpha + \beta + k)\Gamma(\alpha)}. \tag{2.37}$$

The cumulative probability function of the beta distribution is

$$\Psi(x) = \frac{\mathrm{B}_x(\alpha, \beta)}{\mathrm{B}(\alpha, \beta)}. \tag{2.38}$$

Gamma

The density function of the gamma distribution reads

$$\psi(x) = \frac{x^{\alpha-1}}{\Gamma(\alpha)\beta^\alpha} e^{-\frac{x}{\beta}} \tag{2.39}$$

for $x \geqslant 0$ and some $\alpha, \beta > 0$. For $\alpha = n$ and $\beta = \frac{1}{\lambda}$, the waiting time until n events have occurred in a Poisson process is gamma distributed according to (2.39). Expectation and variance of the gamma distribution are

$$E[X] = \alpha\beta, \tag{2.40}$$

$$V[X] = \alpha\beta^2. \tag{2.41}$$

Its cumulative is

$$\Psi(x) = 1 - \frac{\Gamma(\alpha, x/\beta)}{\Gamma(\alpha)}. \tag{2.42}$$

Chi-square

Define X as the sum of the squares of ν independently drawn standard normal variates, i.e.

$$X := \sum_{k=1}^{\nu} z_i^2 \quad \text{with } z_i \sim \mathcal{N}(0, 1). \tag{2.43}$$

The variate X follows the law of the χ^2 distribution density with ν degrees of freedom

$$\psi(x) = \frac{x^{\frac{\nu}{2}-1}}{\Gamma\left(\frac{\nu}{2}\right) 2^{\frac{\nu}{2}}} e^{-\frac{x}{2}} \tag{2.44}$$

and has the cumulative probability function

$$\Psi(x) = 1 - \frac{\Gamma\left(\frac{\nu}{2}, \frac{x}{2}\right)}{\Gamma\left(\frac{\nu}{2}\right)}. \tag{2.45}$$

In general, ν doesn't need to be an integer. The expectation and variance are

$$E[X] = \nu, \tag{2.46}$$

$$V[X] = 2\nu. \tag{2.47}$$

The χ^2 distribution is a special case of the gamma distribution with $\alpha = \frac{\nu}{2}$ and $\beta = 2$.

Student's t

Take two independent variates Y and Z. The first is a standard normal variate $Y \sim \mathcal{N}(0, 1)$ and the second is drawn from a χ^2 distribution with ν degrees of freedom, i.e. $Z \sim \chi_\nu^2$. Then, the quotient

$$X := \frac{Y}{\sqrt{Z/\nu}} \tag{2.48}$$

satisfies Student's t distribution

$$\psi(x) = \frac{\Gamma\left(\frac{\nu+1}{2}\right)}{\sqrt{\nu\pi}\,\Gamma\left(\frac{\nu}{2}\right)} \left[1 + \left(\frac{x^2}{\nu}\right)\right]^{-\frac{\nu+1}{2}} = \frac{\left(1 + x^2/\nu\right)^{-\frac{\nu+1}{2}}}{\sqrt{\nu}\,B\left(\frac{\nu}{2}, \frac{1}{2}\right)}. \tag{2.49}$$

All the moments up to order ν exist. Since the distribution is symmetric around 0, its expectation is 0. For $\nu > 2$, the variance and higher order even moments for $k < \nu$ are

$$V[X] = \frac{\nu}{\nu - 2}, \tag{2.50}$$

$$E\left[X^k\right] = \frac{\Gamma\left(\frac{\nu+1}{2}\right)\Gamma\left(\frac{\nu-k}{2}\right)}{\sqrt{\pi}\,\Gamma\left(\frac{\nu}{2}\right)}. \tag{2.51}$$

For $x \leqslant 0$, the cumulative probability function is

$$\Psi(x) = \frac{B_{\frac{v}{v+x^2}}\left(\frac{v}{2}, \frac{1}{2}\right)}{2B\left(\frac{v}{2}, \frac{1}{2}\right)} \tag{2.52}$$

and for $x > 0$ it is given by virtue of its symmetry as $\Psi(x) = 1 - \Psi(-x)$.

Cauchy

The Cauchy (also known as Lorentz) distribution is defined by the density function

$$\psi(x) = \frac{1}{\pi} \frac{1}{1 + x^2} \tag{2.53}$$

and its cumulative probability function is

$$\Psi(x) = \frac{1}{\pi} \arctan(x) + \frac{1}{2}. \tag{2.54}$$

The Cauchy distribution is symmetric around zero and thus all of its odd moments are zero[2]. None of the even moments exist.

Lognormal

Define

$$X := e^{\sigma z} \tag{2.55}$$

with z being a standard normal variate $z \sim \mathcal{N}(0, 1)$. The variate X follows the *lognormal* distribution

$$\psi(x) = \frac{e^{-\frac{1}{2}\frac{\ln^2 x}{\sigma^2}}}{\sigma x \sqrt{2\pi}}, \tag{2.56}$$

$$\Psi(x) = N\left(\frac{\ln x}{\sigma}\right). \tag{2.57}$$

The expectation, variance and moments are

$$E[X] = e^{\frac{1}{2}\sigma^2}, \tag{2.58}$$

$$V[X] = e^{\sigma^2}\left(e^{\sigma^2} - 1\right), \tag{2.59}$$

$$E\left[X^k\right] = e^{\frac{1}{2}k^2\sigma^2}. \tag{2.60}$$

The lognormal distribution is probably the most important function in computational finance since it is the solution to the stochastic differential equation describing geometric

[2]This is assuming that the moments are defined by Riemann integration. This is important since the half-sided integrals $\int_{x=0}^{\pm\infty} x^{2k+1}\psi(x)\,dx$ for some $k \in \mathbb{N}_0$ diverge for the Cauchy distribution and thus Lebesgue integration would not result in finite moments of odd order.

Brownian motion, which in turn is almost always the first easy choice when the evolution of non-negative quantities is to be modelled.

Generalised Beta 2

The *generalised beta distribution of the second kind* [BM87, CDM90], or GB2 for short, is given by a four-parameter density function

$$\psi(x) = \frac{|a|x^{ap-1}}{b^{ap}\mathrm{B}(p,q)\left[1+(x/b)^a\right]^{p+q}} \tag{2.61}$$

for $a, b, p, q, x > 0$. The cumulative of the GB2 distribution can be written as

$$\Psi(x) = \frac{\mathrm{B}_{-(\frac{x}{b})^a}(p, 1-p-q)}{(-1)^p\,\mathrm{B}(p,q)}. \tag{2.62}$$

Note that

$$(-1)^{-c}\,\mathrm{B}_{-y}(c,d) = (-1)^{-c-1}\int_0^{-y} t^{c-1}(1-t)^{d-1}\,\mathrm{d}t - \int_0^y s^{c-1}(1\mid s)^{d-1}\,\mathrm{d}s \tag{2.63}$$

for $c > 0$ and $d < (1-c)$ is a real positive number and can be evaluated very efficiently, e.g. by the aid of an adaptive Gauss–Lobatto method [GG00b, GG00a, Gan92].

The moments of the GB2 distribution are

$$E\left[X^k\right] = b^k\frac{\mathrm{B}\,(p+k/a, q-k/a)}{\mathrm{B}(p,q)}. \tag{2.64}$$

One of the very useful features of the GB2 distribution is that it allows for a large variety of shapes that are *nearly lognormal*, which is desirable when density functions are used for the extrapolation of volatility smiles of traded options.

Pareto

The *Pareto distribution* is skewed and heavy-tailed and frequently used to model rare events. Its density function is

$$\psi(x) = \frac{a}{x^{a+1}} \tag{2.65}$$

for $x \geqslant 1$ and $a > 0$ and its cumulative probability function is

$$\Psi(x) = 1 - \frac{1}{x^a}. \tag{2.66}$$

All moments of order v with $v < a$ exist and are given by

$$E\left[X^k\right] = \frac{a}{a-k}. \tag{2.67}$$

Generalised Pareto

As a generalisation of (2.65) we have

$$\psi(x) = \frac{ab^a}{x^{a+1}} \tag{2.68}$$

for $x \geqslant b$ and $a > 0$ and its cumulative probability function is

$$\Psi(x) = 1 - \left(\frac{b}{x}\right)^a. \tag{2.69}$$

The moments are

$$E\left[X^k\right] = \frac{ab^k}{a - k} \tag{2.70}$$

for $k < a$.

Weibull

This distribution density is given by

$$\psi(x) = \gamma \frac{x^{\gamma-1}}{\beta} e^{-\frac{x^\gamma}{\beta}} \tag{2.71}$$

for $x \geqslant 0$ and $\gamma, \beta > 0$ and its cumulative probability function is

$$\Psi(x) = 1 - e^{-\frac{x^\gamma}{\beta}}. \tag{2.72}$$

The moments are

$$E\left[X^k\right] = \beta^{\frac{k}{\gamma}} \Gamma\left(1 + \frac{k}{\gamma}\right). \tag{2.73}$$

The Weibull distribution is sometimes also referred to as the *Frechet* distribution.

Gumbel

The *Gumbel* probability density is

$$\psi(x) = abe^{-(be^{-ax} + ax)} \tag{2.74}$$

for $a, b > 0$ and $x \in \mathbb{R}$. Its cumulative is

$$\Psi(x) = e^{-be^{-ax}}. \tag{2.75}$$

The first three moments of the Gumbel distribution are

$$E[X] = \frac{1}{a}(\ln b + C_e), \tag{2.76}$$

$$E\left[X^2\right] = \frac{1}{a^2}\left(\ln^2 b + 2C_e \ln b + C_e^2 + \frac{\pi^2}{6}\right), \tag{2.77}$$

$$E\left[X^3\right] = \frac{1}{a^3}\left(\ln^3 b + 3C_e \ln^2 b + \left(3C_e^2 + \frac{\pi^2}{2}\right)\ln b + C_e^3 + C_e\frac{\pi^2}{2} + 2\zeta(3)\right). \tag{2.78}$$

The number $\zeta(3) \approx 1.2020569$ is also known as Apéry's constant.

Generalised Lambda

The *generalised lambda distribution* is also known as the *asymmetric lambda distribution*. It exists in two forms of parametrisation: the original form by Ramberg and Schmeiser [RS74, RDTM79] and a later rewritten formulation [FMKL88, KDM96].

Unlike most other distributions, it is directly defined in terms of the inverse of the cumulative. In the original parametrisation [RS74], this reads

$$\Psi^{-1}(u) = \lambda_1 + \frac{1}{\lambda_2}\left(u^{\lambda_3} - (1-u)^{\lambda_4}\right) \tag{2.79}$$

for $u \in [0, 1]$. Its density is parametrically given by $x = \Psi^{-1}(u)$ and

$$\psi(x) = \left[\frac{d}{du}\Psi^{-1}(u)\right]^{-1} = \left[\frac{\lambda_3}{\lambda_2}u^{\lambda_3-1} + \frac{\lambda_4}{\lambda_2}(1-u)^{\lambda_4-1}\right]^{-1}. \tag{2.80}$$

The generalised lambda distribution is very popular for the fitting of data due to its tremendous flexibility. With the right choice of parameters it can be used to approximate almost all of the previously mentioned distributions.

The moments of the generalised lambda distribution can be calculated directly as

$$E\left[X^k\right] = \int_0^1 \left(\Psi^{-1}(u)\right)^k du. \tag{2.81}$$

The first three moments are

$$E[X] = \frac{1}{\lambda_2}\left(\lambda_1\lambda_2 + \frac{1}{\lambda_3+1} - \frac{1}{\lambda_4+1}\right), \tag{2.82}$$

$$E\left[X^2\right] = \frac{1}{\lambda_2^2}\left(\lambda_1^2\lambda_2^2 + \frac{1}{2\lambda_3+1} + \frac{1}{2\lambda_4+1} + \frac{2\lambda_1\lambda_2}{\lambda_3+1} - \frac{2\lambda_1\lambda_2}{\lambda_4+1} - 2\,B(\lambda_3+1, \lambda_4+1)\right), \tag{2.83}$$

$$E\left[X^3\right] = \frac{1}{\lambda_2^3}\left(\lambda_1^3\lambda_2^3 + \frac{3\lambda_1^2\lambda_2^2}{1+\lambda_3} + \frac{3\lambda_1\lambda_2}{2\lambda_3+1} + \frac{1}{3\lambda_3+1} - \frac{1}{3\lambda_4+1} - \frac{3\lambda_1^2\lambda_2^2}{\lambda_4+1} + \frac{3\lambda_1\lambda_2}{2\lambda_4+1}\right.$$

$$\left. - 3\,B(2\lambda_3+1, \lambda_4+1) - 6\lambda_1\lambda_2 B(\lambda_3+1, \lambda_4+1) + 3\,B(\lambda_3+1, 2\lambda_4+1)\right). \tag{2.84}$$

2.4 KOLMOGOROV'S STRONG LAW

This fundamental result by Andrey Nikolaevich Kolmogorov was established in the 1920s and is the main mathematical justification for the use of Monte Carlo simulations.

Convergence Almost Surely

Let $X_1, X_2, X_3, \ldots$ be a sequence of random variates, such as, for instance, the running average of a Monte Carlo simulation. If, given some ξ, for all $\varepsilon, \eta > 0$ there exists an n_0 such that

$$Pr[|X_n - \xi| > \varepsilon, \ \forall n > n_0] < \eta \tag{2.85}$$

then we say that the sequence $\{X_n\}$ *converges almost surely* to ξ, which is denoted as

$$X_n \xrightarrow{\text{a.s.}} \xi. \tag{2.86}$$

Kolmogorov's Strong Law of Large Numbers

Given a sequence of *iid*, i.e. *independent identically distributed*, variates ξ_i with expectation

$$E[\xi_i] = \mu \tag{2.87}$$

define their running sum and average as

$$S_n := \sum_{i=1}^{n} \xi_i, \tag{2.88}$$

$$X_n := \frac{1}{n} S_n. \tag{2.89}$$

Then

$$X_n \xrightarrow{\text{a.s.}} \mu. \tag{2.90}$$

2.5 THE CENTRAL LIMIT THEOREM

The central limit theorem is one of the cornerstones of statistics and probability theory. It was first formulated by Laplace. Since then, many great mathematicians such as Chebyshev, Markov, Lyapunov, Khinchin, Lindeberg, and Lévy have given extensions and variations of it. For the sake of brevity, only a rather simplified form is outlined below.

Given a sequence of iid variates ξ_i with expectation and variance

$$E[\xi_i] = \mu, \tag{2.91}$$

$$V[\xi_i] = \sigma \tag{2.92}$$

define the running sum S_n as in equation (2.88). Then, for increasing n, the composite variate

$$X_n := \frac{S_n - n\mu}{\sigma\sqrt{n}} \tag{2.93}$$

converges in distribution to the standard normal distribution. We denote this as

$$X_n \overset{\text{i.d.}}{\longrightarrow} \mathcal{N}(0, 1). \tag{2.94}$$

A practical example for this is the approximation of a Gaussian variate by summing up 12 uniform $(0, 1)$ variates. Since the variance of uniform variates amounts to $\frac{1}{12}$, the denominator in equation (2.93) equals unity and the approximation is simply the sum of 12 uniforms minus 6. Note that this is not a highly accurate approximation and should only be used to establish ballpark estimates. A diagram is given in Figure 2.1 for comparison[3].

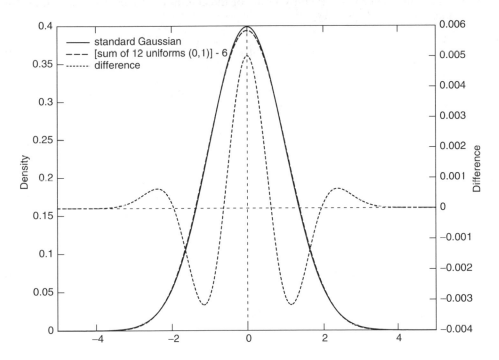

Figure 2.1 Approximating a standard normal variate by taking 12 $\mathcal{U}(0, 1)$ variates and subtracting 6. The uniform number generator used for this diagram is the Mersenne twister (see section 7.5).

2.6   THE CONTINUOUS MAPPING THEOREM

Given a sequence (X_n, Y_n) that converges in distribution to (X, Y), i.e.

$$(X_n, Y_n) \overset{\text{i.d.}}{\longrightarrow} (X, Y) \tag{2.95}$$

---

[3] My thanks to Dr. Carl Seymour for carrying out the calculations for this diagram.

and given a continuous map $\phi(x, y)$, then

$$\phi(X_n, Y_n) \xrightarrow{\text{i.d.}} \phi(X, Y). \tag{2.96}$$

2.7 ERROR ESTIMATION FOR MONTE CARLO METHODS

Given a Monte Carlo estimator $\hat{v}$ as the average of many individual draws of the random variate V, i.e.

$$\hat{v}_N = \frac{1}{N} \sum_{i=1}^{N} v_i \tag{2.97}$$

we know that each individual evaluation of the estimator itself, for large N, behaves approximately like a normal variate by virtue of the central limit theorem. Assuming that the variance of V is σ^2, this means

$$\hat{v}_N \xrightarrow{\text{i.d.}} \mathcal{N}\left(\mu, \frac{\sigma}{\sqrt{N}}\right). \tag{2.98}$$

Since $\hat{v}_N$ approaches a normal distribution, a statistical measure for the uncertainty in any one simulation result of $\hat{v}_N$ is given by the standard deviation of $\hat{v}_N$, namely

$$\sqrt{V[\hat{v}_N]} = \frac{\sigma}{\sqrt{N}}. \tag{2.99}$$

In general, we don't actually know the variance σ^2 of the random variate V whose expectation we are trying to estimate. However, by virtue of the combination of the central limit and the continuous mapping theorems, we can use the variance of the simulation instead as an estimate for σ^2:

$$\hat{\sigma}_N = \sqrt{\left(\frac{1}{N} \sum_{i=1}^{N} v_i^2\right) - \left(\frac{1}{N} \sum_{i=1}^{N} v_i\right)^2}. \tag{2.100}$$

This leads us to the definition of the *standard error*:

$$\epsilon_N = \frac{\hat{\sigma}_N}{\sqrt{N}}. \tag{2.101}$$

Whenever the standard error is used as an error measure, it is important to remember that it is only of statistical nature. Any single simulation can yield a result well outside the standard error. As a matter of fact, since the total probability mass within one standard deviation either side of the centre of the standard normal distribution is only around 68.3%, approximately every third simulation based on random numbers will have a result outside the standard error margin around the correct solution! In addition, the standard error itself is subject to a statistical error margin. It can be shown, however, that the standard deviation of the standard error scales as $\hat{\sigma}_N^2/N$ and is thus much less significant than the statistical nature of the standard error as a measure for expected accuracy.

2.8 THE FEYNMAN–KAC THEOREM

This theorem by R. Feynman and M. Kac [Fey48, Kac51] connects the solutions of a specific class of partial differential equations to an expectation which establishes the mathematical link between the PDE formulation of the diffusion problems we encounter in finance, and Monte Carlo simulations.

Given the set of stochastic processes

$$\mathrm{d}X_i = b_i \, \mathrm{d}t + \sum_{j=1}^{n} a_{ij} \, \mathrm{d}W_j \quad \text{for } i = 1, \dots, n \tag{2.102}$$

with formal solution

$$X_i(T) = X_i(t) + \int_t^T b_i \, \mathrm{d}t + \int_t^T \sum_{j=1}^{n} a_{ij} \, \mathrm{d}W_j \tag{2.103}$$

any function $V(t, X)$ with boundary conditions

$$V(T, X) = f(X) \tag{2.104}$$

that satisfies the partial differential equation

$$\frac{\partial V}{\partial t} + g + \frac{1}{2} \sum_{i,j=1}^{n} c_{ij} \frac{\partial^2 V}{\partial X_i \partial X_j} + \sum_{i=1}^{n} b_i \frac{\partial V}{\partial X_i} = kV \tag{2.105}$$

with

$$c_{ij} := \sum_{k=1}^{n} a_{ik} a_{jk} \tag{2.106}$$

can be represented as the expectation

$$V(t, X) = E\left[f(X_T) \mathrm{e}^{-\int_t^T k \mathrm{d}u} + \int_t^T g \, \mathrm{e}^{-\int_t^s k \mathrm{d}u} \, \mathrm{d}s \right]. \tag{2.107}$$

Hereby, all of the coefficients a_{ij}, b_i, k and g can be functions both of time t and the state vector $X(t)$. As with most mathematical theorems, there is a whole host of additional conditions for good behaviour of all the coefficients and functions involved and the reader is referred to, for example, Karatzas and Shreve [KS91] (p. 366).

2.9 THE MOORE–PENROSE PSEUDO-INVERSE

The Moore–Penrose pseudo-inverse [GK65, Alb72, PTVF92] of a matrix $A \in \mathbb{R}^{m \times n}$ is a very robust way of attempting to solve linear systems that for a variety of reasons may be singular or near-singular. It is based on the method of *singular value decomposition* of A given by

$$
\left(\begin{array}{c} A \end{array} \right) = \left(\begin{array}{c} U \end{array} \right) \cdot \left(\begin{array}{cccc} \lambda_1 & & & \\ & \lambda_2 & & \\ & & \ddots & \\ & & & \ddots \\ & & & & \lambda_n \end{array} \right) \cdot \left(\begin{array}{c} V^\top \end{array} \right).
$$

(2.108)

The entries λ_i of the diagonal matrix Λ in the centre of the right-hand side are called the *singular values*, and are guaranteed to be positive. The matrices U and V are each columnwise orthonormal. Now, define the diagonal matrix Θ of the same dimensions as Λ by setting its diagonal entries to

$$
\theta_i := \begin{cases} \dfrac{1}{\lambda_i} & \text{for} \quad \lambda_i > \epsilon \\ 0 & \text{for} \quad \lambda_i \leqslant \epsilon \end{cases}
$$

(2.109)

for some suitable roundoff threshold ϵ (which can reasonably safely also be set to exactly zero). We thus obtain the Moore–Penrose pseudo-inverse:

$$
A_{\text{MP}}^{-1} := V \cdot \Theta \cdot U^\top.
$$

(2.110)

Using the Moore–Penrose pseudo-inverse to solve a linear system $Ax = b$ will result in a least-square fit whenever the system is overdetermined and thus strictly speaking has no solution. For underdetermined systems, it will find the one solution that has no projection onto the nullspace of A. In other words, it will find the solution of least norm and thus avoid the accidental amplification or contribution of noise.

The Moore–Penrose pseudo-inverse is the method of choice whenever our objective is to find a vector (or matrix) x that best fits

$$
Ax = b
$$

(2.111)

for some vector (or matrix) b with the least possible L_2-norm for x. In most situations when we encounter a singular or ill-conditioned system of this nature, this is precisely what suits us best.

An excellent reference for further details and the numerical method to compute the singular value decomposition of any matrix is [PTVF92].

3
Stochastic Dynamics

In all aspects of life, we face having to take into account the unknown future. In the world of finance we very often want to quantify the uncertainty of the future, or at least the financial impact of the universe's possible evolutions we may incur. The mathematical way to describe that a quantity could evolve in various ways with associated probabilities as time passes by is to say that it is subject to *stochastic dynamics*. Great mathematicians have worked in this area and today we owe a tremendous debt to Gauss, Wiener, Brown, Levy, Itô, and many others for path-breaking discoveries on stochastic processes and stochastic calculus. In this chapter, I briefly summarise some of the more important ones the quantitative analyst commonly encounters. This list is not comprehensive by far, it is merely a little reminder of the whole zoology of stochastic processes studied by mathematicians.

3.1 BROWNIAN MOTION

Brownian motion is ubiquitous in quantitative finance. Wherever we model the evolution of something into the future, the simplest assumption is to say that over any one time step the outcome only depends on the present value of the quantity (Markov property) and that all time steps are equal, i.e. that the structure of the evolution process is the same at all times into the future (stationarity). If in addition to that we demand that the quantity must evolve continuously (without jumps), we necessarily will have to use a Brownian process as the underlying stochastic driver of the quantity we wish to model. The reason for this is that the above set of properties *already defines Brownian motion*, which makes it a beautifully simple concept. This is best summarised in the following theorem taken from [Har90].

Theorem 3.1
If Y is a continuous process with stationary independent increments, then Y is a Brownian motion.

Harrison continues:

> 'This beautiful theorem shows that Brownian motion can actually be defined by stationary independent increments and path continuity alone, with normality following as a consequence of these assumptions. This may do more than any other character-ization to explain the significance of Brownian motion for probabilistic modeling.'

A standard Brownian motion is often also referred to as a *standard Wiener process* owing to the fact that it was N. Wiener in the 1920s who started the mathematical analy-sis of Brownian motion. A Wiener process is formally often represented by the differ-ential increment dW or dW_t (indicating that this is the increment of the Wiener process happening at time t), and this notation is adopted throughout this chapter. A standard Wiener process has the following properties.

1. The expectation of the differential increment dW_t at any one point in time t is zero:

$$E[dW_t] = 0. \tag{3.1}$$

2. The variance of the differential increment dW_t at any one point in time t is equal to the associated differential increment in time:

$$V[dW_t] = E\left[dW_t^2\right] - (E[dW_t])^2 = E\left[dW_t^2\right] = dt. \tag{3.2}$$

This means that the sum of increments, i.e. the value of the process variable W_t, is normally distributed with zero mean and a standard deviation of $\sqrt{t}$:

$$W_t = \int_{s=0}^{t} dW_s \sim \mathcal{N}(0, \sqrt{t}). \tag{3.3}$$

In the design of Monte Carlo algorithms we make frequent use of a more general formulation of the second property of a Wiener process:

$$\int_{t=0}^{T} f(t)\, dW_t \sim \mathcal{N}\left(0, \sqrt{\int_{t=0}^{T} f(t)^2\, dt}\right). \tag{3.4}$$

This results immediately from the fact that the variance of a Wiener process is linearly additive. Equation (3.4) is of fundamental importance in many applications since it enables us to bypass the numerical solution of the stochastic integral on the left-hand side and directly draw variates that represent the distribution of the entire expression.

3.2   ITÔ'S LEMMA

One of the most important mathematical tricks from stochastic calculus that we use for the purpose of transforming stochastic differential equations is *Itô's lemma*. In crude terms, it is the direct consequence of the variance of a Wiener process increment over any infinitesimal time step given by equation (3.2). Itô's lemma states that the total differential of any given function $f(X)$ depending on a stochastic variable $X \in \mathbb{R}^n$ subject to the system of stochastic differential equations

$$dX_i = b_i(t, X)\, dt + \sum_{k=1}^{n} a_{ik}(t, X)\, dW_{kt} \tag{3.5}$$

is given by

$$df = \left(\sum_{i=1}^{n} (\partial_{X_i} f) b_i + \frac{1}{2} \sum_{i,j,k,l=1}^{n} (\partial_{X_i X_j}^2 f) a_{ik} \rho_{kl} a_{jl}\right) dt + \sum_{i,k=1}^{n} (\partial_{X_i} f) a_{ik}\, dW_k \tag{3.6}$$

where

$$\rho_{kl} = \frac{E[dW_k\, dW_l]}{dt} \tag{3.7}$$

is the instantaneous correlation of dW_{kt} and dW_{lt}.

3.3   NORMAL PROCESSES

Normal processes are of paramount importance in financial applications. This is not only due to the fact that they are generally very amenable to analytical evaluations, but also that they are very often considered to be a very good starting point for a realistic modelling of the problem at hand. An example is the celebrated Vasicek model of a mean-reverting evolution of the short interest rate towards a long-term equilibrium distribution [Vas77]. This model can be formulated by the stochastic differential equation

$$dr = a(\theta - r)\, dt + \sigma\, dW \qquad (3.8)$$

with a, θ and σ being constants. Given an initial value for r, i.e. $r_0 = r(0)$, the distribution of $r(t)$ can be calculated explicitly. In order to do so, we utilise the so-called method of *variation of constants*. The first step is to solve the homogeneous differential equation

$$dr_h = a(\theta - r_h)\, dt \qquad (3.9)$$

to obtain

$$r_h(t) = \theta + c \cdot e^{-at} \qquad (3.10)$$

for some constant c. We now assume that the solution of equation (3.8) is of the same form as (3.10), only that c is not a constant. In other words, we use the Ansatz

$$r = \theta + c \cdot e^{-at} \qquad (3.11)$$

and then compare

$$dr = d\left(\theta + c \cdot e^{-at}\right) = a(\theta - r)\, dt + e^{-at}\, dc \qquad (3.12)$$

with the original equation (3.8), which gives us

$$dc = e^{at}\sigma\, dW \qquad (3.13)$$

and thus

$$r(t) = \theta + (r_0 - \theta)e^{-at} + e^{-at}\sigma \int_{s=0}^{t} e^{as}\, dW_s. \qquad (3.14)$$

By virtue of equation (3.4), we can immediately write down the distributional behaviour of $r(t)$ as

$$r(t) = \theta + (r_0 - \theta)e^{-at} + \sigma\sqrt{\frac{1 - e^{-2at}}{2a}}\, z \qquad (3.15)$$

with z being a standard normal variate or, equivalently

$$r(t) \sim \mathcal{N}\left(\theta + (r_0 - \theta)e^{-at},\ \sigma\sqrt{\frac{1 - e^{-2at}}{2a}}\right). \qquad (3.16)$$

For very small values of the mean-reversion speed a, the Taylor expansion of the standard deviation is $\sigma\sqrt{t}$. Thus, initially, the short rate r appears to diffuse like a standard Wiener process, albeit with a drift. For large values of t, however, the distribution converges to a stationary form of $\mathcal{N}\left(\theta, \sigma/\sqrt{2a}\right)$. This highlights that mean-reverting processes of the type of equation (3.8) (also known as Ornstein–Uhlenbeck processes) converge to an equilibrium state for the distribution over long time scales.

Equation (3.8) can be extended to allow for a, θ and σ to be a function of t. The distribution resulting from a so-generalised Ornstein–Uhlenbeck process is still Gaussian and can be derived analytically as outlined above, i.e.

$$\mathrm{d}f = a(t)\left[\theta(t) - f\right]\mathrm{d}t + \sigma(t)\,\mathrm{d}W_t \qquad (3.17)$$

leads to

$$f(t) = \mathrm{e}^{-A(t)}\left(f_0 + \int_0^t a(s)\theta(s)\mathrm{e}^{A(s)}\,\mathrm{d}s\right) + \mathrm{e}^{-A(t)}\int_0^t \sigma(s)\mathrm{e}^{A(s)}\,\mathrm{d}W_s \qquad (3.18)$$

with $A(s) := \int_0^s a(u)\,\mathrm{d}u$ and the distribution reads

$$f(t) \sim \mathcal{N}\left(\left[\mathrm{e}^{-A(t)}\left(f_0 + \int_0^t a(s)\theta(s)\mathrm{e}^{A(s)}\,\mathrm{d}s\right)\right],\ \left[\mathrm{e}^{-A(t)}\sqrt{\int_0^t \sigma^2(s)\mathrm{e}^{2A(s)}\mathrm{d}s}\right]\right).$$
$$(3.19)$$

3.4 LOGNORMAL PROCESSES

The immediately natural extensions of normal processes are all those that can be mapped back to a normal process. For instance, if we were interested in modelling a quantity S that is subject to a mean-reversion effect, but cannot become negative, we could set $f := \ln S$ and describe the behaviour of S indirectly by saying that f satisfies equation (3.17). If we are then still interested in the explicit form of the stochastic differential equation governing the dynamics of S, we can apply Itô's lemma to the inverse transformation $S = \mathrm{e}^f$ to derive $\mathrm{d}S$. This is exactly how we obtain the following stochastic differential equation for a mean-reverting lognormal process:

$$\frac{\mathrm{d}S}{S} = \left(a(t)\left[\theta(t) - \ln S\right] + \frac{1}{2}\sigma^2(t)\right)\mathrm{d}t + \sigma(t)\,\mathrm{d}W_t. \qquad (3.20)$$

The distribution of $\ln S$ is obviously given by (3.19).

3.5 THE MARKOVIAN WIENER PROCESS EMBEDDING DIMENSION

Most systems of stochastic differential equations that we use for modelling financially relevant quantities are of the form

$$\mathrm{d}\boldsymbol{f} = \boldsymbol{b}(t, \boldsymbol{f})\,\mathrm{d}t + A(t, \boldsymbol{f})\cdot\mathrm{d}\boldsymbol{W}_t \qquad (3.21)$$

with $\boldsymbol{f}, \boldsymbol{b} \in \mathbb{R}^n$, $\boldsymbol{W}_t \in \mathbb{R}^m$, $A \in \mathbb{R}^{n\times m}$ and $m \leqslant n$. The function $\boldsymbol{b}(t, \boldsymbol{f})$ is frequently called the *drift* of the stochastic process, and the matrix $A(t, \boldsymbol{f})$ may be called the *driving matrix* or, following the nomenclature of Karatzas and Shreve [KS91], the *dispersion matrix*.

Clearly, when viewed as embedded in the full state space dimensionality n, stochastic systems of the kind (3.21) are by definition *Markovian*, since none of the terms depend on the past or the future. Still, the reader may have come across the phrase that certain models are *not* Markovian, even though they can be described by an equation like (3.21). This slightly misleading notion usually arises when it is intended to express the fact that it is not possible to construct a recombining tree for f in the Wiener process dimensionality m. Of course, for all processes of the form (3.21) it is theoretically possible to construct a recombining tree when the embedding dimensionality of the tree is chosen to be n. However, one cannot in general reduce the embedding dimension of the tree to m. Whenever it is possible, though, the full system (3.21) may be called *Markovian Wiener process embedding dimension reducible*, or simply *reducible*. A process of the type of equation (3.21) is reducible if there is a bijection

$$f(t) \iff W_t. \tag{3.22}$$

In other words, given knowledge of the exact state of the m-dimensional driving Wiener process at any one time, it must be possible to identify exactly the values of all state variables in the vector f. This means that the process for f must not depend on the path that W took to get to its state at time t. Only then can we assign unique transition densities to each branch of the m-dimensional recombining tree[1].

The above considerations arise naturally in the context of Heath–Jarrow–Morton models [HJM92a] of the yield curve. It can be shown that HJM models for the instantaneous forward rates $f(t, T)$ at time t for time T are reducible only for a very specific choice of the instantaneous volatility function $\sigma(t, T)$, and the specific choice leads to what is sometimes referred to as the *generalised Hull–White* model. Otherwise, the Markovian embedding dimension of any HJM forward rate model is infinite, even though only a few driving Wiener processes may be involved! Another yield curve modelling family that is not reducible is given by the Brace–Gatarek–Musiela/Jamshidian market models which always require as many dimensions as there are market rates in the model due to the specific state dependence of the BGM/J drift terms. For those problems, Monte Carlo methods are the numerical technique of choice since the difficulties involved with high-dimensionality are negligible for Monte Carlo methods, whilst for trees and lattice methods only a few dimensions are realistically tractable.

3.6 BESSEL PROCESSES

A *Bessel* process R_t of dimension ν is given by the L_2-norm of a ν-dimensional Wiener process and probably owes its name to the spherical symmetry imposed by the L_2-norm:

$$R_t := \|W_t\| = \sqrt{\sum_{i=1}^{\nu} W_{i\,t}^2}. \tag{3.23}$$

---

[1]The discussion can equally be adapted to cater for a PDE formulation of the solution technique. It is only for the sake of clarity and convenience that we restrict the explanation to trees.

It can be shown[2] that a Bessel process of dimension ν satisfies the stochastic differential equation

$$dR_t = \frac{\nu - 1}{2} \frac{dt}{R_t} + dW_t \tag{3.24}$$

generated by a one-dimensional standard Wiener process dW_t.

3.7 CONSTANT ELASTICITY OF VARIANCE PROCESSES

The *constant elasticity of variance* process [Bec80, Sch89] is given by

$$df = \sigma f^\gamma dW_t \quad \text{for } \gamma \geqslant 0 \tag{3.25}$$

whereby I have omitted any drift terms. It has been used extensively throughout all areas of financial modelling, including equity, interest rates, commodities and many other financial values. The reason that the CEV process is very popular is that it can reproduce a slightly curved implied volatility skew for plain vanilla options priced on the basis of it. For $\gamma < 1$, the skew is negative with options at low strikes having a higher implied volatility than those at high strikes. For $\gamma > 1$, the skew resulting from the CEV process is positive and describes the option prices observed in some commodity markets reasonably well. The formal solutions for the SDE (3.25) can be found in [BS96]. Alternatively, in the context of the BGM modelling framework for interest rates, a good summary of the properties of the CEV process and simple Call and Put option pricing formulae resulting from it can also be found in [AA00]. As for Monte Carlo simulations of the process (3.25), we will come back to the CEV process in section 4.3.

The CEV process has a direct relation to the Bessel process. The transformation

$$R := \frac{1}{1 - \gamma} f^{1-\gamma} \tag{3.26}$$

turns the SDE of the CEV process into that of a Bessel process of dimension

$$\nu = \frac{1 - 2\beta}{1 - \beta}. \tag{3.27}$$

This means that, for $0 \leqslant \beta \leqslant \frac{1}{2}$, the CEV process is equivalent to a Bessel process of a fractional dimension between 0 and 1, and can thus be absorbed at zero. For $\beta > \frac{1}{2}$, however, the CEV process corresponds to a Bessel process of *negative dimension* and cannot attain zero.

An interesting question in the context of section 3.5 is if a system of n equations of type (3.25) is reducible to the dimensionality m of the driving Wiener process $W_t \in \mathbb{R}^m$. Clearly for $\gamma = 0$ or $\gamma = 1$, the process is reducible since we then have the standard normal or lognormal process, respectively. In general, however, as we discussed in section 3.5, for this to be the case, we must be able to write

$$f(t) = F(W_t, t) \quad \text{for } f \in \mathbb{R}^n \quad \text{and} \quad W \in \mathbb{R}^m \quad \text{with } m \leqslant n \tag{3.28}$$

---

[2] See [KS91] p. 159, eq (3.16).

for some function $F(W_t, t)$. The application of Itô's lemma to F then yields

$$dF = \partial_W F \, dW + \left(\partial_t F + \tfrac{1}{2}\partial^2_{WW} F\right) dt = df = f^\gamma \, dW = F^\gamma \, dW. \qquad (3.29)$$

This means

$$\partial_W F = F^\gamma \qquad (3.30)$$

whose solution is

$$F = \left((1-\gamma)W + F_0^{(1-\gamma)}\right)^{\frac{1}{1-\gamma}} + g(t) \qquad (3.31)$$

for some function $g(t)$ with $\gamma \neq 1$, which we had already excluded anyway. The second condition to be satisfied by F that resulted from (3.28) is

$$\partial_t F + \tfrac{1}{2}\partial_{WW} F = 0 \qquad (3.32)$$

which, together with (3.31), implies

$$\dot{g}(t) = -\tfrac{1}{2}\gamma F^{2\gamma-1}. \qquad (3.33)$$

This last equation can only hold if g is a constant and $\gamma = 0$ because otherwise we would have a pure function of t on the left-hand side, and a function of t *and* W on the right-hand side, which is clearly a contradiction. In other words, the CEV process is path-dependent, and a multi-dimensional CEV process driven by fewer Wiener processes than there are CEV state variables cannot be reduced.

3.8   DISPLACED DIFFUSION

Another process formulation that also gives rise to an implied volatility skew, in fact very similar to that of the CEV process, is the *displaced diffusion* process [Rub83]

$$dS = \mu S \, dt + \sigma_{\text{displaced diffusion}}(S + \theta) \, dW. \qquad (3.34)$$

If we use the map

$$\theta = -\log_2(\gamma) \cdot S_0 \qquad (3.35)$$

the displaced diffusion process can be used as a very good numerical proxy for the skew one would obtain from the CEV process, only with a somewhat more pronounced curvature (which is probably desirable). Unlike the CEV process, though, the displaced diffusion process is extremely easy to solve and numerically fast. Clearly we need to rescale the volatility similarly to how we translate from relative to absolute volatilities:

$$S_0 \cdot \sigma_{\text{lognormal}} = (S_0 + \theta) \cdot \sigma_{\text{displaced diffusion}}. \qquad (3.36)$$

As can be seen from (3.35), for $\gamma = 1$, the displaced diffusion process becomes ordinary geometric Brownian motion, i.e. a lognormal process. For $\gamma = \tfrac{1}{2}$ the skew of the displaced diffusion process is approximately that of the square root process, and in the limit $\gamma \to 0$ we arrive at the normal evolution, similar to the CEV equation (3.25).

The evolution of S subject to (3.34) out to a time horizon T is given by

$$S_T = (S_0 + \theta) \cdot e^{\left[\left(\mu - \frac{1}{2}\sigma_{dd}^2\right)T + \sigma_{dd}\sqrt{T}z\right]} - \theta \qquad \text{with } z \sim \mathcal{N}(0, 1). \qquad (3.37)$$

In the context of statistics, the distribution of S_T is also known as a *Johnson I distribution* [JKB94, Joh49, Whe80].

4

Process-driven Sampling

In financial engineering and option pricing, we frequently wish to calculate the expectation of functionals of the time evolution of one or more underlying assets. In order to do this, one typically has to simulate a stochastic process and evaluate a pricing functional for each simulated path. In this chapter, some of the key concepts involved in this task are explained. Also, I will demonstrate how different methods work and recommend which technique is best for which class of problem.

4.1 STRONG VERSUS WEAK CONVERGENCE

The numerical approximation of the solution of a stochastic differential equation amounts to a computing scheme that creates a sequence of numbers representing the time-discretisation of a specific sample path of a mathematically defined stochastic process. For ordinary differential equations, there is a natural meaning to the concept of *convergence* of a numerical method to the solution. For SDEs, the situation is different. The concept of *strong* convergence can be seen as the equivalent to convergence for ODEs since it requires that the numerical approximation to a given path of the stochastic process matches the truly exact solution at any point along the path. However, the solution to a stochastic differential equation at any time horizon, unlike ODEs, is not a single number but a (possibly multi-dimensional) *distribution*. As for this distribution, we are often not interested in obtaining its exact functional shape but rather in the expectation of some function (typically a payoff profile) over that distribution.

A time-discretised approximation Y_δ of steps not larger than δ is said to be of general *strong* convergence order γ if for any time horizon T the approximation $Y_\delta(T)$ is guaranteed to converge to the exact solution $X(T)$ in expectation by absolute difference as

$$E\big[\,|\,X(T) - Y_\delta(T)\,|\,\big] \leqslant c\,\delta^\gamma \qquad (4.1)$$

for all δ smaller than some positive δ_0 and some constant c.

In contrast to the strong convergence criterion by absolute difference, *weak* convergence of order β only requires that the numerically calculated expectation of any function $g(\cdot)$ which is $2(\beta + 1)$ times continuously differentiable and of polynomial growth converges to the exact equivalent. In other words, for any $g \in C_P^{2(\beta+1)}$

$$\big|\,E\big[g\,(X(T))\big] - E\big[g\,(Y_\delta(T))\big]\,\big| \leqslant c\,\delta^\beta \qquad (4.2)$$

must hold for all δ smaller than some positive δ_0 and some constant c.

A consequence of the above definitions of strong and weak convergence is that many schemes of a given strong convergence order are of a higher weak convergence order. An example of this is the standard Euler scheme which, whilst being an order $\frac{1}{2}$ strong scheme, is also an order 1 weak scheme, given suitable smoothness and growth conditions on the drift and diffusion coefficients. It is therefore not surprising that in general any method of higher convergence order for the strong criterion also turns out to be of superior performance for the purpose of option pricing. Another point of interest is that, for many schemes, the convergence order, weak or strong, which they are guaranteed to have for any general SDE may actually be exceeded for specific stochastic differential equations. In particular, for the kind of SDEs that we encounter in finance this is often the case.

4.2 NUMERICAL SOLUTIONS

Whilst there are a great many different kinds of numerical schemes for the solution of stochastic differential equations, and the best reference is almost certainly the book by Kloeden and Platen [KP99], I now briefly introduce and discuss the Euler and the Milstein schemes. The starting point in both cases is the following general form of a stochastic differential equation:

$$dX = a \, dt + b \, dW. \tag{4.3}$$

Note that both a and b can be functions of the process variable X and time. In the multi-dimensional case of m state variables X_i driven by d independent Wiener processes, we have

$$dX_i = a_i(t, X) \, dt + \sum_{j=1}^{d} b_{ij}(t, X) \, dW_j. \tag{4.4}$$

4.2.1 The Euler Scheme

Denote the numerical approximation to the solution of (4.3) for a scheme over equal steps of size Δt at time $n \cdot \Delta t$ as $Y(t_n)$. The Euler scheme is then given by

$$Y(t_{n+1}) = Y(t_n) + a(t_n, Y(t_n)) \, \Delta t + b(t_n, Y(t_n)) \, \Delta W. \tag{4.5}$$

The Euler scheme is of strong convergence order $\frac{1}{2}$ which means we can always fall back on this workhorse of a numerical procedure to test any other method.

In financial applications, we are often interested to represent the evolution of an asset by a stochastic process. The most common assumption is probably that of geometric Brownian motion:

$$\frac{dS}{S} = (r - d) \, dt + \sigma \, dW. \tag{4.6}$$

In this case, the Euler scheme becomes

$$S(t_{n+1}) = S(t_n) \cdot \{1 + (r - d)\Delta t + \sigma \Delta W\} \tag{4.7}$$

$$= S(t_n) \cdot \left\{1 + \sigma z \sqrt{\Delta t} + (r - d)\Delta t\right\} \quad \text{with} \quad z \sim \mathcal{N}(0, 1).$$

In the multi-dimensional case, the Euler scheme is

$$Y_i(t_{n+1}) = Y_i(t_n) + a_i(t_n, Y(t_n)) \, \Delta t + \sum_{j=1}^{d} b_{ij}(t_n, Y(t_n)) \, \Delta W_j. \tag{4.8}$$

4.2.2 The Milstein Scheme

The Milstein scheme involves the addition of the next order terms of the Itô–Taylor expansion of equation (4.3). This gives

$$Y(t_{n+1}) = Y(t_n) + a(t_n, Y(t_n)) \, \Delta t + b(t_n, Y(t_n)) \, \Delta W + \tfrac{1}{2} bb' \left[\Delta W^2 - \Delta t \right] \qquad (4.9)$$

with

$$b' = \frac{\partial b(t, X)}{\partial X}. \qquad (4.10)$$

For the case of geometric Brownian, this results in

$$S(t_{n+1}) = S(t_n) \cdot \left\{ 1 + \left(r - d - \tfrac{1}{2}\sigma^2 \right) \Delta t + \sigma \Delta W + \tfrac{1}{2}\sigma^2 (\Delta W)^2 \right\} \qquad (4.11)$$

$$= S(t_n) \cdot \left\{ 1 + \sigma z \sqrt{\Delta t} + \left(r - d + \tfrac{1}{2}\sigma^2 \left[z^2 - 1 \right] \right) \Delta t \right\}.$$

Although the Milstein scheme is definitely manageable in the one-dimensional case, its general multi-dimensional extension is not as straightforward as one may expect. It requires not only the drawing of standard normal variates for the simulation of the standard Wiener process increments ΔW for each dimension, but additional ones to account for the Itô integrals involving the mixing terms $\sum_{j=1}^{d} b_{ij}(t, X) \, dW_j$.

4.2.3 Transformations

Let us have a closer look at the difference between the Milstein scheme and the Euler scheme for geometric Brownian motion. The additional terms of the Milstein scheme amount to adding

$$\tfrac{1}{2}\sigma^2 \left[\Delta W^2 - \Delta t \right]$$

to the terms in the braces on the right-hand side of (4.7). If we compare the two schemes for geometric Brownian motion with the exact analytical solution

$$S(t_{n+1}) = S(t_n) \cdot e^{\left(r - d - \frac{1}{2}\sigma^2 \right) \Delta t + \sigma \Delta W} \qquad (4.12)$$

we find that the Milstein scheme essentially just adds all the terms that make the scheme exact up to order $\mathcal{O}(\Delta t)$ in expectation and variance. We could have achieved almost the same effect by simply transforming the original equation for geometric Brownian motion (4.6) to logarithmic coordinates by application of Itô's lemma to obtain

$$d \ln S = \left(r - d - \tfrac{1}{2}\sigma^2 \right) dt + \sigma \, dW. \qquad (4.13)$$

This similarity is not coincidental. In fact, in particular for the equations we deal with in finance, it is almost always preferable to transform the original SDE to a more amenable form and then simply use the original Euler scheme.

Let us now demonstrate the similarity between the Milstein scheme and a suitably chosen transformation using the example of a mean-reverting square-root process

$$dv = a(\theta - v) \, dt + \lambda \sqrt{v} \, dW. \qquad (4.14)$$

This is essentially the Cox–Ingersoll–Ross interest rate model [CIR85] if we interpret v as the short rate. This kind of process is also popular to describe the behaviour of stochastic volatility, see e.g. [Hes93]. The Milstein discretisation scheme of (4.14) is

$$\Delta v = \left[a(\theta - v) - \tfrac{1}{4}\lambda^2\right] \Delta t + \lambda\sqrt{v}\sqrt{\Delta t}\, z + \tfrac{1}{4}\lambda^2 \Delta t\, z^2 \qquad (4.15)$$

where we have substituted $\sqrt{\Delta t}\, z$ with $z \sim \mathcal{N}(0, 1)$ for the Wiener process increment ΔW. Now, let us consider a generic function u of v, i.e. $u = u(v)$. Itô's lemma gives us the stochastic differential equation for u:

$$du = \left[\frac{\partial u}{\partial v}a(\theta - v) + \frac{1}{2}\frac{\partial^2 u}{\partial v^2}\lambda^2 v\right] dt + \frac{\partial u}{\partial v}\lambda\sqrt{v}\, dW. \qquad (4.16)$$

We should now make a fortuitous choice of $u(v)$ so that the new equation is better behaved. This is done by ensuring that the term in front of the driving process becomes independent on the state variable. In other words, we choose

$$\frac{\partial u}{\partial v} \propto \sqrt{v}^{-1} \quad \text{or specifically} \quad u = \sqrt{v}. \qquad (4.17)$$

This gives us

$$du = \frac{1}{2u}\left[a(\theta - u^2) - \frac{1}{4}\lambda^2\right] dt + \frac{1}{2}\lambda\, dW \qquad (4.18)$$

and finally we have the following Euler scheme for the transformed SDE:

$$\Delta u = \frac{1}{2u}\left[a(\theta - u^2) - \frac{1}{4}\lambda^2\right] \Delta t + \frac{1}{2}\lambda\sqrt{\Delta t}\, z. \qquad (4.19)$$

In order to compare the convergence order in v using the Euler scheme in the transformed equation and the Milstein scheme in the original equation, we now calculate

$$(v(u + \Delta u_{\text{Euler}}) - v(u)) - \Delta v_{\text{Milstein}} = \left((u + \Delta u_{\text{Euler}})^2 - u^2\right) - \Delta v_{\text{Milstein}} \qquad (4.20)$$

$$= 2u\,\Delta u_{\text{Euler}} + \Delta u^2 - \Delta v_{\text{Milstein}}$$

$$= 0 + \mathcal{O}(\sqrt{\Delta t}^3).$$

The above relationship between a transformation to an SDE whose stochastic term no longer contains the state variable and the Milstein scheme holds in general. Given the general SDE

$$dv = a(t, v)\, dt + b(t, v)\, dW \qquad (4.21)$$

the Milstein scheme is

$$\Delta v = \left[a - \tfrac{1}{2}b\,\partial_v b\right] \Delta t + b\sqrt{\Delta t}\, z + \tfrac{1}{2}b\,\partial_v b\,\Delta t\, z^2 \qquad (4.22)$$

with $z \sim \mathcal{N}(0, 1)$. For a general transformation $u = F(v)$ to a new state variable u and the inverse transformation $v = G(u)$, the SDE (4.21) becomes

$$du = \left[F'a + \tfrac{1}{2}F''b^2\right] dt + F'b\, dW \qquad (4.23)$$

by virtue of Itô's lemma. Given the choice

$$F'(v) = \frac{1}{b(t,v)} \quad \text{which leads to} \quad F''(v) = -\frac{1}{b^2}\partial_v b \quad (4.24)$$

the Euler scheme in the transformed variable reads

$$\Delta u = \left[\frac{a}{b} - \frac{1}{2}\partial_v b\right]\Delta t + \sqrt{\Delta t}\, z. \quad (4.25)$$

In order to compare, we calculate the Taylor expansion of the inverse transformation

$$v(u+\Delta u) = v(u) + G'(u)\Delta u + \tfrac{1}{2}G''(u)\Delta u^2 + \mathcal{O}(\Delta u^3). \quad (4.26)$$

Since

$$\frac{dv}{du} = \left(\frac{du}{dv}\right)^{-1}, \quad \text{i.e.} \quad G'(u) = \frac{1}{F'(G(u))} = b(t, G(u)) \quad (4.27)$$

and thus

$$G''(u) = G'\partial_v b = b\,\partial_v b \quad (4.28)$$

we have

$$v(u+\Delta u) - v(u) = \left[a - \tfrac{1}{2}b\,\partial_v b\right]\Delta t + b\sqrt{\Delta t}\,z + \tfrac{1}{2}b\,\partial_v b\,\Delta t\,z^2 + \mathcal{O}(\Delta t^{\frac{3}{2}}). \quad (4.29)$$

As we can see, the Euler scheme in the transformed equation leads to a procedure that is equal in convergence up to order $\mathcal{O}(\Delta t)$ (inclusive) to the Milstein scheme in the original variable. An additional benefit of transformations that removes all dependence of the multiplicative factor in front of the driving Wiener process increments on the state variables is that the resulting equations become readily amenable to a particularly simple predictor–corrector scheme. Since this predictor–corrector scheme is of weak convergence order 1 for the transformed variable, we typically obtain an integration scheme of weak convergence order higher than 1 for the original state variable without the need for a complicated integration algorithm that requires the drawing of more normal variates than we have driving Wiener processes over any one time step.

4.2.4 Predictor–Corrector

One way to describe the idea behind predictor–corrector methods for stochastic differential equations is as follows. Given a time-discretised approximation to a general SDE such as equation (4.4), we know that taking an Euler step as in (4.8) ignores the fact that the coefficients a_i and b_{ij} *actually change along the path over the time step* Δt. Now, if that is so, wouldn't it be better to use an approximate average value for those coefficients along the path over the finite time step Δt? Since the values of the coefficients depend on the state variables themselves, which we don't know, we need to approximate those first. The simplest predictor–corrector scheme, which incidentally is of weak convergence order 1, is thus as follows. First take an Euler step as in equation (4.8) to arrive at the *predictor*

$$\bar{Y}_i(t_{n+1}) = Y_i(t_n) + a_i(t_n, \boldsymbol{Y}(t_n))\,\Delta t + \sum_{j=1}^{d} b_{ij}(t_n, \boldsymbol{Y}(t_n))\,\Delta W_j. \tag{4.30}$$

Next, select two weighting coefficients α and η in the interval $[0, 1]$, usually near $\frac{1}{2}$, and calculate the *corrector*

$$Y_i(t_{n+1}) = Y_i(t_n) + \left\{\alpha\,\bar{a}_i(t_{n+1}, \bar{\boldsymbol{Y}}(t_{n+1}); \eta) + (1 - \alpha)\bar{a}_i(t_n, \boldsymbol{Y}(t_n); \eta)\right\} \Delta t \tag{4.31}$$

$$+ \sum_{j=1}^{m} \left\{\eta\,b_{ij}(t_{n+1}, \bar{\boldsymbol{Y}}(t_{n+1})) + (1 - \eta)b_{ij}(t_n, \boldsymbol{Y}(t_n))\right\} \sqrt{\Delta t}\, z_j$$

with

$$\bar{a}_i(t, \boldsymbol{Y}; \eta) := a_i(t, \boldsymbol{Y}) - \eta \sum_{j=1}^{m} \sum_{k=1}^{d} b_{kj}(t, \boldsymbol{Y})\partial_{Y_k} b_{ij}(t, \boldsymbol{Y}). \tag{4.32}$$

Clearly, this scheme is very easy to implement, in particular for the special case that the coefficients b_{ij} don't depend on the state variables.

4.3 SPURIOUS PATHS

Anyone who implements the straightforward Euler scheme (4.7) for geometric Brownian motion will notice a strange thing occurring every now and then: some paths cross zero! Clearly, geometric Brownian motion should never even reach the point zero, let alone cross it. The reason why this happens is simple. The scheme (4.7) is only an approximation and only guaranteed to converge to the mathematically consistent description of the geometric Wiener process in the limit of ever smaller time steps Δt. In any simulation with a finite step size, it is only a matter of time until you draw a normal variate z that satisfies

$$z < -\frac{1 + (r - d)\Delta t}{\sigma\sqrt{\Delta t}} \tag{4.33}$$

and thus makes $S(t_{n+1})$ negative. For geometric Brownian motion, this phenomenon disappears when we use an Euler discretisation of the transformed stochastic differential equation (4.13). However, for other processes such as the CEV process

$$dS = \mu S\,dt + S^\gamma\,dW \tag{4.34}$$

the transformation to a constant coefficient in front of the Wiener process does not solve the problem. Setting

$$u = \frac{1}{1 - \gamma} S^{1-\gamma} \tag{4.35}$$

results in the transformed SDE

$$du = \left\{\mu\left[(1 - \gamma)u\right]^{\frac{\gamma}{\gamma-1}} - \frac{1}{2}\frac{\gamma}{(1 - \gamma)}\frac{1}{u}\right\} dt + dW. \tag{4.36}$$

For $\gamma \in (0, 1)$, this gives an Euler scheme that for certain paths, specifically for u approaching zero, can result in u crossing the zero line, which is clearly inconsistent with the continuous description of the CEV process (4.34). After all, for a generic real value of γ, there is no real value of S that satisfies the inverse transformation

$$S = \left[(1 - \gamma)u \right]^{\frac{1}{1-\gamma}} \tag{4.37}$$

for $u < 0$. The solution to this puzzle is both unexpected and surprisingly simple: the CEV process (4.34) with $\gamma < \frac{1}{2}$ has a positive probability of absorption at zero[1]! Thus, the easiest way to fix the Euler scheme for (4.36) is to assume that any path that reaches or crosses zero actually represents a path that is absorbed at zero, and treat it exactly in that way. In fact, numerical tests of this way of handling the zero crossing show that they give the correct probability for absorption at zero for the CEV process, which is known analytically.

4.4 STRONG CONVERGENCE FOR EULER AND MILSTEIN

In order to demonstrate the difference in strong convergence behaviour between the Euler and the Milstein schemes, we begin by thinking about a *single* path of a standard Wiener process. In any numerical scheme, we can only ever handle a time-discretised version of a stochastic process. A practical criterion of the strong convergence behaviour of a numerical method is how finely we have to discretise to achieve a satisfactory accuracy. A sequence of subsequently refined discretisations of one and the same standard Wiener path starting at $W(0) = 0$ from $t = 0$ to $t = 1$ is shown in Figure 4.1. The straight line in the front of the figure is effectively a single step discretisation. The second line consists

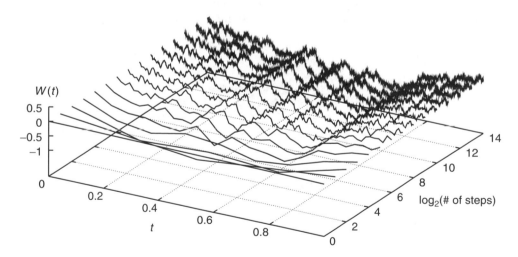

Figure 4.1 Increasing refinement in the discretised representation of one specific standard Wiener path

---

[1]To be precise, it can be reflecting or absorbing at zero depending both on the parameter γ and the chosen boundary conditions [BS96].

of two straight segments, the first one from $t = 0$ to $t = \frac{1}{2}$, and the second one from $t = \frac{1}{2}$ to $t = 1$, starting and ending in precisely the same points at $t = 0$ and $t = 1$ as the previous line. The third line then shares the exact same locations at $t = 0$, $t = \frac{1}{2}$ and $t = 1$ with the second line, but consists of four straight segments, introducing new abscissas at $t = \frac{1}{4}$ and $t = \frac{3}{4}$. This sequence of iterated refinement to construct in the limit a path that is continuous but non-differentiable everywhere is also known as the *Brownian bridge* and was, incidentally, used historically for the first ever constructive proof of the existence of the mathematical concept of Brownian motion by N. Wiener in the 1920s. More details of the constructive mathematics are given in section 10.8.3.

Each of the discretisations depicted in Figure 4.1 can be seen as a sequence of Wiener path increments ΔW for a given time step size Δt. The application of all of the discretisations in Figure 4.1 in the Euler scheme (4.7) then gives another sequence of increasingly refined approximations for the idealised geometric Brownian motion corresponding to the driving Wiener path. This is shown in Figure 4.2. Note that the paths of ever increasingly refined numerical approximations of the geometric Brownian motion are no longer guaranteed to end in the same point at $t = 1$, or indeed at any point. It is the convergence to the exact solution at $t = 1$ which we will later use as a criterion for convergence.

Equally to using the Wiener path increments in the Euler scheme, we can instead apply them to the Milstein scheme (4.11). The result is shown in Figure 4.3. Again, none of the individual discretised paths need to be in exactly the same place at any point along the paths. However, in the limit of ever refining discretisations, the numerical scheme is guaranteed to converge to the exact solution. A real test for the strong convergence behaviour would have to demonstrate the power law (4.1). However, at this point we only show what the improvement of the Milstein scheme over the Euler method means for the convergence to the value of the geometric Brownian process at the time horizon $T = 1$ for the increasingly refined discretisations in Figure 4.4. Clearly, the Milstein scheme

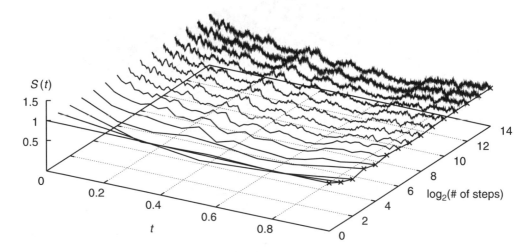

Figure 4.2 Increasing refinement of a geometric Brownian path integrated from the Wiener path shown in Figure 4.1 using the Euler scheme given by equation (4.7) with $(r - d) = 1.1\%$ and $\sigma = 81.6\%$

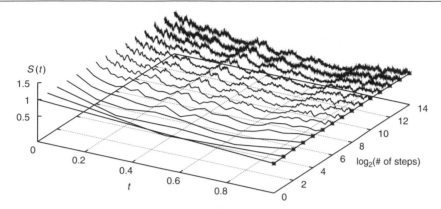

Figure 4.3 Increasing refinement of a geometric Brownian path integrated from the Wiener path shown in Figure 4.1 using the Milstein scheme given by equation (4.11) with $(r - d) = 1.1\%$ and $\sigma = 81.6\%$

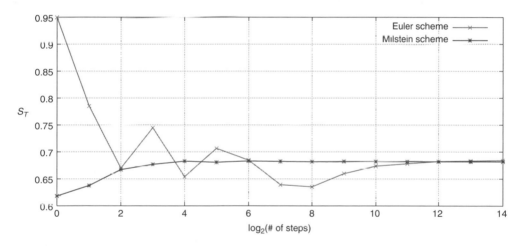

Figure 4.4 Comparison of pathwise convergence behaviour in the terminal value of the spot (S_T) for a geometric Brownian path integrated from the Wiener path shown in Figure 4.1 using the Euler and Milstein schemes given by equations (4.7) and (4.11)

appears to be the superior method. Since we know the analytical solution of the SDE for geometric Brownian motion (4.6), we can gain additional insight into why this is so. The exact solution is

$$S_T = S_0 \cdot e^{\left(r - d - \frac{1}{2}\sigma^2\right)T + \sigma z \sqrt{T}}. \tag{4.38}$$

From this, we can immediately see that the Milstein scheme is, in expectation and variance, unlike the Euler method, consistent with an $\mathcal{O}(\Delta t)$ Taylor expansion of the exact solution. Of course we would in practice almost always use an exact solution when it is available. Exceptions may be cases where the generation of sample paths from a numerical approximation is more efficient whilst sufficiently accurate, or when we simply wish to test an analytical solution by different means.

5
Correlation and Co-movement

Correlation, or more generally co-movement, is one of the single greatest challenges facing quantitative analysts and risk managers today. Its effects are present in many calculations that are widely taken for granted. The pricing of many derivative contracts such as quantos, rainbows, options on baskets and many others depends on some kind of co-dependence assumptions. Also, any (investment) bank's self-assessment of exposure, frequently calculated as the Value at Risk (VaR) quantile, depends strongly on the assumptions about co-dependence between all of the involved market risk factors. To model the co-movement of all the market observables constituting an entire organisation's risk in an adequate way is still deemed untractable, and most companies resort to the use of historical data in order to estimate their firm-wide capital needs. Since historical data can only ever show you risk with respect to (co-)movements that already occurred in the past, but is oblivious to hitherto unseen co-dependent market moves, and also doesn't know about new developments in the markets, scenario analysis is usually added to assess the riskiness of a company's standing. The scenarios used for these analyses in turn are almost never constructed anywhere nearly along the lines of approach taken for derivatives pricing. Whilst the constructed scenarios virtually always represent the breakdown of linearly correlated (log)normal evolution, correlated (geometric) Brownian motion is still the default method for modelling the interdependence between the various underlyings affecting the value of a derivatives contract. This inconsistency becomes even more startling if we take into account that only moves of a few standard deviations, rarely more than two to three, are considered for scenario analyses whose purpose is to complement a VaR calculation. On the other hand, the quoted volatility smile and skew surfaces indicate that derivatives traders are sometimes concerned with moves in excess of four or sometimes even five standard deviations. The desire of exotic derivatives traders for their pricing tools to realistically model the co-dependence of the financial observables that are the underlyings of a given exotic deal is motivated by the fact that whilst hedging is possible with respect to moves in the underlyings, correlation or co-dependence is still largely impossible to protect against[1]. A simple way to summarise the problem of unhedgeable quantities is '*If you can't hedge it, you better guess it right*'. The most prominent reason for the proliferation of the assumption of linear correlation for the pricing of exotic derivatives is its ease of use and (approximate) tractability. In fact, there are few analytical approximations for exotic derivatives of several underlyings that do not use the assumption of linear correlation, if any. And when it comes to numerical solutions, the only methods that realistically and in a feasible way allow the modelling of several underlyings that co-depend in any fashion other than linear correlation are probably Monte Carlo methods, and this is what this chapter is about.

---

[1] Some types of correlation are starting to become almost tradable, such as Nikkei/USD.

5.1   MEASURES FOR CO-DEPENDENCE

Marginal Distributions

Given the joint distribution density $\psi(x, y)$ of the two variables x and y, the *marginal* distribution density function of x is defined as

$$\psi_x(x) = \int \psi(x, y) \, dy \tag{5.1}$$

and analogously

$$\psi_y(y) = \int \psi(x, y) \, dx. \tag{5.2}$$

The marginal distribution density of any one of the two variables is nothing other than the probability density disregarding the value of the second variable.

Independence

Two variates x and y are considered *independent* if their joint distribution density function separates into the product of their individual distribution density functions, i.e.

$$\psi(x, y) = \psi_x(x)\psi_y(y). \tag{5.3}$$

Linear Correlation

We recall from equation (2.8) that the *linear correlation* $\rho_{xy} := Corr[x, y]$ of two variates x and y is defined as

$$\rho_{xy} = \frac{Cov[x, y]}{\sqrt{V[x]\,V[y]}}$$

$$= \frac{\displaystyle\int xy\psi(x, y)\,dx\,dy - \int x\psi_x(x)\,dx \int y\psi_y(y)\,dy}{\sqrt{\displaystyle\int x^2\psi_x(x)\,dx - \left[\int x\psi_x(x)\,dx\right]^2}\sqrt{\displaystyle\int y^2\psi_y(y)\,dy - \left[\int y\psi_y(y)\,dy\right]^2}}. \tag{5.4}$$

Linear correlation is a good measure for the co-dependence of normal variates. For distributions that are nearly normal, it still serves well to measure to what extent two marginal distributions depend on each other. However, the further we go away from the normal distribution, the more misleading the concept of linear correlation becomes. An extreme example is the case when the variate pair (x, y) can take on the possible combinations $\{(0, 1), (0, -1), (1, 0), (-1, 0)\}$ with equal probability $\frac{1}{4}$, as illustrated in Figure 5.1. The linear correlation of the co-dependent variates x and y for this discrete distribution is identically zero, which is clearly misleading. In fact, they are strongly dependent in this case. Given the variate x to be zero, we have two possible combinations for y: plus or minus one. However, for x to be non-zero, y is fully determined: it has to be zero. In

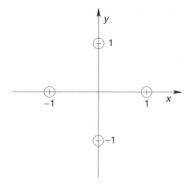

Figure 5.1 An example of a discrete distribution of two variates with zero correlation but strong dependence

strongly non-normal distributions like this example, linear correlation can actually conceal the strong co-dependence information contained in the full joint distribution.

Another problem with linear correlation is that it misleads one to believe that given the marginal distributions and the correlation of two variates, we have all there is to know about the joint distribution. A special case when knowledge of the marginal distribution densities $\psi_x(x)$ and $\psi_y(y)$ of two random variates x and y, and their correlation ρ_{xy}, is sufficient to reconstruct the joint distribution density $\psi(x, y)$ in a natural (but not unique) way is when both x and y are normal variates: an obvious candidate for the joint distribution is then the bivariate normal distribution[2]. In general, though, the inference

$$\psi_x(x), \ \psi_y(y), \ \rho_{xy} \Longrightarrow \psi(x, y)$$

cannot be made. What's more, for a given pair $\psi_x(x)$ and $\psi_y(y)$, there may not even be a joint distribution density $\psi(x, y)$ for every possible $\rho_{xy} \in [-1, 1]$. Finally, it should be mentioned that the correlation coefficient of two variates x and y is not invariant under non-linear transformations. An explicit example of this will be given in section 5.2.1. The linear correlation coefficient as defined in equation (5.4) above is sometimes also referred to as *Pearson's r*.

Spearman's Rho

Spearman's rho is closely linked to the concept of linear correlation. It is, in fact, defined as the linear correlation coefficient of the probability-transformed variates, i.e. of the variates transformed by their own cumulative marginal distribution functions. In other words, given two variables $x \in \mathbb{R}$ and $y \in \mathbb{R}$, their marginal distribution densities $\psi_x(x)$ and $\psi_y(y)$, their respective cumulative marginal distributions

$$\Psi_x(x) := \int_{-\infty}^{x} \psi_x(x') \, dx', \tag{5.5}$$

$$\Psi_y(y) := \int_{-\infty}^{y} \psi_y(y') \, dy' \tag{5.6}$$

---

[2]As explained later in section 5.2, this would correspond to the co-dependence structure being formed by the Gaussian copula. However, we could equally use any other copula to govern the co-dependence of the two marginally normally distributed variates x and y as long as the given correlation number is attainable by the co-dependence structure of two Gaussian densities under the chosen copula.

and their joint distribution density function $\psi(x, y)$, we have

$$\rho_S := \frac{\iint \Psi_x(x)\Psi_y(y)\psi(x, y)\,dx\,dy - \int \Psi_x(x)\psi_x(x)\,dx \int \Psi_y(y)\psi_y(y)\,dy}{\sqrt{\int \Psi_x(x)^2\psi_x(x)\,dx - \left[\int \Psi_x(x)\psi(x)\,dx\right]^2}\sqrt{\int \Psi_y(y)^2\psi_y(y)\,dy - \left[\int \Psi_y(y)\psi(y)\,dy\right]^2}}.$$

(5.7)

Since

$$\int \Psi_x(x)\psi_x(x)\,dx = \int_0^1 u\,du = \frac{1}{2}$$

(5.8)

and

$$\int \Psi_x(x)^2\psi_x(x)dx = \int_0^1 u^2\,du = \frac{1}{3}$$

(5.9)

Spearman's rho can be expressed as

$$\rho_S := 12\iint \Psi_x(x)\Psi_y(y)\psi(x, y)\,dxdy - 3.$$

(5.10)

Since Spearman's rho is defined on the cumulative probability functions of the individual variates, it is independent with respect to variable transformations[2], whether linear or not.

Kendall's Tau

Kendall's tau is a co-dependence measure that focuses on the idea of *concordance* and *discordance*. Two separately drawn pairs (x, y) and (x', y') from the same joint distribution density are considered to be concordant if both members of one pair are larger than the respective members of the other pair. They are said to be discordant if $x > x' \wedge y < y'$ or $x < x' \wedge y > y'$. Kendall's tau is defined as the difference between the probabilities of two such pairs being concordant and discordant, i.e.

$$\tau_K := Pr\left[(x - x')(y - y') > 0\right] - Pr\left[(x - x')(y - y') < 0\right].$$

(5.11)

Naturally, this means that $\tau_K \in [-1, 1]$. If we define the distributional densities and cumulative probabilities of x and y as in the previous section, and in addition

$$\Psi(x, y) := \int\!\!\!\int_{x',y'=-\infty}^{x,y} \psi(x', y')\,dx'\,dy'$$

(5.12)

it can be shown that an alternative formula for Kendall's tau for continuous distribution densities is

$$\tau_K = 4\iint \Psi(x, y)\psi(x, y)\,dxdy - 1.$$

(5.13)

---

[2]Provided they are not pathologically malicious.

Since Kendall's tau is defined on the joint cumulative probability, it is also invariant with respect to transformations[4].

Kendall's tau and Spearman's rho belong to the category of *rank correlations*. Rank correlations have the nice property that for any two marginal distribution densities $\psi_x(x)$ and $\psi_y(y)$, there always exists a joint distribution density $\psi(x, y)$ for every possible value in $[-1, 1]$ of the rank correlation.

5.2 COPULÆ

copula /'kɒpjʊlə/ *n.* (*pl.* **copulas**) *Logic & Gram.* a connecting word, esp. a part of the verb *be* connecting a subject and predicate. □ **copular** *adj.* [L (as co-, *apere* fasten)]

copulate /'kɒpjʊ,leɪt/ *v.intr.* (often foll. by *with*) have sexual intercourse.

A *copula* of two variables x and y is a cumulative probability function defined directly as a function of the marginal cumulative probabilities of x and y. A copula is thus a way to specify the co-dependence between two variates entirely independently on their individual marginal distribution. By this definition, a copula of n variables is a function $C : [0, 1]^n \rightarrow [0, 1]$. Reusing the definitions (5.5), (5.6) and (5.12) we can thus identify

$$\Psi(x, y) = C\big(\Psi_x(x), \Psi_y(y)\big). \tag{5.14}$$

For strictly increasing cumulative marginals $\Psi_x(x)$ and $\Psi_y(y)$, we can also write

$$C(u, v) = \Psi\left(\Psi_x^{-1}(u), \Psi_y^{-1}(v)\right). \tag{5.15}$$

The copula of independent variables, not surprisingly, is given by

$$C_{\text{independent}}(u, v) = u \cdot v. \tag{5.16}$$

By virtue of the definition on the cumulative marginal distribution functions, the copula of a set of variables (x, y) is invariant with respect to a set of strictly increasing transformations $(f(x), g(y))$. The differential of a copula is sometimes written by the notation $dC(u, v)$, which is to mean

$$dC(u, v) = \psi\left(\Psi_x^{-1}(u), \Psi_y^{-1}(v)\right) \left|\frac{\partial(u, v)}{\partial(x, y)}\right| du\, dv \tag{5.17}$$

with $u = \Psi_x(x)$ and $v = \Psi_y(y)$. In this notation, Kendall's tau appears as

$$\tau_K = 4 \iint_{[0,1]^2} C(u, v)\, dC(u, v) - 1. \tag{5.18}$$

Naturally, all of the above definitions extend to more than just two variables. Note that a sensible copula must be a function of all the cumulative marginal probabilities, and some kind of control parameters that determine the strength of co-dependence of the individual variables.

---

[4]Again: as long as they are reasonably benign.

Here is a puzzle for you: What does the following piece of code do and how is it connected to the excerpt from a dictionary at the beginning of section 5.2?

```
/d { rand 2147483647. div } def /r { d d d add add } def /normal { r r r r add add add 6
sub } def /T 415 def /dt 1 def /sigma .5 def /a -.25 def 0 0 dt T { pop dup a mul dt mul
sigma dt sqrt mul normal mul add dup dt exch rlineto add } for
```

5.2.1   The Gaussian Copula

The short explanation of the Gaussian copula mechanism is: generate a vector of correlated normal variates, transform them back to uniform variates by the aid of the cumulative normal probability function, and then map the variates into their individual marginal distributions using their respective inverse cumulative marginal probability functions. In other words, if we wish to construct the variate vector x subject to a vector of individual marginal distribution densities $\boldsymbol{\psi}_x(x) = \left(\psi_{x_1}(x_1), \psi_{x_2}(x_2), \ldots, \psi_{x_n}(x_n)\right)^\top$ coupled by the Gaussian copula controlled by the correlation matrix R, we need to proceed as follows.

- Find a suitable pseudo-square root A of R such that $R = A \cdot A^\top$. More on this in Chapter 6.
- Draw a vector $z \in \mathbb{R}^n$ of uncorrelated standard normal variates.
- Compute $\tilde{z} := A \cdot z$.
- Map $\tilde{z}$ back to a vector of uniform variates $v \in [0, 1]^n$ by setting $v_i = N(\tilde{z}_i)$.
- Construct the variate vector x by use of the inverse cumulative probability functions $x_i := \Psi_{x_i}^{-1}(v_i)$.

It is important to remember that the correlation coefficient governing the Gaussian copula can be very different from the linear correlation of the elements of the variate vector x. I give below two specific examples for this effect. First, however, there is one further point to mention. It can be shown [LMS01, Kau01] that Kendall's tau of two variables connected by a Gaussian copula with correlation coefficient ρ is given by

$$\tau_K = \frac{2}{\pi} \arcsin \rho. \tag{5.19}$$

Examples for the density of the Gaussian copula as defined in (5.17) are shown[4] in Figure 5.2.

Two Uniform Variates under the Gaussian Copula

Let us assume that for some purpose we would like to have two uniform variates that are correlated. Our first thought of constructing correlated uniforms is to transform two uncorrelated uniform variates u_1 and u_2 to the standard normal distribution by setting $z_i = N^{-1}(u_i)$, applying the conventional correlation transformation

$$\tilde{z}_1 = z_1, \tag{5.20}$$

$$\tilde{z}_2 = \rho z_1 + \sqrt{1 - \rho^2} z_2 \tag{5.21}$$

for some correlation coefficient $\rho \in [-1, 1]$ and transforming back to the unit square by the aid of $\tilde{u}_i = N(\tilde{z}_i)$. Naïvely, we now expect the co-dependent uniform variates to have a linear correlation coefficient in the range $[-1, 1]$. But little do we know... .

---

[4]The colour code in this and subsequent density diagrams, although only visible in the electronic version of this book on the accompanying CD, is as follows: red signifies the lowest density, i.e. 0, and purple the highest density, which is usually only a tiny little speck in the diagram. In all figures, the colours are non-linearly scaled with the density such that the centre point at $(0.5, 0.5)$ always has the same turquoise colour throughout all of the density figures.

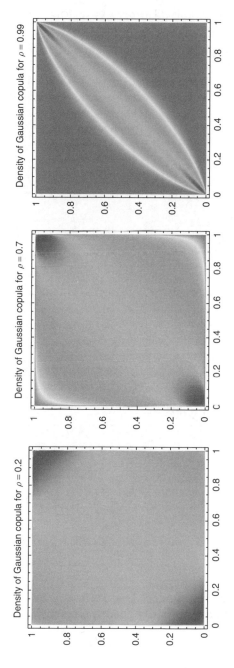

Figure 5.2 The Gaussian copula density as given by equation (5.17). For $\rho = 0$, the density is identically equal to 1 on the unit square. The density for negative values of ρ corresponds to the density for the same absolute value by a rotation of $90°$

The linear correlation η between the two dependent uniform variates can be calculated as

$$\eta(\rho) = 12 \iint N(z_1)N\left(\rho z_1 + \sqrt{1 - \rho^2}z_2\right) \varphi(z_1)\varphi(z_2)\, dz_1 dz_2 - 3. \qquad (5.22)$$

Straightforward calculus shows that

$$\eta \in [-1, 1] \quad \text{for } \rho \in [-1, 1].$$

Near the origin, we have

$$\eta(\rho) \approx \frac{3}{\pi}\rho \quad \text{for } |\rho| \ll 1. \qquad (5.23)$$

A diagram of $\eta(\rho)$ is shown in Figure 5.3.

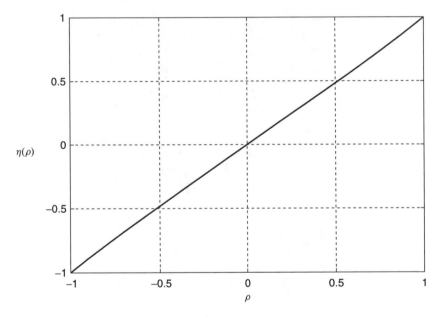

Figure 5.3   The linear correlation $\eta(\rho)$ of two uniform variates connected by a Gaussian copula of correlation coefficient ρ

Don't be misled by the apparently straight line: there is a little bit of curvature there, although a straight line would certainly be a good approximation for it.

Two Exponential Variates under the Gaussian Copula

In certain areas in finance, we are interested in the modelling of the time elapsed until a certain event happens for the first time. When we model a given event A using a Poisson process of intensity λ_A as explained in section 2.3, we have the following distribution density for the time T_A until arrival:

$$T_A \sim \lambda_A e^{-\lambda_A T_A}. \tag{5.24}$$

Random draws for T_A can be generated from a uniform variate u_A by setting

$$T_A = -\frac{\ln(1 - u_A)}{\lambda_A}. \tag{5.25}$$

When we model the co-dependent arrival of two events A and B using a Gaussian copula with correlation coefficient ρ, we can calculate the linear correlation $\zeta(\rho)$ for T_A and T_B as

$$\zeta(\rho) = \iint \ln(1 - N(z_1)) \ln\left(1 - N\left(\rho z_1 + \sqrt{1 - \rho^2} z_2\right)\right) \varphi(z_1)\varphi(z_2) \, dz_1 dz_2 - 1. \tag{5.26}$$

Again, we can evaluate analytically what interval $\zeta(\rho)$ is confined to:

$$\zeta \in \left[1 - \frac{\pi^2}{6}, 1\right] \quad \text{for } \rho \in [-1, 1]$$

where $1 - \frac{\pi^2}{6} \approx -0.6449341$. However, as we can see in Figure 5.4, the correlation transformation is not quite as nearly linear as it was for two uniform variates.

5.2.2   The t-Copula

The t-copula is conceptually very similar to the Gaussian copula. It is given by the cumulative distribution function of the marginals of correlated t-variates. The simplest way to explain the t-copula is probably by the aid of an algorithm that would create uniform variates under a t-copula [ELM01].

- Select a standard correlation matrix R that is to govern the co-dependence of the copula.
- Find a suitable pseudo-square root A of R such that $R = A \cdot A^\top$.
- Draw a vector $z \in \mathbb{R}^n$ of uncorrelated standard normal variates.
- Compute $\tilde{z} := A \cdot z$.
- Draw an independent χ_ν^2-variate s. For ν an integer, this can be done by drawing ν independent Gaussians, and summing their squares.
- Set $x := \sqrt{\frac{\nu}{s}} \tilde{z}$.
- Map x back to a vector of uniform variates $v \in [0, 1]^n$ using the cumulative probability function of Student's t distribution given in equation (2.52).

The so-generated uniform variates can then be transformed to any set of marginal distributions by use of their respective inverse cumulative probability functions, just as for the Gaussian copula. The t-copula shares with the Gaussian copula the feature that two variates, which are connected using either of the two copulae with a given correlation

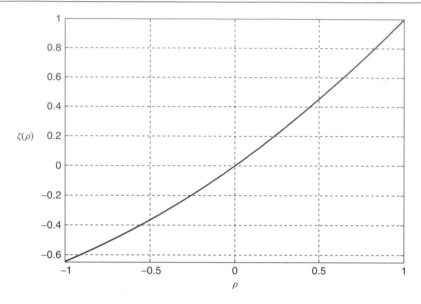

Figure 5.4   The linear correlation $\zeta(\rho)$ of two exponential variates connected by a Gaussian copula of correlation coefficient ρ.

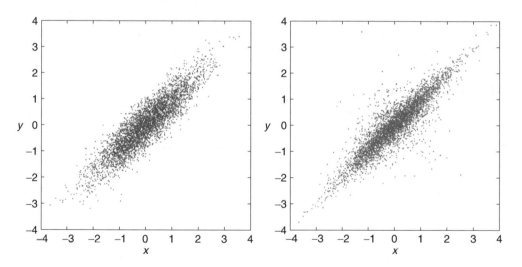

Figure 5.5   Both figures show data that are marginally normally distributed. The figure on the left depicts ordinary correlated normal variates with $\rho = 0.9$, and the figure on the right was created from data under a t_2-copula, also with $\rho = 0.9$.

coefficient ρ, have a Kendall's tau coefficient given by equation (5.19). An example for the difference from both copulae is shown in Figure 5.5. Note how the t-copula generates apparently higher correlation for large co-movements of equal sign, at the expense of giving rise to a higher density near the origin, and a noticeable set of what looks like significant outliers.

5.2.3 Archimedean Copulae

All members of this class of copulae have in common that they are generated by a strictly decreasing convex function $\phi(u)$ which maps the interval $(0, 1]$ onto $[0, \infty)$ such that $\lim_{\epsilon \to 0} \phi(\epsilon) = \infty$ and $\phi(1) = 0$. An Archimedean copula is generated from a given function $\phi(u)$ by

$$C(u, v) = \phi^{-1}\left(\phi(u) + \phi(v)\right). \tag{5.27}$$

Two uniform variates u and v under any Archimedean copula can be produced by the following algorithm.

- Draw two independent uniform variates s and q.
- Solve

$$q = t - \frac{\phi(t)}{\phi'(t)} \tag{5.28}$$

for t.
- Set

$$u := \phi^{-1}\left(s\phi(t)\right), \tag{5.29}$$

$$v := \phi^{-1}\left((1-s)\phi(t)\right). \tag{5.30}$$

For further details and a proof see [ELM01]. An example of a copula generator for which the above algorithm can be applied directly is

$$\phi(u) = \left(u^{-1} - 1\right)^{\theta} \tag{5.31}$$

for $\theta \geq 1$ since then the solution to equation (5.28) is immediately given by

$$t = \frac{1+\theta}{2} - \sqrt{\left(\frac{1+\theta}{2}\right)^2 - \theta q}. \tag{5.32}$$

It is possible to extend Archimedean copulae to higher dimensions. However, these extensions are rather restrictive with respect to the co-dependence structure since they do not allow for one parameter per pair of variates, unlike the Gaussian copula and the t-copula. This is probably the major disadvantage of Archimedean copulae. For algorithms on the generation of variates under a higher dimensional Archimedean copula, see [ELM01, FV97].

The Gumbel Copula

The Gumbel copula (sometimes also referred to as the Gumbel–Hougaard copula) is controlled by a single parameter $\theta \in [1, \infty)$. It is generated by

$$\phi_{\text{Gumbel}}(u) = (-\ln u)^{\theta} \tag{5.33}$$

and thus defined as

$$C_{\text{Gumbel}}(u, v) = e^{-\left[(-\ln u)^{\theta} + (-\ln v)^{\theta}\right]^{\frac{1}{\theta}}}. \tag{5.34}$$

The Gumbel copula gives rise to a stronger dependence in the upper tail of the joint distribution density, as can be seen in Figure 5.6. Kendall's tau of the Gumbel copula can be shown [GR00] to be

$$\tau_{\text{Gumbel}} = 1 - \frac{1}{\theta}. \tag{5.35}$$

The Clayton Copula

This copula is also known under the names Pareto, Cook–Johnson or Oakes copula, and is generated by the definition

$$\phi_{\text{Clayton}}(u) = \frac{(u^{-\theta} - 1)}{\theta} \tag{5.36}$$

for $\theta \in [-1, \infty) \setminus \{0\}$ and reads

$$C_{\text{Clayton}}(u, v) = \max\left(\left[u^{-\theta} + v^{-\theta} - 1 \right]^{-\frac{1}{\theta}}, 0 \right). \tag{5.37}$$

The Clayton copula gives rise to a stronger dependence in the lower tail of the joint distribution density, as can be seen in Figure 5.7. Kendall's tau of the Clayton copula is

$$\tau_{\text{Clayton}} = \frac{\theta}{\theta + 2}. \tag{5.38}$$

The Frank Copula

The Frank copula is given by

$$\phi_{\text{Frank}}(u) = -\ln\left[\frac{(e^{-\theta u} - 1)}{(e^{-\theta} - 1)} \right] \tag{5.39}$$

and

$$C_{\text{Frank}}(u, v) = -\frac{1}{\theta} \ln\left(1 + \frac{\left(e^{-\theta u} - 1\right)\left(e^{-\theta v} - 1\right)}{\left(e^{-\theta} - 1\right)} \right) \tag{5.40}$$

for $\theta \in \mathbb{R} \setminus \{0\}$. The Frank copula enhances the upper and lower tail dependence equally, as can be seen in Figure 5.8. For negative values of θ, this copula is able to produce negative co-dependence similar to the Gaussian copula for negative ρ. Not only that, it also displays the invariances with respect to $(u, v) \rightarrow (1 - u, 1 - v)$ and $(u, v; \theta) \rightarrow (1 - u, v; -\theta)$, as does the Gaussian copula, which is demonstrated in Figure 5.8. For the Frank copula, Kendall's tau is

$$\tau_{\text{Frank}} = 1 - 4\frac{(1 - D_1(\theta))}{\theta} \tag{5.41}$$

with $D_k(x)$ for some positive integer k being the Debye function [AS84, Mac96] defined as

$$D_k(x) = \frac{k}{x^k} \int_0^x \frac{s^k}{e^s - 1} \, ds. \tag{5.42}$$

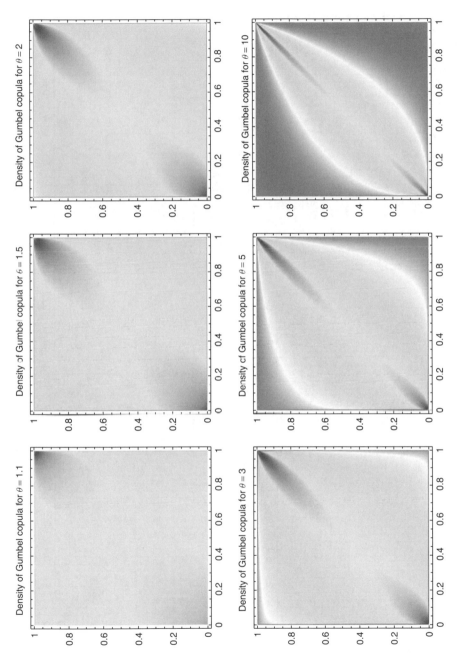

Figure 5.6 The Gumbel copula density as given by equation (5.17). For $\theta = 1$, the density is identically equal to 1 on the unit square

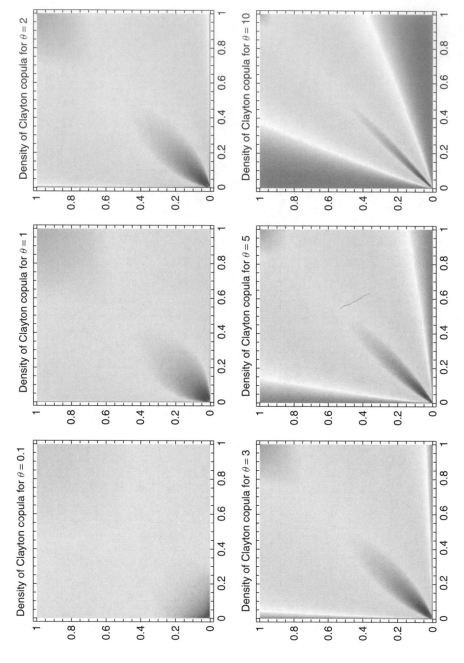

Figure 5.7 The Clayton copula density as given by equation (5.17). For $\theta = 0$, the density is identically equal to 1 on the unit square

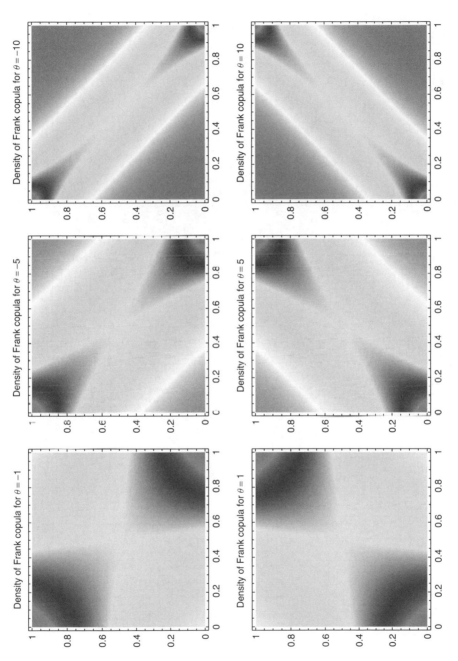

Figure 5.8 The Frank copula density as given by equation (5.17). For $\theta \to \pm 0$, the density approaches the uniform density on the unit square

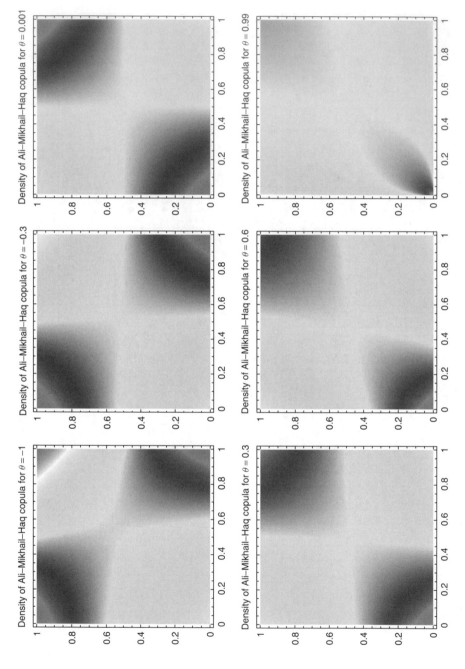

Figure 5.9 The Ali–Mikhail–Haq copula density as given by equation (5.17). For $\theta = 0$, the density is uniformly 1 on the unit square

The Ali–Mikhail–Haq Copula

This copula is generated by [AMH78]

$$\phi_{\text{Ali–Mikhail–Haq}}(u) = \ln\left(\frac{1 - \theta(1 - u)}{u}\right) \tag{5.43}$$

and has the form

$$C_{\text{Ali–Mikhail–Haq}}(u, v) = \frac{uv}{1 - \theta(1 - u)(1 - v)} \tag{5.44}$$

for $\theta \in [-1, 1]$. The Ali–Mikhail–Haq copula enhances the lower tail dependence for positive θ, and displays some strong negative co-dependence for $\theta < 0$, as shown in Figure 5.9. Kendall's tau is [FV97]

$$\tau_{\text{Ali–Mikhail–Haq}} = \left(\frac{3\theta - 2}{\theta}\right) - \frac{2}{3}\left(1 - \frac{1}{\theta}\right)^2 \cdot \ln(1 - \theta). \tag{5.45}$$

A generalisation of the Ali–Mikhail–Haq copula to two parameters, known as the Fang–Fang–Rosen copula [GR00, FFvR00], is given by

$$\phi_{\text{Fang–Fang–Rosen}}(u) = \ln\left(\frac{1 - \theta\left(1 - u^{\frac{1}{\kappa}}\right)}{u^{\frac{1}{\kappa}}}\right). \tag{5.46}$$

6
Salvaging a Linear
Correlation Matrix

The problem of how to specify a correlation matrix occurs in several important areas of finance. A few of the important applications are the specification of a (possibly time-dependent) instantaneous correlation matrix in the context of the BGM interest-rate option models, stress testing and scenario analysis for market risk management purposes, or the specification of a correlation matrix amongst a large number of obligors for credit derivative pricing or credit risk management.

Ad hoc correlation matrices, those calculated from incomplete data and those taken from news services, sometimes don't comply with the requirement of symmetry and positive semi-definiteness. Whilst it is easy to amend the symmetry requirement by manual intervention, it is not always straightforward to see how to adjust the given correlation matrix to become usable for factor analysis or simulation purposes. What's more, there are many situations when it is desirable to carry out a calculation not only for a single input matrix, but for a whole set of modified versions of the original matrix. Examples of this include comparative pricing in order to ascertain the extent of correlation exposure for multi-asset derivatives, but also the assessment of portfolio risk. In many of these cases, we end up with a matrix that is no longer positive semi-definite, and often there is no clear way to remedy this.

In practice, the problem of an invalid correlation matrix, i.e. one that has negative eigenvalues, can also very easily arise in the context of risk analysis for equity portfolios. This is because there are frequently asynchronous gaps in the historical stock exchange time series. The chance that slight inconsistencies in the data from which historical correlation coefficients are calculated can lead to negative eigenvalues grows rapidly as the size of the correlation matrix increases. This has recently been pointed out by Ju and Pearson [JP99]. Intuitively, it can be understood to be an effect of the characteristic polynomial that determines the eigenvalues becoming of higher order as the dimension of the correlation matrix grows, and thus displaying a stronger non-linear response to slight changes in the polynomial's coefficients. Since equity index or portfolio analysis typically involves many underlying assets, the risk of negative eigenvalues of the correlation matrix calculated from historical data is particularly large.

In this chapter, I describe two methods based solely on mathematical grounds which can be used to best match an invalid correlation matrix given the constraint of positive semi-definiteness. Not only are these guaranteed to give a solution, but in addition we also have a measure of to what extent we are matching the target matrix. Both methods are centred around the idea of decomposing a covariance matrix C into its *pseudo-square root*, which is to mean any matrix A such that $C = A \cdot A^{\top}$. For scalars, A would be an actual square root of C, but for matrices the concept of a square root is ill-defined, whence I use the term *pseudo-square root*.

6.1 HYPERSPHERE DECOMPOSITION

The starting point is the well-known result from linear algebra that every $n \times n$ matrix M given by

$$M = WW^\top \tag{6.1}$$

for any $W \in \mathbb{R}^{n \times n}$ is positive semi-definite and conversely, every positive semi-definite matrix $M \in \mathbb{R}^{n \times n}$ can be decomposed as in equation (6.1).

The *hypersphere decomposition* method for the construction of a valid correlation matrix

$$\hat{C} = BB^\top \tag{6.2}$$

that best matches a given, *not* positive semi-definite, target matrix C is to view the elements of the row vectors of matrix B in equation (6.2) as coordinates lying on a unit hypersphere [RJ00]. If we denote by b_{ij} the elements of the matrix B, the key is to obtain the $n \times n$ coordinates b_{ij} from $n \times (n-1)$ angular coordinates θ_{ij} according to

$$b_{ij} = \cos\theta_{ij} \cdot \prod_{k=1}^{j-1} \sin\theta_{ik} \qquad \text{for } j = 1, \ldots, n-1,$$

$$b_{ij} = \prod_{k=1}^{j-1} \sin\theta_{ik} \qquad\qquad \text{for } j = n. \tag{6.3}$$

For an arbitrary set of angles $\{\theta_{ij}\}$, a matrix $\hat{C}$ formed from B as in equation (6.2) satisfies all the given constraints required of a correlation matrix by construction. In particular, thanks to the trigonometric relationship (6.3) and to the fact that the radius of a unit hypersphere is always equal to one, the main diagonal elements are guaranteed to be unity, which is shown in section 6.5.

In general, matrix $\hat{C}$ will bear no resemblance to the target matrix C. However, after using the above transformation and defining a suitable error measure ε in the resulting approximate correlation matrix $\hat{C}$

$$\varepsilon = \|C - \hat{C}\| \tag{6.4}$$

one can use an optimisation procedure over the angles θ_{ij} to find the best possible fit given the chosen error measure. Sensible choices for the error measure are as follows.

- The sum of squares of the elements of the difference matrix $(C - \hat{C})$:

$$\chi^2_{\text{elements}} := \sum_{ij} (c_{ij} - \hat{c}_{ij})^2. \tag{6.5}$$

Since both C and $\hat{C}$ have unit diagonal elements, this error norm is equal to twice the sum of squares of errors in the free correlation coefficients.

- The elementwise sum of squares of errors in the sorted sets of eigenvalues of C and $\hat{C}$:

$$\chi^2_{\text{eigenvalues}} := \sum_i (\lambda_i - \hat{\lambda}_i)^2. \tag{6.6}$$

Naturally, the above suggestions are only examples and various other choices are conceivable. If, in particular, a risk manager felt that certain portions of the target correlation matrix C should be recovered with particularly high accuracy, then correspondingly large weights could be assigned to the relative elements $(c_{ij} - \hat{c}_{ij})^2$.

The fundamental benefits of this method are twofold. Firstly, when the underlying space over which the optimisation is carried out is expressed in terms of angle vectors describing coordinates on a unit hypersphere, no constraints have to be satisfied. Secondly, the approach presented in the next section requires no iterations and provides a solution very similar to the one obtained using error metric (6.5). It can therefore be used to provide the starting point for the search procedure.

6.2 SPECTRAL DECOMPOSITION

This method is based on the idea that the spectrum, i.e. the set of eigenvalues, is the most significant criterion to be preserved in a matrix when we amend it to meet certain constraints[1]. It is a particularly useful approach for the given problem since the violated constraint itself is that an eigenvalue is negative.

Given the right-hand-side eigensystem S of the real and symmetric matrix C and its associated set of eigenvalues[2] $\{\lambda_l\}$ such that

$$C \cdot S = S \cdot \Lambda \quad \text{with } \Lambda = \text{diag}(\lambda_i) \tag{6.7}$$

define the non-zero elements of the diagonal matrix Λ' as

$$\Lambda' \; : \; \lambda'_i = \begin{cases} \lambda_i : \lambda_i \geqslant 0, \\ 0 : \lambda_i < 0. \end{cases} \tag{6.8}$$

If the target matrix C is not positive semi-definite, it has at least one negative eigenvalue, whence at least one of the λ'_i will be zero.

Also, define the non-zero elements of the diagonal scaling matrix T with respect to the eigensystem S by

$$T \; : \; t_i = \left[\sum_m s_{im}^2 \lambda'_m \right]^{-1}. \tag{6.9}$$

Now, let[3]

$$B' := S\sqrt{\Lambda'} \tag{6.10}$$

and

$$B := \sqrt{T} B' = \sqrt{T} S \sqrt{\Lambda'}. \tag{6.11}$$

---

[1]This method is also known as principal component analysis.

[2]The combination of Householder reduction to tridiagonal form and the QL algorithm with implicit shifts for tridiagonal matrices provides a very efficient way of computing the eigenvalues and eigenvectors of real symmetric matrices. The Numerical Recipes [PTVF92] routines `tred2`, `tqli` and `eigsrt` can be used in that order to carry out the decomposition.

[3]Please note that the notation $\sqrt{D}$ for a diagonal matrix D with non-negative elements is a symbolic description of the diagonal matrix whose non-zero elements are the positive roots of the diagonal elements of D.

For normalised row vectors of S, the truncation of the negative eigenvalues results in row vectors of B' that are not of unit length. This is rectified in equation (6.11) by the aid of matrix T which contains the required normalisation factors. By construction

$$\hat{C} := B B^\top \tag{6.12}$$

is now both positive semi-definite and has unit diagonal elements, since its elements are

$$
\begin{aligned}
\hat{c}_{ij} &= \sum_{klmnp} \left(\sqrt{T}\right)_{ik} \cdot s_{kl} \cdot \left(\sqrt{\Lambda'}\right)_{lm} \cdot \left(\sqrt{\Lambda'}\right)_{mn} \cdot s_{pn} \cdot \left(\sqrt{T}\right)_{pj} \\[2mm]
&= \sum_l \sqrt{t_i} \cdot s_{il} \cdot \lambda'_l \cdot s_{jl} \cdot \sqrt{t_j} \\[2mm]
&= \frac{\displaystyle\sum_l s_{il} s_{jl} \lambda'_l}{\sqrt{\displaystyle\sum_m s_{im}^2 \lambda'_m \cdot \sum_k s_{jk}^2 \lambda'_k}} .
\end{aligned} \tag{6.13}
$$

A procedural description of the above method may clarify what actually has to be done.

- Calculate the eigenvalues λ_i and the right-hand-side eigenvectors s_i of C.
- Set all negative λ_i to zero.
- Multiply the column vectors s_i by the square roots of their associated corrected eigenvalues λ'_i and arrange them as the columns of B'.
- Finally, B results from B' by normalising the *row vectors* of B' to unit length.

By following this procedure we obtain an acceptable correlation matrix which is intuitively similar to the target one (the more so, the fewer the eigenvalues which have to be set to zero). The crucial point, however, is not so much the plausibility of the metric but the fact that empirically I have always observed the results obtained using equations (6.7) to (6.12) to be very similar to those from the angular method discussed in section 6.1. How close the results are in practice is shown in section 6.4. This is significant because one can use the result of the method described here either as an accurate approximation to the best (in a χ^2_{elements} sense) solution, or as the starting point for the optimisation discussed in section 6.1, thereby substantially reducing the computational burden of the hypersphere decomposition approach.

6.3   ANGULAR DECOMPOSITION OF LOWER TRIANGULAR FORM

The form given in equation (6.3) is the most general decomposition B of any valid correlation matrix $\hat{C}$ such that $\hat{C} = B B^\top$. However, any so-derived matrix B can be transformed by a generic orthogonal matrix O without any change of the effective correlation matrix given by the product $B B^\top$. The group of all possible orthogonal matrices $O \in \mathbb{R}^{n \times n}$ represents all possible rotations and reflections. Ignoring the latter and just taking into account all possible rotation matrices, we end up with $[n \times (n-1)]/2$ degrees of freedom in the rotation matrices given by the same number of rotation angles. By virtue of these degrees of freedom, we can rotate every decomposition matrix B such that the transformed decomposition matrix $B' := BO$ is of lower triangular form. We can thus, without loss of generality, formulate the following reduced form for the hypersphere decomposition B' of $\hat{C}$:

$$b'_{11} = 1,$$

$$b'_{ij} = \prod_{k=1}^{j-1} \sin\theta_{ik} \cdot \cos\theta_{ij} \quad \text{for} \quad j = 1, \ldots, i-1,$$

$$b'_{ij} = \prod_{k=1}^{j-1} \sin\theta_{ik} \qquad\qquad \text{for} \quad j = i, \tag{6.14}$$

$$b'_{ij} = 0 \qquad\qquad\qquad \text{for} \quad j = i+1, \ldots, n.$$

The above reduced form is identical to (6.3) if we choose $\theta_{ij} = 0$ for all $j \geqslant i$. In matrix form, the lower triangular decomposition (6.14) thus looks as follows:

$$B' = \begin{pmatrix} 1 & 0 & 0 & 0 & 0 & \cdots \\ \cos\theta_{21} & \sin\theta_{21} & 0 & 0 & 0 & \cdots \\ \cos\theta_{31} & \sin\theta_{31}\cos\theta_{32} & \sin\theta_{31}\sin\theta_{32} & 0 & 0 & \cdots \\ \cos\theta_{41} & \sin\theta_{41}\cos\theta_{42} & \sin\theta_{41}\sin\theta_{42}\cos\theta_{43} & \sin\theta_{41}\sin\theta_{42}\sin\theta_{43} & 0 & \cdots \\ \vdots & \vdots & \vdots & \vdots & \vdots & \ddots \end{pmatrix}. \tag{6.15}$$

One of the advantages of the completely general decomposition (6.3) was that the result of the spectral decomposition and truncation (6.11) could be used directly in a bootstrapping procedure to calculate good initial values for the angles θ_{ij} for the subsequent optimisation procedure. In order to start off the optimisation in the case of the reduced form, the result of the spectral decomposition and truncation can still be used as follows. First, we reconstitute the effective correlation matrix $\hat{C}$ as given in equation (6.12) from the spectrally truncated approximation (6.11). Then, we calculate the Cholesky decomposition of $\hat{C}$ (which can be done very efficiently [PTVF92]). Since the Cholesky decomposition is of lower triangular form, it can then be used directly to back out good initial guesses for the reduced number $[n \times (n-1)]/2$ of angles that specify the matrix B' as given in equations (6.14) and (6.15), respectively. The advantage of the reduction by 50% of the number of free parameters in the optimisation procedure is obvious: halving the dimension of the optimisation domain decreases the number of entries in any involved Jacobian or Hessian matrix by a factor of four, which should give rise to a speed-up factor of the same order of magnitude.

6.4 EXAMPLES

A risk manager retrieves from the middle office's reporting system the following correlation matrix of three world equity indices:

$$\tilde{C} = \begin{pmatrix} 1 & 0.9 & 0.7 \\ 0.9 & 1 & 0.4 \\ 0.7 & 0.4 & 1 \end{pmatrix}.$$

The eigenvalues of $\tilde{C}$ are $\{2.35364,\ 0.616017,\ 0.0303474\}$ and the correlation matrix can be split up as

$$\tilde{C} = \tilde{B}\tilde{B}^{\top}$$

with

$$\tilde{B} = \begin{pmatrix} 0.98742 & 0.08718 & -0.13192 \\ 0.88465 & 0.45536 & 0.10021 \\ 0.77203 & -0.63329 & 0.05389 \end{pmatrix}.$$

The risk manager is aware of the VaR calculated under the assumption of this correlation between the three indices. In order to assess the change in VaR resulting from a decrease in correlation between two of the three underlying variables, the risk manager wishes to adjust the matrix to

$$C = \begin{pmatrix} 1 & 0.9 & 0.7 \\ 0.9 & 1 & 0.3 \\ 0.7 & 0.3 & 1 \end{pmatrix}.$$

Unfortunately, the eigenvalues of C' are now $\{2.29673,\ 0.710625,\ -0.00735244\}$, and despite its plausible appearance, matrix C' is no longer an acceptable correlation matrix. This highlights how a minor change can lead to the violation of the requirement of positive semi-definiteness of a correlation matrix. The system will now fail when trying to construct a split-up matrix B for the purpose of Monte Carlo simulations[4] in order to calculate the VaR under the new assumptions.

Using the method outlined in section 6.1 with the error measure chosen to be χ^2_{elements} as given by equation (6.5), we can calculate

$$\hat{B} = \begin{pmatrix} 0.99804 & 0.06265 & 0 \\ 0.86482 & 0.50209 & 0 \\ 0.74020 & -0.67239 & 0 \end{pmatrix}$$

with

$$\hat{C} = \hat{B}\hat{B}^{\top} = \begin{pmatrix} 1 & 0.89458 & 0.69662 \\ 0.89458 & 1 & 0.30254 \\ 0.69662 & 0.30254 & 1 \end{pmatrix}.$$

and a total error of $\chi^2_{\text{elements}} = 0.946 \times 10^{-4}$.

In comparison, the method outlined in section 6.2 above yields

$$\hat{B} = \begin{pmatrix} 0.99805 & 0.06238 & 0 \\ 0.86434 & 0.50292 & 0 \\ 0.73974 & -0.67290 & 0 \end{pmatrix}$$

---

[4]Recall that the construction of correlated normal variates from a vector of uncorrelated normal variates z is done by the transformation $x = B \cdot z$ with $C = BB^{\top}$.

to give us

$$\hat{C} = \hat{B}\hat{B}^{\top} = \begin{pmatrix} 1 & 0.89402 & 0.69632 \\ 0.89402 & 1 & 0.30100 \\ 0.69632 & 0.30100 & 1 \end{pmatrix}.$$

One can notice that not only the total error of $\chi^2_{\text{elements}} = 1.0 \times 10^{-4}$ but also the individual elements are remarkably close to the values obtained by optimisation. Despite the fact that there is in general no guarantee that the results of the two methods are as close together as in this example, I have always found very good agreement between the two approaches.

6.5 ANGULAR COORDINATES ON A HYPERSPHERE OF UNIT RADIUS

The ith row vector of B as specified by equation (6.3) is given by

$$(b_{i1}, \ b_{i2}, \ \ldots, \ b_{i\,n-1}, \ b_{in})$$

$$= \left(\cos\theta_{i1}, \ \sin\theta_{i1}\cos\theta_{i2}, \ \ldots, \ \prod_{k=1}^{n-2} \sin\theta_{ik}\cos\theta_{i\,n-1}, \ \prod_{k=1}^{n-2} \sin\theta_{ik}\sin\theta_{i\,n-1} \right). \quad (6.16)$$

The sum of squares $\sum_{j=1}^{j=n} b_{ij}^2$ will definitely be unity if the recursive relation

$$\sum_{k=j+1}^{k=n} b_{ik}^2 = b_{ij}^2 \cdot \frac{\sin^2\theta_{ij}}{\cos^2\theta_{ij}} \quad (6.17)$$

holds, since then

$$\sum_{k=2}^{k=n} b_{ik}^2 = b_{i1}^2 \cdot \frac{\sin^2\theta_{i1}}{\cos^2\theta_{i1}} = \cos^2\theta_{i1} \cdot \frac{\sin^2\theta_{i1}}{\cos^2\theta_{i1}} = \sin^2\theta_{i1} \quad (6.18)$$

and thus

$$\sum_{k=1}^{k=n} b_{ik}^2 = b_{i1}^2 + \sum_{k=2}^{k=n} b_{ik}^2 = \cos^2\theta_{i1} + \sin^2\theta_{i1} = 1. \quad (6.19)$$

To start the induction, we see that equation (6.17) is satisfied for $j = n - 1$ since then we have

$$\prod_{k=1}^{n-2} \sin^2\theta_{ik}\sin^2\theta_{i\,n-1} = \prod_{k=1}^{n-2} \sin^2\theta_{ik}\cos^2\theta_{i\,n-1} \cdot \frac{\sin^2\theta_{i\,n-1}}{\cos^2\theta_{i\,n-1}}. \quad (6.20)$$

It remains to be shown that

$$b_{ij}^2 = \frac{\cos^2\theta_{ij}}{\sin^2\theta_{ij}} \cdot \sum_{k=j+1}^{k=n} b_{ik}^2 \quad (6.21)$$

for $j < n - 1$. Using the recursive relation (6.17) itself, we obtain

$$
\begin{aligned}
b_{ij}^2 &= \frac{\cos^2 \theta_{ij}}{\sin^2 \theta_{ij}} \cdot \left(b_{i\,j+1}^2 + \sum_{k=j+2}^{k=n} b_{ik}^2 \right) \\
&= \frac{\cos^2 \theta_{ij}}{\sin^2 \theta_{ij}} \cdot \left(b_{i\,j+1}^2 + \frac{\sin^2 \theta_{i\,j+1}}{\cos^2 \theta_{i\,j+1}} \cdot b_{i\,j+1}^2 \right) \\
&= \frac{\cos^2 \theta_{ij}}{\sin^2 \theta_{ij} \cos^2 \theta_{i\,j+1}} \cdot b_{i\,j+1}^2,
\end{aligned}
$$

i.e.

$$
b_{i\,j+1} = b_{ij} \cdot \frac{\sin \theta_{ij}}{\cos \theta_{ij}} \cos \theta_{i\,j+1} \tag{6.22}
$$

which is identical to the construction description (6.3) for $j < n-1$. Hence, all row vectors of B are of unit length. The elements of $\hat{C} = B B^{\top}$ are the pairwise scalar products of the row vectors of B. Since the scalar product of two vectors of unit length is by definition contained in $[-1, 1]$, $\hat{C}$ satisfies the requirements of unit diagonal elements, symmetry and all elements being contained in $[-1, 1]$.

7
Pseudo-random Numbers

For all Monte Carlo methods, we need an underlying number generator. This driving engine has to supply us with variate vectors which in the limit of infinitely many draws satisfy a given joint multivariate distribution density function. This is typically done by transformation of draws from the uniform distribution of equal probability for all numbers in the interval (0, 1). Note that, unlike most textbook definitions of numerically generated uniform numbers, both 0 and 1 are explicitly excluded since for most of the desired target distributions at least one of the two endpoints maps to either $+\infty$ or $-\infty$, which clearly poses a numerical problem.

Traditionally, Monte Carlo techniques used to depend on a number generation method that mimics *randomness* as well as possible, and a great deal of effort has gone into number theoretical research for this purpose. Generations of number theoreticians have focused on ever more refined and intricate ways of constructing random numbers, whilst others devised ever more sophisticated tests for randomness [Knu81]. The reason for all of this hard work is that a machine that is designed to follow instructions in a deterministic way, such as a computer, *cannot* produce anything that *actually is random*. This was beautifully expressed by John von Neumann in his statement which has become known as 'the original sin of random number generation':

> 'Anyone who considers arithmetical methods of producing random digits is, of course, in a state of sin.'
>
> John von Neumann, 1951 [vN51]

A more mathematical way to express this fundamental failure of randomness of computer-generated digits is that due to the algebraic nature of their generation, there always exists a high-dimensional embedding space $\mathbb{R}^d$ such that vector draws v whose elements are sequential draws from a one-dimensional number generation engine can appear as systematically aligned in a lower dimensional manifold. One example of such a high-dimensional embedding is clearly given by the periodicity of the number generator, which is why modern methods pay great attention to this feature and achieve very long periodicities. However, this continuous chase for ever more random numbers is somehow doomed because for any new method that satisfies all known tests, one can always construe a new test criterion for randomness which will prove it to be non-random:

> 'Every random number generator will fail in at least one application.'
>
> Donald E. Knuth, 1969

It is for this reason that computer-generated random numbers are referred to as *pseudo-random* numbers [Sob94]. They simply cannot be random.

Recently, there have been several attempts to overcome the very last bit of non-randomness left in modern pseudo-random number generators. Devices have been constructed that link the output signal of radioactive decay processes or light intensities of so-called 'lava lamps' through encryption algorithms to digit scramblers. To some extent, these approaches ought to be taken with the proverbial pinch of salt since the benefits that can be gained from the additional level of randomisation can hardly be in any proportion to the extreme effort and thus cost involved. This is certainly true for applications of Monte Carlo methods in finance, but may be different when it comes to security critical encryption uses of random numbers.

This chapter is not meant to be an exhaustive overview of available pseudo-random number generation methods. There are many excellent books on this subject alone [Knu81, PTVF92, Tez95, Nie92], and the reader is referred to them for details of individual number generators. Section 7.1 is mainly for the entertainment of those who always wondered about the difference between chaos and randomness, but never dared to ask. In section 7.2, a little historical detour to the beginnings of computer-generated pseudo-random numbers is taken. Then, in section 7.3, I briefly outline the most basic principle of pseudo-random number generation. Following that, I acknowledge the probably most frequently used number generators around, namely *Ran0* to *Ran3* as denoted in [PTVF92].

7.1 CHAOS

The general principle of pseudo-random number generation is as follows. Given the current value of one or more (usually internally stored) state variables, apply a mathematical iteration algorithm to obtain a new set of values for the state variables, and use a specific formula to obtain a new uniform (0, 1) variate from the current values of all the state variables. This kind of process is mathematically also known as a *discrete-time dynamical system*.

A simple example of a one-dimensional discrete dynamical system is the *logistic map*. It was originally used by P. F. Verhulst in 1845 to model the development of a population in a limited environment [May76], and is known as a consequence of its *non-linearity* to produce chaotic dynamics for certain choices of parameters. The logistic map gives rise to discrete dynamics by the following algorithm. Given a number $x_n \in (0, 1)$, we have

$$x_{n+1} = \mu x_n (1 - x_n) \qquad (7.1)$$

for some $\mu \in (0, 4]$, which is shown in Figure 7.1. For any value of μ and x_0, the system (7.1) will converge to a so-called *attractive invariant set*. This means, skipping some initial transient behaviour, the system (7.1) will only produce iterates that take on values from this invariant set. As long as the invariant set is (finitely) piecewise continuous, we can remap it relatively easily to the interval (0, 1), and thus obtain the desired uniform (0, 1) variates (whereby we have not yet ascertained to what extent these meet the requirement of serial decorrelation, etc.). The first question that arises is what value of μ should we use. For this purpose, I plot in Figure 7.2 the invariant set of values of μ from 0 to 4. As we can see in the figure, the most promising value for μ is 4 since then the entire interval (0, 1) appears to be filled homogeneously. In fact, the value $\mu = 4$ can be shown to give rise to a *strange attractor* for the dynamical system (7.1), and to fill the uniform interval (0, 1) with Lebesgue measure 1 [GH83]. Does this mean we can use the logistic map as a pseudo-random number generator? Sadly, no. There are two substantial problems with it, and I shall now briefly look at them individually.

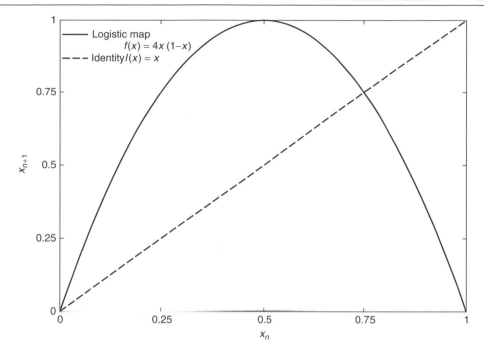

Figure 7.1 The logistic map for $\mu = 4$.

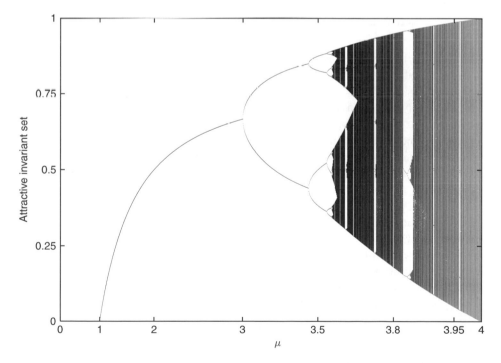

Figure 7.2 The attractive invariant set of the logistic map for values of μ from 0 to 4. Note that the abscissa has been scaled according to $\mu \rightarrow -\ln(4.25 - \mu)$.

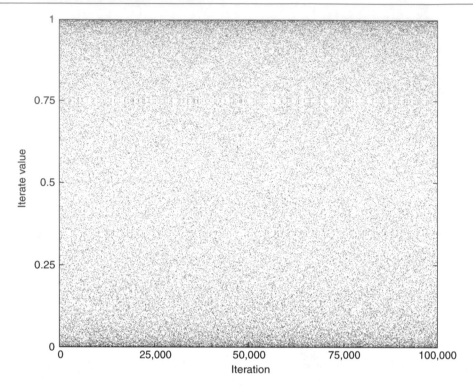

Figure 7.3   Iterates from the logistic map at $\mu = 4$.

First, have a look at Figure 7.3. What you see are iterates from the logistic map for $\mu = 4$. Admittedly, they look rather random indeed, and it is this similarity between chaos and randomness which gives rise to the common misunderstanding that chaotic systems behave randomly. Now, have a closer look at the ordinate level of 0.75. There is clearly some kind of structure. What happens is that any iterate that comes very close to 0.75 is succeeded by more iterates nearby. We see from equation (7.1) that $x^* = \frac{3}{4}$ is actually a fixed point under the logistic map for $\mu = 4$. However, this fixed point is not stable under the dynamics of (7.1). This means that any point in an arbitrarily small vicinity of x^* is gradually repelled from the fixed point, until it eventually starts orbiting all over the unit interval again. As a consequence, a number generator based on the logistic map would never return the value 0.75, but instead, whenever it happens to come close to this value, there will be a number of variates following with values very nearby, displaying a temporary *near-periodicity*. What's more, there are actually uncountably infinitely many other values that are also excluded by the map. Firstly, there are all of the predecessors of 0.75, i.e. all the values that would actually end up right on 0.75 under the iteration rule (7.1). Going back from $x^* = \frac{3}{4}$ one iteration we have $\left\{\frac{1}{4}, \frac{3}{4}\right\}$. One more backwards iteration gives us $\left\{\frac{1}{2} - \frac{\sqrt{3}}{4}, \frac{3}{4}, \frac{1}{2} + \frac{\sqrt{3}}{4}\right\}$. In each iteration that we look backwards out from x^*, we have from then on two new predecessors of the unstable fixed point for each one that we already had. Therefore, there are $\lim_{i \to \infty} 2^i$ many points excluded from the attractive invariant set of the logistic map for $\mu = 4$. What we are left with after taking all

of those points out of the unit interval is what is known as a *Cantor set*. It is impossible
to map a Cantor set back to a continuous interval with any sensible function that could
be used on a computer. Also, the predecessors of x^* are not the only points that are
being avoided by the logistic map. In addition, there are also all the points that represent
short periodic orbits (i.e. fixed points of the iterated map), and they also have domains of
temporary near-periodicity in their vicinity. Take for instance the value $x_0 = \frac{1}{8}(5 - \sqrt{5})$.
Its iterate is $x_1 = \frac{1}{8}(5 + \sqrt{5})$, which in turn leads back to $x_2 = \frac{1}{8}(5 - \sqrt{5}) = x_0$, and thus
we have a period-2 orbit. This period-2 orbit is unstable and therefore we have another
set of repelling points embedded in the chaotic attractive invariant set for $\mu = 4$. Equally,
there are points forming short periodic orbits for many other cycle lengths, and all of
them are unstable at $\mu = 4$. This is one of the most defining points of chaotic motion:
embedded inside the attractive invariant set of chaotic dynamics, known as a *strange
attractor*, there is always an infinity of unstable periodic orbits.

The second problem with a non-linear dynamical system such as the logistic map is
that of the non-uniformity of the *invariant measure*. For a random number generator, the
invariant measure $\psi(x)$ is simply the probability density that the next draw will be in
the interval $[x, x + dx]$, and for a discretely iterated system it is the long-term average
of points arriving in that interval. The attentive reader may have noticed that the points
in Figure 7.3 are a lot denser at the top and bottom of the diagram. This is a symptom
of the fact that for $\mu = 4$ the invariant measure of the logistic map is given by

$$\psi_{\mu=4}(x) = \frac{1}{\pi \sqrt{x(1 - x)}} \tag{7.2}$$

[vN51, GH83], which is singular at $x = 0$ and $x = 1$. Nonetheless, if we transform from
x to the new variable α by setting

$$x = \sin^2\left(\frac{\pi}{2}\alpha\right) \Longleftrightarrow \alpha = \frac{2}{\pi} \arcsin \sqrt{x} \tag{7.3}$$

we can calculate the density $\eta(\alpha)$ of the new variable α on $(0, 1)$ according to

$$\psi(x)\, dx = \eta(\alpha)\, d\alpha, \tag{7.4}$$

$$\eta(\alpha) = \psi(x(\alpha)) \frac{dx}{d\alpha}$$

$$= \frac{\pi \sin\left(\frac{\pi}{2}\alpha\right) \cos\left(\frac{\pi}{2}\alpha\right)}{\pi \sqrt{x(1 - x)}}$$

$$= 1. \tag{7.5}$$

In other words, the transformed variable α is uniformly distributed on $(0, 1)$, and thus we
might be able to use it as a generator for uniform $(0, 1)$ pseudo-random numbers. Alternatively, we could use the untransformed variates x and correct the probability density
associated with each draw as explained in section 9.2, and thus avoid the evaluation of an
inverse trigonometric function[1]. However, the issue of embedded unstable periodic orbits
and all their pre-iterates, i.e. all the points that would map onto them, cannot be removed

---

[1] Albeit that it may not be worth the trouble, see section 14.6.

in any way that we can implement on computers[2]. In the early days of Monte Carlo simulations on electronic computers, these islands of regularity in the stream of generated numbers were not considered a major issue, since they can be shown to be of Lebesgue measure zero, and the very iteration formula (7.1) for $\mu = 4$ was used [UvN47, vN51] as an alternative to the mid-square method mentioned in section 7.2. However, since the mid-1940s, a lot of progress has been made in the area of non-linear dynamics, and the phenomenon of temporary near-periodic behaviour in the vicinity of unstable periodic orbits (also known as *intermittency*) is much better understood. For financial simulations, we definitely don't want to employ a sequence that displays features of such obvious involuntary regularity as shown in Figure 7.3.

7.2   THE MID-SQUARE METHOD

The first ever algorithm for the computer generation of pseudo-random numbers was proposed by John von Neumann, and is known as the *mid-square method* [Ham51]. The procedure is as follows. Take a uniform $(0, 1)$ number x_0 in a four-digit representation. The next variate x_{n+1} is calculated from x_n by taking the square of x_n and extracting the middle four digits. In other words, from $x_0 = 0.9876$ we obtain

$$x_0^2 = 0.97\,\underbrace{5353}\,76$$

$$x_1 = 0.5353$$

$$x_1^2 = 0.28\,\underbrace{6546}\,09$$

$$x_2 = 0.6546$$

and so on. Unfortunately, this procedure is very likely to end up in a short periodic orbit or at 0, depending on the initial value x_0, which was recognised early on [For51]. In fact, for the above starting value it is absorbed at 0 after 50 iterations. Even when a starting value is used that does not enter a short periodic orbit soon, and does not map into 0, this method tends to produce a disproportionate frequency of small numbers [Sob94].

7.3   CONGRUENTIAL GENERATION

The most commonly used pseudo-random number generation methods are essentially piecewise linear, or piecewise affine, to be precise. The basic idea is to produce integer values m_n on a given interval $[0, M - 1]$, and to return a uniform $(0, 1)$ variate u_n by rescaling[3]. The next integer variate is calculated by

$$m_{n+1} = (a\,m_n + c) \qquad \text{mod } M. \tag{7.6}$$

Note that equation (7.6) is piecewise affine with the same multiplier over all pieces. Thus, it preserves the volume of any given subinterval of $[0, M - 1]$, which is why it is called a *congruential generator*. Unlike the non-linear methods that were presented

---

[2]Mathematically, this may be possible by defining a function that is discontinuous everywhere, but such a function cannot easily be implemented on a computer.

[3]The common method for rescaling is to set $u_n = m_n/M$. Since m_n can, however, take on the value 0, which we usually want to avoid, I recommend rescaling according to $u_n = (m_n + 1)/(M + 1)$.

above, there is no absorption into a fixed point or short periodic orbit for congruential generators. In fact, since all calculations are carried out using integer arithmetics, and since a and M must be chosen to be co-prime, the system (7.6) cannot give rise to fixed points at all. The constant a is typically chosen to be sufficiently large in order to have any two close initial values very quickly wrap around the unit interval repeatedly and thus appear to be decorrelated. This in turn means that the iteration map (7.6) consists of many nearly vertical lines. For all the specific examples of the multiplier a discussed below, the iteration map would actually appear to be a completely filled unit square, unless the diagram is enlarged greatly, which is why I omit to show it. Incidentally, the transformation (7.3) of the logistic map (7.1) for $\mu = 4$ results in the iteration scheme

$$\alpha_{n+1} = \begin{cases} 2\alpha_n & \text{for } \alpha_n < \frac{1}{2} \\ 2 - 2\alpha_n & \text{for } \frac{1}{2} \leqslant \alpha_n \leqslant 1 \end{cases} \tag{7.7}$$

which has the same structural features as

$$\alpha_{n+1} = (2\,\alpha_n) \qquad \text{mod } 1. \tag{7.8}$$

The small multiplier 2 in this form makes it somewhat clearer that the logistic map displays the feature of comparatively slow separation of two initial values near unstable periodic orbits or near the fixed point at $x^* = \frac{3}{4}$ in Figure 7.3.

Frequently, the constant c in equation (7.6) is chosen to be zero, whence we commonly encounter the name *linear congruential generator*. There is a lot of literature on good choices for a and M, and not all of it is trustworthy. In IBM's early computing days, it used to deliver its mainframe systems equipped with its infamous *RANDU* generator which uses $a = 65,539$, $M = 2^{31}$ and $m_0 = 1$. This generator has meanwhile repeatedly been reported to be highly inadequate [PTVF92, Sob94, FMM77, Tcz95][4]. Sadly, it has been copied to a variety of other computer systems, including even the Russian ES system [Sob94]. Since it is well conceivable that other computer manufacturers have slipped up similarly[5], and since there is according to Murphy's law a tendency for mistakes to proliferate, I advise the reader never to rely on black box number generators that come with any one system and allegedly have been tested. Note that this kind of mistake is extremely easy to make. Again, please don't trust any number generator that you can't find a proper reference to, even if it looks sophisticated and similar to the trustworthy ones given in, for example, [PTVF92].

Not all is doom and gloom, however. A simple choice for the constructing multiplier and modulus that does work is $a = 5^{17}$, $M = 2^{40}$ and $m_0 = 1$, which has been used successfully in Russian 40-bit computers [Sob94]. Its period is 2^{38}.

---

[4][Sob94] reports that IBM's RANDU uses $M = 2^{29}$, whilst [PTVF92] and [Tez95] report it to use $M = 2^{31}$. I don't know which is accurate or whether it makes a difference. I simply advise the reader to avoid any number generator that uses the multiplier $a = 65,539$.

[5][PTVF92] reports that *one popular 32-bit PC-compatible compiler* comes with a severely flawed pseudo-random number generator. Apparently, a reasonable number generator has been used as the basis for the compiler vendor's own design which was to add a byte swapping mechanism. This kind of action is always a dangerous thing to do and in this case ruined the number generator.

7.4   Ran0 TO Ran3

The seminal masterpiece by Press, Teukolsky, Vetterling and Flannery [PTVF92] is a very good source of reliable number generators that have been well tested and are well understood. The simplest of their suggested number generators, Ran0, is given by equation (7.6) with $a = 7^5 = 16\,807$, $c = 0$ and $M = 2^{31} - 1$. This choice of parameters was proposed by Park and Miller [PM88] as a minimal standard generator and goes back to IBM's *GGL generator* [Tez95, LGM69] from 1969. There are some technicalities involved with the issue of overcoming the roundoff problem in the multiplication in (7.6) for the given parameters on 32-bit computers. This is typically done with the aid of Schrage's method, and the reader is referred to [PTVF92] for details.

Ran1 is an enhancement of Ran0 using a careful shuffling algorithm. Note that any kind of enhancement of a pseudo-random number generator has to be done with utmost care, and should be left to number theoreticians. The reason is that any non-linear alteration or modification of the numbers given by one number generator is more than likely to result in disaster[6]. The message here is: kids, don't do this at home!

Ran2 is based on the idea of coupling two linear congruential generators, to construct one of a much longer period [L'E88]. Finally, there is Ran3 which is based on a subtractive method suggested by Knuth [Knu81]. I won't go into details for either of them because I don't think I could explain them any better than is already done in [PTVF92].

7.5   THE MERSENNE TWISTER

Another random number generator technique that has become increasingly popular recently is the *Mersenne twister*. The name is to indicate that the period of the sequence is a Mersenne number, i.e. a prime number that can be written as $2^n - 1$ for some $n \in \mathbb{N}$, and that it belongs to the class of 'Twisted Generalized Feedback Shift Register' sequence generators. The period of the Mersenne twister as published [MN98] and available [MN97] is $2^{19,937} - 1$. In order to give you a feeling for this number, imagine that we started at the time of the creation of the universe a computer producing 1 billion numbers per second[7] from the Mersenne twister sequence. The fraction of the full period that this computer would have produced by now is a decimal number with 5975 digits of zeros behind the decimal point, prior to any non-zero digits. In other words, this computer could continue to draw numbers for many thousand lifecycles of your average solar system between its formation and collapse into a black hole before beginning to repeat the sequence. Clearly, for all practical purposes, this number generator can be assumed to have infinite periodicity.

The Mersenne twister sequence is guaranteed to have equidistribution properties in at least 623 dimensions. As George Marsaglia put it in 1968, 'Random numbers fall mainly in the planes', for all random number sequences there exists an embedding dimensionality in which, in the right projection, all sample points appear to lie in hyperplanes. This can have fatal consequences for a Monte Carlo calculation if the problem that is evaluated just

---

[6]You may, if you want, compare it to the problem of interaction of two individually chaotic systems (although randomness is *not* chaos, as was demonstrated in the previous sections), which in most cases gives rise to stable periodic behaviour.

[7]Even though at the time of writing computers running at 1 GHz CPU clock frequency are readily available, software running on such fast hardware could only produce Mersenne twister numbers at a rate of less than 100 million draws per second.

so happens to be susceptible to the used sequence's regularity. The higher the embedding dimension is which produces those patterns, the safer will be the underlying number generator for general purpose use. I do not intend to go into details about the internal mechanics of this particular generator; suffice it to say that it tries to utilise as much of the existing number theory as possible to produce a reliable number generator. To quote the authors themselves:

> 'MT uses many existing ideas. In particular, we are thankful to the following persons. N. Yoneda, P. L'Ecuyer, R. Couture, H. Niederreiter, P. Hellekalek, M. Fushimi, S. Tezuka, Y. Kurita, D. Knuth, H. Leeb, S. Wegenkittl, T. Cooper, M. Rieffel, H. Enomoto, and many persons who gave us valuable comments, including the users of TT800, a previous twisted generator.'

In all of my tests and experiences this sequence engine performed well. Since code is freely available for it [MN97], and since it is no slower than any of the other pseudo-random number generators[8], it is recommended to integrate it into your general purpose library. It is certainly worth having it, even if only as a backup should you ever wish to cross-test results against a number generator whose code base was not taken from the seminal reference 'Numerical Recipes in C' [PTVF92].

7.6 WHICH ONE TO USE?

All of them, or at least more than one of them. Sadly, many people who use Monte Carlo methods underestimate the importance of the underlying number generator greatly, or have some kind of deep trust in whoever built the number generator they are using from within a black box. This is not to say that the sequence generator is the most difficult part of the design of a Monte Carlo procedure, on the contrary. It is, however, one link in a chain of techniques that together comprise a Monte Carlo simulation, and the nature of chains is that they are only as strong as their weakest link. Unlike some add-on parts of the chain such as control variates, etc. which are supposed to just add strength with their weak performance not breaking the fundamentals of the calculation, the reliability of the number generator is crucial. I hope that by the end of this chapter the reader is sufficiently aware of the basic principles ensuring that, as a matter of fact, *all pseudo-random number generators are flawed*. How suitable they still are for any one application depends on the very problem that is being tackled, and it is virtually impossible to foresee where a number generator may break down. Therefore, I advise any user of Monte Carlo methods to have a small library of number generators available, and rather than rerunning a calculation with a new seed for any one generator, flick a switch that makes the simulation use a different number construction method altogether. That's the way to do it.

---

[8]It is in fact faster than most other reliable pseudo-random number generators.

8

Low-discrepancy Numbers

In the light of the fundamental difficulties involved in the generation of truly random numbers mentioned in Chapter 7, we may ask ourselves why do we need randomness? The answer lies with the need to represent multi-dimensional joint distributions. As an easy example, let us consider the incremental path construction of standard Brownian motion

$$W(t_{i+1}) = W(t_i) + \sqrt{\Delta t_i}\, z_i \qquad (8.1)$$

with $z_i \sim \mathcal{N}(0, 1)$ over the time interval $[0, t_n]$ for $i = 0, \ldots, n-1$. Evidently, any serial correlation between the drawn normal variates z_i will give rise to a bias or undesirable regularity in the constructed path. If many paths constructed in this way are used as the basis for the valuation of a path-dependent financial derivative, for instance, any serial correlation is likely to give rise to a mispricing. We can, however, view this kind of problem from a different perspective. What we are really sampling here is a function of a vector argument z whose elements are to be taken from an n-dimensional standard normal distribution. In this formulation, there is absolutely no reason why subsequent draws of n-dimensional vector variates z would have to be serially uncorrelated. The need for perfect decorrelation and thus randomness is merely an artefact of the custom to construct multi-dimensional vector variates from one and the same underlying one-dimensional number generator. For number generation methods that allow for a given dimensionality of the problem at hand, taking previous vector draws into account, and thus making subsequent vector draws serially correlated in order to avoid the inevitable clusters and gaps of (pseudo-)random numbers, can actually aid the equidistribution property of the number sequence generator. This is the essential idea behind the concept of low-discrepancy numbers.

Unlike pseudo-random numbers, *low-discrepancy numbers* aim *not* to be serially uncorrelated, but instead to take into account which points in the domain to be sampled have already been probed. The mathematical foundations of low-discrepancy sequences go back to H. Weyl in 1917 [Sob94] and many number theoreticians have worked in this field, although I name but a few of the better known sequences: Halton, Faure, Haselgrove, Niederreiter and Sobol' [Sob67, Sob76, BF88, BFN94, Nie88, Nie96, Nie92, Tez95]. Low-discrepancy numbers have become a popular tool for financial Monte Carlo calculations since the early 1990s [BMW92].

It has been shown that number sequences can be generated that enable us to do quasi-Monte Carlo calculations which, given certain smoothness conditions of the function to be integrated, converge not as one over the square root of the number of samples taken, i.e. $\propto 1/\sqrt{N}$, but instead much more closely to one over N, namely $\propto c(d)[(\ln N)^d/N]$. This, even for a large dimensionality d, is asymptotically much faster than $\propto 1/\sqrt{N}$. The only problem is that the coefficient $c(d)$ can depend on the dimensionality and thus for any one high-dimensional calculation we cannot know in advance if the use of low-discrepancy numbers will be beneficial with respect to the accuracy required for the specific computation. At this point, number-theoretical results alone no longer tell us if any particular low-discrepancy sequence will give a speed-up in convergence and we have to rely on empirical results.

In this chapter, I first explain the number-theoretical concept of *discrepancy*. Then, I introduce the Halton sequence which is probably the easiest low-discrepancy number generation method to describe. Next, I discuss the Sobol' sequence. Following that, I briefly discuss the Niederreiter (1988) method. For further details and other low-discrepancy number generation methods the reader is advised to refer to the books by Tezuka [Tez95] and Niederreiter [Nie92]. Then, some empirical evidence will be given that Sobol' numbers, if adequately initialised, can be used in high dimensions, conversely to common belief. I will also try to explain the origin of what I think is a misunderstanding in the literature that they begin to fail as and when you start using dimensionalities above a few dozen.

8.1   DISCREPANCY

A measure for how inhomogeneously a set of d-dimensional vectors $\{r_i\}$ is distributed in the unit hypercube is the so-called *discrepancy*. A simple geometrical interpretation of the number-theoretical definition is as follows. Generate a set of N multivariate draws $\{r_i\}$ from a selected uniform number generation method of dimensionality d. All of these N vectors describe the coordinates of points in the d-dimensional unit hypercube $[0, 1]^d$. Now, select a sub-hypercube $S(y)$ by choosing a point y delimiting the upper right corner of the hyper-rectangular domain from $\mathbf{0}$ to y. In other words, the sub-hypercube S can be written as $S(y) = [0, y_1) \times \cdots \times [0, y_d)$. Next, let $n_{S(y)}$ denote the number of all those draws that are in $S(y)$, i.e.

$$n_{S(y)} = \sum_{i=1}^{N} \mathbf{1}_{\{r_i \in S(y)\}}$$

$$= \sum_{i=1}^{N} \prod_{k=1}^{d} \mathbf{1}_{\{y_k \geqslant r_{ik}\}}. \tag{8.2}$$

In the limit $N \to \infty$, we clearly require perfect homogeneity from the sequence generator, which means

$$\lim_{N \to \infty} \frac{n_{S(y)}}{N} = \prod_{i=1}^{d} y_i \tag{8.3}$$

for all $y \in [0, 1]^d$. The above equation simply results from the fact that for a perfectly homogeneous and uniform distribution on a unit hypercube the probability of being in a subdomain is equal to the volume of that subdomain, and the volume V of $S(y)$ is given by the right-hand side of equation (8.3). With these definitions, we can now compare $n_{S(y)}/N$ with $V(S(y))$ for any one given y. In order to obtain a measure for the global discrepancy of the number generator, we still need to choose an error norm over all possible y in the unit hypercube. With respect to the L_2-norm, this gives us

$$T_N^{(d)} = \left(\int_{[0,1]^d} \left(\frac{n_{S(y)}}{N} - \prod_{k=1}^{d} y_k \right)^2 \mathrm{d}y \right)^{\frac{1}{2}}. \tag{8.4}$$

Another frequently used discrepancy measure is the one resulting from the above procedure involving the L_∞-norm:

$$D_N^{(d)} = \sup_{y \in [0,1]^d} \left| \frac{n_{S(y)}}{N} - \prod_{k=1}^{d} y_k \right|. \tag{8.5}$$

Clearly, by the nature of the underlying norms used for the respective definitions of $T_N^{(d)}$
and $D_N^{(d)}$, we have

$$D_N^{(d)} \geqslant T_N^{(d)}. \tag{8.6}$$

For numerical tests, the L_∞ discrepancy is rather cumbersome to evaluate. However, as
demonstrated in appendix section 8.8.1, the discrepancy with respect to the L_2-norm can
be evaluated with the explicit formula

$$\left(T_N^{(d)} \right)^2 = \frac{1}{N^2} \sum_{i,j=1}^{N} \prod_{k=1}^{d} \left(1 - \max(r_{ik}, r_{jk}) \right) - \frac{2^{1-d}}{N} \sum_{i=1}^{N} \prod_{k=1}^{d} \left(1 - r_{ik}^2 \right) + 3^{-d} \tag{8.7}$$

where r_{ik} is the kth element of r_i. In appendix section 8.8.2, I show that the *expected*
squared discrepancy for truly random numbers is

$$E\left[T_N^{(d)\,2} \right] = \frac{1}{N} \left(2^{-d} - 3^{-d} \right). \tag{8.8}$$

We now arrive at the number-theoretical definition of low-discrepancy sequences. A
sequence in $[0,1]^d$ is called a *low-discrepancy* sequence if for all $N > 1$ the first N
points in the sequence satisfy

$$D_N^{(d)} \leqslant c(d) \frac{(\ln N)^d}{N} \tag{8.9}$$

for some constant $c(d)$ that is only a function of d.

8.2 HALTON NUMBERS

The idea behind Halton numbers is to use the representation of a given *generating* integer
γ in a different number base for each dimension. Of course, the mentioned integer has
to be a different one for each new vector draw. An easy and natural choice for this
constructing integer is simply the number n for the nth draw, $\gamma(n) := n$, but any other
choice using a new integer with each draw, such as the Gray code $G(n)$ discussed in
section 8.3.3, would work, too. In order to prevent any asymptotic pairwise periodicity,
the number bases are chosen to be the prime numbers, of which one has to be precalculated
for each dimension. The algorithm to construct a new vector draw of Halton numbers is
as follows.

1. For each of the required dimensions $i = 1, \ldots, d$, find the representation of $\gamma(n)$ in
    the associated prime number base p_i, i.e. find the coefficients a_k in

$$\gamma(n) = \sum_{k=1}^{m_{ni}} a_{ki} p_i^{k-1} \tag{8.10}$$

with all of the $a_{ki} < p_i$ and m_{ni} chosen large enough to make sure that all non-zero digits of $\gamma(n)$ in the number base p_i are accounted for.

2.   To construct the coordinate u_{ni} for dimension i of the nth uniform vector draw, the sequence of calculated coefficients is now inverted and used as multipliers of fractions in the number base p_i, i.e.

$$u_{ni} = \sum_{k=1}^{m_{ni}} a_{ki} p_i^{-k}. \tag{8.11}$$

For instance, if we choose the prime numbers 2,3,5,7 as the basis in the four dimensions of a four-dimensional Halton sequence, the 37th draw is constructed as follows for $\gamma(n) = n$:

Base	$n = 37_{10}$ in base		u_{ni}
2	100101_2	$0.101001_2 = 1 \cdot 2^{-1} + 0 \cdot 2^{-2} + 1 \cdot 2^{-3} + 0 \cdot 2^{-4} + 0 \cdot 2^{-5} + 1 \cdot 2^{-6}$	$= 0.640625$
3	1101_3	$0.1011_3 =$ $\quad 1 \cdot 3^{-1} + 0 \cdot 3^{-2} + 1 \cdot 3^{-3} + 1 \cdot 3^{-4}$	$= 0.382716$
5	122_5	$0.221_5 =$ $\quad 2 \cdot 5^{-1} + 2 \cdot 5^{-2} + 1 \cdot 5^{-3}$	$= 0.488000$
7	52_7	$0.25_7 =$ $\quad 2 \cdot 7^{-1} + 5 \cdot 7^{-2}$	$= 0.387755$

An actual implementation of the algorithm to create the next draw of the Halton sequence is given in Code Example 8.1. The variable `sequenceCounter` is the index of the next

```
const vector<double>& Halton::nextUniformVector( void ) {
    unsigned long b, i, k;
    double f, h;
    for (++sequenceCounter, i = 0;  (i < dimensionality);  ++i) {
        for ( k = sequenceCounter, b = primeNumbers[i], f = 1., h = 0.;  (k);  k/=b ) {
            f /= b;
            h += (k%b)*f;
        }
        sequenceVector[i] = h;
    }
    return sequenceVector;
}
```

Code Example 8.1   Code sample for the generation of the next vector draw of the Halton sequence

vector draw, i.e. it represents n in the discussion above. The precalculated prime numbers are stored in the array `primeNumbers`.

8.3   SOBOL' NUMBERS

The construction of Sobol' numbers [Sob67] is somewhat more involved. Again, a set of incommensurate basis numbers is used. This time, however, a different kind of multiplication determines the meaning of *incommensurate*. Whereas for Halton numbers the basis numbers simply had to be incommensurate with respect to ordinary multiplication, for Sobol' numbers the basis numbers are compared with respect to binary multiplication modulo two.

8.3.1   Primitive Polynomials Modulo Two

The theory of Sobol' numbers starts with modular integer arithmetic. Two integers i and j are called *congruent with respect to the modulus m*, i.e.

$$i \triangleq j \qquad \mathrm{mod}\ m \tag{8.12}$$

if and only if the difference $i - j$ is divisible by m. Clearly, the numbers $0, \ldots, m - 1$ are sufficient to represent the result of any multiplication or addition in the modulus m, due to the congruence relation (8.12). For m prime, the combination of addition and multiplication modulo m, plus a neutral element with respect to both, is also called a *finite commutative ring* which is *isomorphic* to a Galois field with m elements, $GF[m]$.

A polynomial $P(z)$ of degree g

$$P(z) = \sum_{j=0}^{g} a_k z^{g-j} \tag{8.13}$$

is considered to be an element of the ring $GF[m, z]$ of polynomials over the finite field $GF[m]$ if we assume all of the coefficients $a_k \in GF[m]$. In other words, all algebra on the coefficients a_k is to be carried out modulo m. This means, for instance, that

$$(z + 1)(z + 1)(z^2 + z + 1) \triangleq z^4 + z^3 + z + 1 \qquad \mathrm{mod}\ 2. \tag{8.14}$$

A polynomial $P(z)$ of positive degree is considered to be *irreducible* modulo m if there are no other two polynomials $Q(z)$ and $R(z)$ which are not constant or equal to $P(z)$ itself such that

$$P(z) \triangleq Q(z)R(z) \qquad \mathrm{mod}\ m. \tag{8.15}$$

An irreducible polynomial modulo m in $GF[m, z]$ is the equivalent to a prime number in the set of integers.

The order of a polynomial $P(z)$ modulo m is given by the smallest positive integer q for which $P(z)$ divides $z^q - 1$, i.e.

$$q = \inf_{q'} \left\{ q' \ \middle| \ z^{q'} - 1 \triangleq P(z)R(z) \qquad \mathrm{mod}\ m \right\} \tag{8.16}$$

for some non-constant polynomial $R(z)$.

An irreducible polynomial $P(z)$ of degree g is also considered to be *primitive* modulo m if its order is $m^g - 1$. Note that not all irreducible polynomials are also primitive, although (especially for $m = 2$) most of them are.

The importance of primitive polynomials modulo two is given by two separate facts. Firstly, algebraic manipulations modulo two, i.e. binary algebra, are particularly well suited to implementation on today's digital computers. Secondly, for any primitive polynomial of degree g there are recurrence relations to obtain a new random bit from g preceding ones [PTVF92]. In other words, the use of a distinct primitive polynomial modulo two for each of the required dimensions of the vector of uniform numbers makes it possible to generate a sequence of vectors in which the sampling happens uniformly over all of the dimensions, but in each dimension we also have uniform use of all the binary digits. For further information on the distinction between irreducibility and primitivity, see for example [Tez95, Chi00]. The calculation of primitive polynomials can be rather involved. Whilst there are limited tables of primitive polynomials available [Wat62, PTVF92, Jäc97], I provide a list of all primitive polynomials modulo two up to degree 27 on the accompanying CD. This amounts to a total number of 8 129 334 primitive polynomials which should be more than enough for all practical applications.

8.3.2   The Construction of Sobol' Numbers

The generation of Sobol' numbers is initially carried out on a set of integers in the interval from 1 to a power of two minus one, say $[1, 2^b - 1]$. As you may imagine, b simply represents the number of bits in an unsigned integer on the given computer and should typically be 32, which amounts to the set of attainable integers being given by all those in the range $[1, 4 294 967 295]$. We will denote the nth draw of one such Sobol' integer in dimension k as x_{nk}. The final conversion to a uniform variate $y_{nk} \in (0, 1)$ is done by dividing x_{nk} by 2^b as a floating point operation, i.e.

$$y_{nk} := \frac{x_{nk}}{2^b}, \quad y_{nk} \in (0, 1), \ x_{nk} \in \mathbb{Z}[1, 2^b - 1]. \tag{8.17}$$

By construction, the only Sobol' variate that could ever be exactly zero[1] is the zeroth draw (more on the meaning of this later), and this holds for all dimensions. Therefore, we can explicitly exclude the possibility that any one of the drawn integers is actually zero by simply skipping the zeroth draw.

For each of the d dimensions, the basis of the number generation is given by a set of so-called *direction integers*, of which there is one for each of the b bits in the binary integer representation. It is conducive for the following to view all of the direction integers as b-wide bit fields. Let us denote the lth direction integer for dimension k as v_{kl}. Additional constraints on the bit field representing v_{kl} are that only the l leftmost[2] bits can be non-zero, and that the lth leftmost bit of v_{kl} must be set. The actual number draws will later on be calculated by binary addition modulo two of some of these direction integers, which makes it clear that each v_{kl} can only affect the l leftmost bits in the drawn integer x_{nk}, and that it definitely influences the lth leftmost bit of x_{nk}.

Binary addition of integers modulo two, which amounts to bitwise addition without carry, is a particularly fast operation on contemporary computers, known as *Exclusive OR*, and is usually abbreviated as XOR. The key to the generation of Sobol' numbers is the calculation of the direction integers. This involves the binary coefficients of a selected primitive polynomial modulo two for each dimension. Let the primitive polynomial modulo two for dimension k be p_k. Denote the degree of this polynomial as g_k. Let the coefficient of the highest monomial in p_k be a_{k0}, and so forth down to $a_{k g_k}$, i.e.

$$p_k(z) = \sum_{j=0}^{g_k} a_{kj} z^{g_k - j}. \tag{8.18}$$

Note the fact that $a_{k0} \equiv 1$ is a simple consequence of $p_k(z)$ being of degree g_k.

---

[1]This means for both the original Sobol' algorithm as well as the Antonov–Saleev modification using the conventional Gray code, but also for all other methods that choose the generating integer $\gamma(n)$ such that $\gamma(0) = 0$.

[2]The leftmost bits in a bit field representing an integer are the most significant ones. On standard contemporary computers, the number of bits in an integer is 32. Thus, an unsigned integer with only the leftmost bit set would correspond to the number $2^{31} = 2 147 483 648$, and all bits being 1 corresponds to 4 294 967 295.

Now we come to the setting up of the direction integers. In each dimension with its associated primitive polynomial p_k, the first g_k direction integers v_{kl} for $l = 1, \ldots, g_k$ can be chosen freely, within the above-mentioned two constraints. All subsequent ones are constructed from the following recurrence relation:

$$v_{kl} = \frac{v_{k(l-g_k)}}{2^{g_k}} \oplus_2 \sum_{j=1}^{g_k} {}^{\oplus_2} a_{kj} v_{k(l-j)} \quad \text{for } l > g_k. \tag{8.19}$$

Hereby, the operator $\oplus_2$ stands for the XOR operation[3], and the notation $\sum^{\cdots \, \oplus_2}_{\cdots}$ indicates a whole sequence of XOR operations, or binary additions without carry, in analogy to the conventional sum operator $\sum$. In other words, the direction integer $v_{k\,(l-g_k)}$ is right-shifted by g_k bits, and then XORed with a selection of the (unshifted) direction integers $v_{k\,(l-j)}$ for $j = 1, \ldots, g_k$ (controlled by which of the coefficients a_{kj} are set), to obtain v_{kl}. Note that the highest order coefficient a_{k0} is not actually used in the recurrence relation (8.19), and that since the lowest order coefficient $a_{k\,g_k}$ is always set, the direction integer $v_{k\,(l-g_k)}$ will always enter v_{kl}. This is the reason why the highest and lowest coefficients of the polynomial p_k are not usually included in its encoding, provided that its degree is known [PTVF92].

If you made it this far, and managed to follow the above explanations, you'll be relieved to see how simple the *actual* construction of the Sobol' integers x_{nk} turns out, given the above preliminaries. Just like for the construction of Halton numbers, we need a new unique generating integer $\gamma(n)$ for each new draw. An easy choice of such an integer for the nth draw is n itself, i.e. $\gamma(n) := n$, which amounts to the original algorithm published by Sobol' [Sob67]. However, any other method of ensuring a new integer for each new draw, such as the Gray code $\gamma(n) := G(n)$, is equally possible. Given the generating integer of the nth draw, the Sobol' integers for all of the d dimensions are given by

$$x_{nk} := \sum_{j=1}^{b} {}^{\oplus_2} v_{kj} \mathbf{1}_{\{j\text{th bit (counting from the right) of } \gamma(n) \text{ is set}\}} \quad \text{with } k = 1..d \tag{8.20}$$

In other words, depending on which bits in the binary representation of $\gamma(n)$ are set, the direction integers are simply XORed, to produce the Sobol' integer x_{nk}. The final transformation to a uniform floating point number in the interval was already given by the simple division in equation (8.17). It may be clear from formula (8.20) that we need to ensure

$$\gamma(n) \neq 0 \tag{8.21}$$

in order to prevent any of the y_{nk} being exactly zero. By the nature of the construction algorithm of the direction integers, no other value for $\gamma(n)$ can result in any x_{nk} and thus y_{nk} being zero, whence condition (8.21) is sufficient to ensure $y_{nk} \neq 0$.

8.3.3   The Gray Code

Antonov and Saleev contributed to Sobol' numbers as we know them today by realising that instead of using the binary representation of the sequence counter n directly, any other

---

[3] Just in case you don't know this already, but still care: the '$\oplus_2$' operation's equivalent in C is '$\hat{\ }$'.

Table 8.1 Possible transitions from 3 to 4 in standard binary representation

$3_{10} = 011_2$	$2_{10} = 010_2$	$0_{10} = 000_2$	$4_{10} = 100_2$
$3_{10} = 011_2$	$2_{10} = 010_2$	$6_{10} = 110_2$	$4_{10} = 100_2$
$3_{10} = 011_2$	$1_{10} = 001_2$	$0_{10} = 000_2$	$4_{10} = 100_2$
$3_{10} = 011_2$	$1_{10} = 001_2$	$5_{10} = 101_2$	$4_{10} = 100_2$
$3_{10} = 011_2$	$7_{10} = 111_2$	$6_{10} = 110_2$	$4_{10} = 100_2$
$3_{10} = 011_2$	$7_{10} = 111_2$	$5_{10} = 101_2$	$4_{10} = 100_2$

unique representation of the sequence counter n can be used too [AS79]. In particular, a bitwise representation of n which switches only one single bit for every increment in n means that only one single XOR operation is to be carried out for the generation of every integer representing the uniform coordinate of the next vector draw. This kind of encoding of integers is known as a Gray code $G(n)$, named after the engineer Frank Gray who patented this method for use with shaft encoders in the 1950s. Gray codes are still used with shaft encoders today, and in many communication applications. They are useful wherever a set of parallel electrical wires is used to indicate a number by the individual voltage state of each line. Frequently, such lines are used to transmit the current state of a counter variable, which would only ever increase by one. In such an application, using any encoding whereby more than one bit can change from one number to the next, the tiniest mistiming in the transition of the high–low states from one number to the next will cause the recipient of the signal not to receive a clean increase, but a rapid and spurious sequence of intermediate numbers. As an example, think of the transition from $3_{10} = 011_2$ to $4_{10} = 100_2$. Due to the inevitably limited accuracy of mechanical or electronic components, the receiver is likely to perceive one of the possible sequences from 3 to 4 given in Table 8.1. Clearly, none of them are desirable. Using a Gray code in the representation of the integers surmounts this problem because exactly one bit changes in any one increase. It turns out that there is no single unique Gray code. The most commonly used choice for the Gray code is

$$G(n) = n \oplus_2 [n/2]. \tag{8.22}$$

In Table 8.2, the Gray code of the integers 1 to 7 is given as an example. An interesting feature of the Gray code is that the single bit that changes from $G(n)$ to $G(n+1)$ is always the rightmost zero bit of the binary representation of n itself. This can readily be verified analytically and is also easy to see in Table 8.2.

As for the generation of Sobol' numbers, they are clearly aided by the use of $G(n)$ instead of n as the constructing integer of the nth vector draw. Imagine we have already generated all of the vector draws out to number $n-1$, and we have kept in memory the uniform integers $x_{(n-1)}$ for all of the required dimensions. Since the Gray code $G(n)$ differs from that of the preceding one $G(n-1)$ by just a single, say the jth, bit (which is the rightmost zero bit of $n-1$), all that needs to be done is a single XOR operation for each dimension in order to propagate all of the $x_{(n-1)}$ to x_n, i.e.

$$x_{nk} = x_{(n-1)k} \oplus_2 v_{jk}. \tag{8.23}$$

Table 8.2   Gray codes

n	n in binary	$[n/2]$ in binary	$G(n)$ in binary	$G(n)$ in decimal
0	000	000	000	0
1	001	000	001	1
2	010	001	011	3
3	011	001	010	2
4	100	010	110	6
5	101	010	111	7
6	110	011	101	5
7	111	011	100	4

8.3.4   The Initialisation of Sobol' Numbers

The attentive reader may have noticed that there is yet some freedom left in the construction of Sobol' numbers, namely the specific choice of the free direction numbers. As we recall from section 8.3.2, given the primitive polynomial p_k of degree g_k associated with the kth dimension, the first g_k direction integers can be chosen freely within certain constraints. All remaining direction integers are then determined by the recurrence equation (8.19). Since the first g_k direction integers thus initialise the entire construction of the sequence, I also call them *initialisation numbers*. The constraints on the lth initialisation number v_{kl} of dimension k are that only the l leftmost bits can be non-zero, and that the lth bit from the left-hand side of the b-wide bit field representing v_{kl} must be 1. Arguably the easiest choice for the initialisation numbers is thus to just have the lth leftmost bit set, and all other bits to be zero, which amounts to what I call *unit initialisation*, i.e.

$$v_{kl} = 2^{b-l}. \tag{8.24}$$

The impact of the initialisation numbers on the homogeneity properties of the entire sequence is not to be underestimated. In 1976, Sobol' published algebraic conditions that link specific choices of initialisation numbers to certain uniformity properties [Sob76]. A low-discrepancy sequence is said to satisfy *property A* if for any binary segment (not an arbitrary subset) of the d-dimensional sequence of length 2^d there is exactly one draw in each of the 2^d hypercubes that result from subdividing the unit hypercube along each of its unit length extensions into half. In other words, assume that in each dimension we divide the interval $[0, 1)$ into the two subintervals $[0, \frac{1}{2})$ and $[\frac{1}{2}, 1)$. This will result in a subdivision of the d-dimensional unit hypercube $[0, 1)^d$ into 2^d sub-hypercubes. Given any sequential section S of length 2^d of the low-discrepancy sequence of d-dimensional uniform variates that starts at some index $m = l2^d$ for some integer l, i.e. $S_l := (u_{l2^d}, u_{l2^d+1}, \ldots, u_{(l+1)2^d-1})$, there must be exactly one $u \in S_l$ that lies in each and every one of the sub-hypercubes of volume 2^{-d} for the sequence generator to satisfy property A. Property A$'$ is similar in its definition in that it refers to sections of length 4^d being required to provide that a single element is contained in each and every sub-hypercube resulting from the subdivision of the unit hypercube into four equal intervals in each dimension. Of course, if we explicitly exclude the point at the origin $u \equiv 0$ (as we would in order to prevent a mapping to infinity when transforming to Gaussian variates), the segment of the sequence starting with the first element will have no point in the sub-hypercube $[0, \frac{1}{2})^d$ and will be most uniform for a length of $2^d - 1$.

The algebraic equations that guarantee properties A and A' can be solved numerically, and there are precalculated tables of initialisation numbers that provide properties A and A' up to certain dimensionalities in the literature. The original article [Sob76], for instance, provides initialisation numbers up to dimension 16 for property A and up to dimension 6 for property A'. Unfortunately, the importance of these properties has not been fully appreciated by many subsequent publications on the subject of usability of Sobol' numbers in higher dimensions, which may be the reason that many authors resort to various forms of enhancements [Owe98] already in very moderate dimensionalities. In finance, however, we often face problems that are of very high dimensionality d. In order to benefit from property A, we would need to carry out a Monte Carlo simulation over a number of iterations of order of magnitude 2^d. The pricing of an Asian option with daily monitoring and one year to maturity, for instance, represents a Monte Carlo integration in 250 dimensions, one for each trading day in the year. Since $2^{250} \simeq 10^{75}$, we would have to iterate as many times as is currently estimated to be the total number of particles in the universe, which is clearly excessive, before we would benefit from property A, not to mention property A'.

However, as we will see in sections 8.5 and 8.6 this is not to say that for high-dimensional problems every set of initialisation numbers will work as well as any other. There is a clear benefit from the choice of initialisation numbers that enables the low-discrepancy sequence to start exploring the volume of the unit hypercube early on, rather than initially just focusing on certain areas. I therefore recommend using initialisation numbers that provide properties A and A' for the lowest dimensions, and for the higher dimensions, at least to ensure that any regularity in the initialisation set is broken up. One choice of initialisation numbers that does the complete opposite is the aforementioned unit initialisation. Although strictly speaking a valid choice of initialisation numbers, unit initialisation leads to surprisingly bad results for Sobol' numbers, and should be avoided. A very simple way to generate initialisation numbers that break the regularity is to use a separate pseudo-random number generator to draw uniform variates from (0, 1), and to initialise as follows. Draw u_{kl}^* from a separate uniform random number generator such that

$$w_{kl} := \mathrm{int}\left[u_{kl}^* \cdot 2^{l-1}\right] \tag{8.25}$$

is odd (simply keep drawing until the condition is met), and set

$$v_{kl} := w_{kl} \cdot 2^{b-l} \quad \text{for } l = 1, \dots, g_k. \tag{8.26}$$

To finish this section I give in Table 8.3 a list of initialisation numbers that have been tested to give property A up to dimension 32 and are guaranteed to provide property A' up to dimension 6 [Sob76]. The columns are as follows: k is the dimension index, g_k is the degree of the associated polynomial, $a_{k0}, \dots, a_{kg_k}$ are the coefficients of the polynomial as in equation (8.18), and v_{kl} are the direction numbers. The freely chosen direction numbers, i.e. the initialisation set, are unshaded and those derived from the recurrence relation (8.19) are shaded. Note that the polynomial associated with dimension 1 is not strictly a primitive polynomial, similar to the number 1 not strictly being a prime number. This is also the reason why the direction numbers for dimension 1 are not given by the recurrence relation (8.19), but are simply $v_{1l} = 2^{b-l}$. Further details can be found in the original literature [Sob67]. As for readily available code to construct Sobol', there is of course the

Table 8.3 Initialisation numbers providing property A up to dimension 32

			v_{kl} for $l=1,\dots,10$									
k	g_k	$a_{k0},\dots,a_{kg_k}$	1×2^{31}	1×2^{30}	1×2^{29}	1×2^{28}	1×2^{27}	1×2^{26}	1×2^{25}	1×2^{24}	1×2^{23}	1×2^{22}
1	0	1	1×2^{31}	1×2^{30}	1×2^{29}	1×2^{28}	1×2^{27}	1×2^{26}	1×2^{25}	1×2^{24}	1×2^{23}	1×2^{22}
2	1	11	1×2^{31}	3×2^{30}	5×2^{29}	15×2^{28}	17×2^{27}	51×2^{26}	85×2^{25}	255×2^{24}	257×2^{23}	771×2^{22}
3	2	111	1×2^{31}	1×2^{30}	7×2^{29}	11×2^{28}	13×2^{27}	61×2^{26}	67×2^{25}	79×2^{24}	465×2^{23}	721×2^{22}
4	3	1011	1×2^{31}	3×2^{30}	7×2^{29}	5×2^{28}	7×2^{27}	43×2^{26}	49×2^{25}	147×2^{24}	439×2^{23}	1013×2^{22}
5	3	1101	1×2^{31}	1×2^{30}	5×2^{29}	3×2^{28}	15×2^{27}	51×2^{26}	125×2^{25}	141×2^{24}	177×2^{23}	759×2^{22}
6	4	10011	1×2^{31}	3×2^{30}	1×2^{29}	1×2^{28}	9×2^{27}	59×2^{26}	25×2^{25}	89×2^{24}	321×2^{23}	835×2^{22}
7	4	11001	1×2^{31}	1×2^{30}	3×2^{29}	7×2^{28}	31×2^{27}	47×2^{26}	109×2^{25}	173×2^{24}	181×2^{23}	949×2^{22}
8	5	100101	1×2^{31}	3×2^{30}	3×2^{29}	9×2^{28}	9×2^{27}	57×2^{26}	43×2^{25}	43×2^{24}	225×2^{23}	113×2^{22}
9	5	101001	1×2^{31}	3×2^{30}	7×2^{29}	7×2^{28}	21×2^{27}	61×2^{26}	55×2^{25}	19×2^{24}	59×2^{23}	761×2^{22}
10	5	101111	1×2^{31}	1×2^{30}	5×2^{29}	11×2^{28}	27×2^{27}	53×2^{26}	69×2^{25}	25×2^{24}	103×2^{23}	615×2^{22}
11	5	110111	1×2^{31}	1×2^{30}	7×2^{29}	3×2^{28}	29×2^{27}	51×2^{26}	47×2^{25}	97×2^{24}	233×2^{23}	39×2^{22}
12	5	111011	1×2^{31}	3×2^{30}	7×2^{29}	13×2^{28}	3×2^{27}	35×2^{26}	89×2^{25}	9×2^{24}	235×2^{23}	929×2^{22}
13	5	111101	1×2^{31}	3×2^{30}	5×2^{29}	1×2^{28}	15×2^{27}	19×2^{26}	113×2^{25}	115×2^{24}	411×2^{23}	157×2^{22}
14	6	1000011	1×2^{31}	3×2^{30}	1×2^{29}	9×2^{28}	23×2^{27}	37×2^{26}	37×2^{25}	97×2^{24}	353×2^{23}	169×2^{22}
15	6	1011011	1×2^{31}	3×2^{30}	3×2^{29}	13×2^{28}	11×2^{27}	7×2^{26}	37×2^{25}	101×2^{24}	463×2^{23}	657×2^{22}
16	6	1100001	1×2^{31}	1×2^{30}	3×2^{29}	5×2^{28}	19×2^{27}	33×2^{26}	3×2^{25}	197×2^{24}	329×2^{23}	983×2^{22}
17	6	1100111	1×2^{31}	1×2^{30}	7×2^{29}	-3×2^{28}	25×2^{27}	5×2^{26}	27×2^{25}	71×2^{24}	377×2^{23}	719×2^{22}
18	6	1101101	1×2^{31}	3×2^{30}	1×2^{29}	3×2^{28}	13×2^{27}	39×2^{26}	7×2^{25}	23×2^{24}	391×2^{23}	389×2^{22}
19	6	1110011	1×2^{31}	3×2^{30}	5×2^{29}	-1×2^{28}	7×2^{27}	11×2^{26}	43×2^{25}	25×2^{24}	187×2^{23}	825×2^{22}
20	7	10000011	1×2^{31}	3×2^{30}	1×2^{29}	7×2^{28}	3×2^{27}	23×2^{26}	79×2^{25}	65×2^{24}	451×2^{23}	321×2^{22}
21	7	10001001	1×2^{31}	3×2^{30}	1×2^{29}	15×2^{28}	17×2^{27}	63×2^{26}	13×2^{25}	113×2^{24}	147×2^{23}	881×2^{22}
22	7	10001111	1×2^{31}	1×2^{30}	3×2^{29}	3×2^{28}	25×2^{27}	17×2^{26}	115×2^{25}	17×2^{24}	179×2^{23}	883×2^{22}
23	7	10010001	1×2^{31}	3×2^{30}	7×2^{29}	9×2^{28}	31×2^{27}	29×2^{26}	17×2^{25}	121×2^{24}	363×2^{23}	783×2^{22}
24	7	10011101	1×2^{31}	1×2^{30}	3×2^{29}	15×2^{28}	29×2^{27}	15×2^{26}	41×2^{25}	249×2^{24}	201×2^{23}	923×2^{22}
25	7	10100111	1×2^{31}	1×2^{30}	1×2^{29}	9×2^{28}	5×2^{27}	21×2^{26}	19×2^{25}	53×2^{24}	319×2^{23}	693×2^{22}
26	7	10101011	1×2^{31}	3×2^{30}	5×2^{29}	5×2^{28}	1×2^{27}	27×2^{26}	33×2^{25}	253×2^{24}	341×2^{23}	385×2^{22}
27	7	10101101	1×2^{31}	1×2^{30}	3×2^{29}	1×2^{28}	23×2^{27}	13×2^{26}	75×2^{25}	29×2^{24}	181×2^{23}	895×2^{22}
28	7	10111001	1×2^{31}	1×2^{30}	7×2^{29}	7×2^{28}	19×2^{27}	25×2^{26}	105×2^{25}	173×2^{24}	509×2^{23}	75×2^{22}
29	7	11000001	1×2^{31}	3×2^{30}	5×2^{29}	5×2^{28}	21×2^{27}	9×2^{26}	7×2^{25}	143×2^{24}	157×2^{23}	959×2^{22}
30	7	11001011	1×2^{31}	1×2^{30}	1×2^{29}	15×2^{28}	5×2^{27}	49×2^{26}	59×2^{25}	71×2^{24}	31×2^{23}	111×2^{22}
31	7	11010011	1×2^{31}	3×2^{30}	5×2^{29}	15×2^{28}	17×2^{27}	19×2^{26}	21×2^{25}	227×2^{24}	413×2^{23}	727×2^{22}
32	7	11010101	1×2^{31}	1×2^{30}	7×2^{29}	11×2^{28}	13×2^{27}	29×2^{26}	3×2^{25}	15×2^{24}	279×2^{23}	17×2^{22}

algorithm in [PTVF92]. Using that source code, and the table of primitive polynomials modulo two on the accompanying CD, and the initialisation method described above for the free direction numbers, it shouldn't be too difficult to create your own high-dimensional Sobol' number generator. Also, there is a commercial library module available from an organisation called BRODA [KS] that can generate Sobol' sequences in up to 370 dimensions. In a way, this module can claim to be a *genuine* Sobol' number generator since Professor Sobol' himself is behind the initialisation numbers that drive the sequence, and he is also linked to the company distributing the library. Just before you get any wrong ideas: I am not affiliated with BRODA in any way whatsoever.

8.4 NIEDERREITER (1988) NUMBERS

H. Niederreiter devised a general framework for number-theoretically constructed sequences of low discrepancy [Nie92]. This contributed greatly to the analysis of the internal mechanisms and helped us to understand the similarities and differences of the various number sequences. He also devised several sequence generation algorithms [Nie88, Nie96], of which only one has been implemented [BFN94]. We refer to these numbers as the Niederreiter (1988) sequence. They are, from a constructional point of view, not too different from Sobol' numbers. They, too, are based on polynomial arithmetic modulo some base m, and the most frequently used base happens to be 2, not least due to the enormous speed and ease in carrying out binary calculations on a modern computer. However, Niederreiter (1988) numbers employ *irreducible* rather than *primitive* polynomials[4]. Despite the fact that they are theoretically supposed to be superior to Sobol' numbers in the limit, from an empirical point of view, where the start-up rather than the asymptotic performance[5] is more relevant, Niederreiter (1988) numbers, in my experience, do not provide quite the same reliability in terms of rapid convergence for high dimensionalities as Sobol' numbers do.

8.5 PAIRWISE PROJECTIONS

The aim of low-discrepancy number generation methods is to provide a source of vector coordinates that covers a given domain as homogeneously and uniformly as possible. The more homogeneous the underlying number generator, the more accurate and rapidly converging will be a Monte Carlo calculation based on it[6].

It has been documented in the literature that low-discrepancy number generators tend to lose their quality of homogeneous coverage as the dimensionality increases. A particularly striking way to demonstrate this is to plot the projection of a given number of vector coordinates drawn from a number generator onto a two-dimensional projection of adjacent dimensions. In Figure 8.1, we show the projection of the first 2047 vector draws of various number generators on several two-dimensional uniform intervals. In the first row, we have

---

[4]Clearly, since all primitive polynomials are also irreducible, one can just use primitive polynomials for the construction of Niederreiter (1988) numbers too. This does not, however, remedy the not-so-good performance of Niederreiter (1988) numbers in high-dimensional applications.

[5]For practical applications, we are more interested in the realised convergence over the first 10,000 or even 500 million draws, and the question as to which number generator will provide a higher rate of convergence in the asymptotic limit of *actually infinitely many draws* is not really of great importance.

[6]A more mathematical form of this statement is known as the Koksma–Hlawka theorem, but since this relationship is sufficiently plausible by sheer common sense, I won't go into the details here.

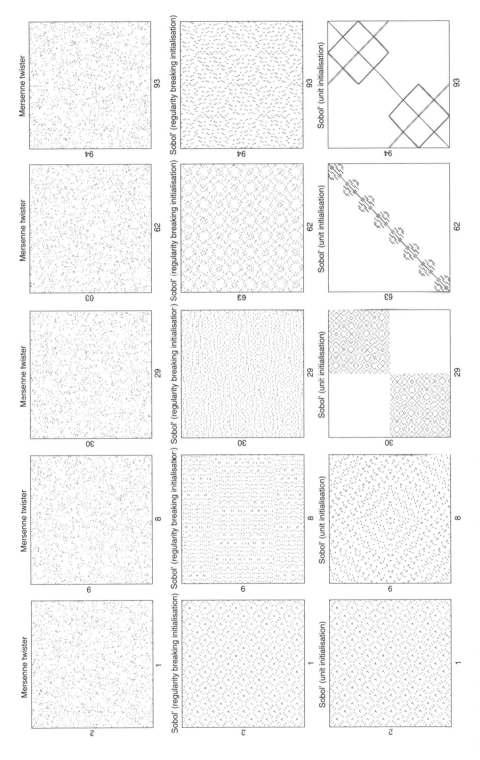

Figure 8.1   Two-dimensional projections of various number generators

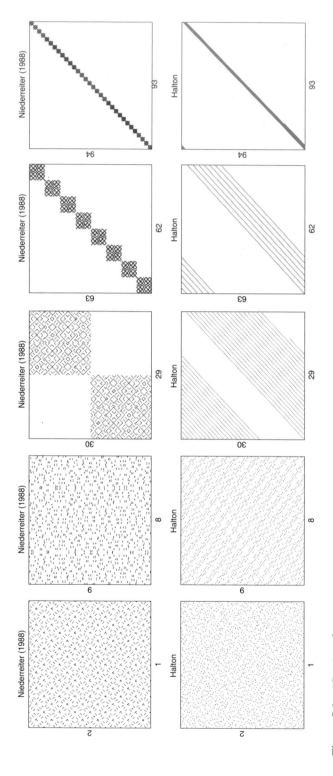

Figure 8.1 (*Continued*)

vector draws from the Mersenne twister as an example of a random pattern for reference. Rows 2 to 5 give the projections of the Sobol' generator (regularity breaking initialisation), Sobol' (unit initialisation), Niederreiter and Halton. In column 1, the projection onto the first two dimensions is shown, followed by dimension 8 versus 9, 29 versus 30, 62 versus 63, 93 versus 94. The particular dimensions shown were selected randomly. These projections are a first indicator that not all low-discrepancy number generators are reliable when fairly high dimensions are required. For the last three low-discrepancy number generators there is clearly a trend towards clusters and gaps as the dimension increases. Sobol' numbers with regularity breaking initialisation, however, do not seem to suffer from this problem.

There have been reports in various publications that Sobol' numbers also suffer the problem of rapid breakdown of homogeneity in higher dimensions. I believe this is due to an unfortunate choice of the initialisation numbers used for their construction. In fact, Sobol' himself has been aware of the importance of careful initialisation at least since the early 1970s [Sob76]. Alas, when the financial sector started using low-discrepancy numbers, this wasn't picked up, whence there is the notion that no low-discrepancy number generator is suitable for high dimensions.

8.6   EMPIRICAL DISCREPANCIES

A more thorough measure for the homogeneity properties of a low-discrepancy number generator than visual inspection of projections is the discrepancy as defined in equations (8.4) or (8.5). In order to provide even harder evidence that suitably initialised Sobol' numbers are indeed reliable, even in significantly high-dimensional applications, I show in Figures 8.2 to 8.9 the discrepancy with respect to the L_2-norm $T_N^{(d)}$ as defined in equation (8.4) for $d = 2, 3, 5, 10, 15, 30, 50, 100$ for various number generators. Note that the line denoted 'expectation for truly random numbers' is actually $\sqrt{E\left[\left(T_N^{(d)}\right)^2\right]}$, as calculated in appendix section 8.8.2.

It can clearly be seen in Figures 8.2 to 8.9 that for low dimensionalities all of the tested low-discrepancy number generators are considerably superior to pseudo-random numbers. However, as the dimensionality increases, this advantage decreases, until around $d = 15$ the Halton method, the Niederreiter sequence and Sobol' with unit initialisation all appear to be significantly inferior to pseudo-random number methods. This underperformance becomes so dramatic for $d = 100$ that there are more than 10 decimal orders of magnitude between the aforementioned three number methods and plain pseudo-random methods. However, for suitably initialised Sobol' numbers, there is no deterioration to the extent that they appear inferior to pseudo-random number generators. It is true that the total discrepancy over all of the equally weighted 100 dimensions as shown in Figure 8.9 makes well-initialised Sobol' numbers appear hardly worth bothering with. At this point, however, we should bear in mind that in most applications in finance we are dealing with problems that have a natural ordering in importance of all the involved dimensions. A very good example of a simulation problem that decomposes into dimensions of strongly varying importance is that of paths describing Brownian motion. Clearly, if the terminal value of the Brownian motion determines the payoff of a derivative contract, it is of particular importance in the valuation problem. How the specific features of Brownian

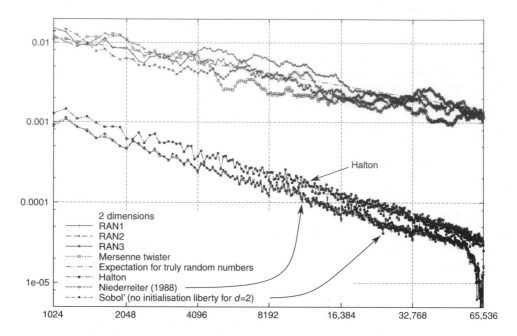

Figure 8.2 $T_N^{(2)}$ as defined in equation (8.4)

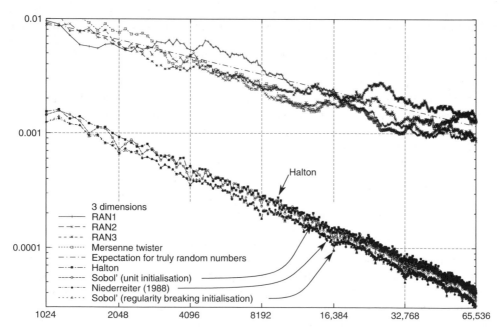

Figure 8.3 $T_N^{(3)}$ as defined in equation (8.4)

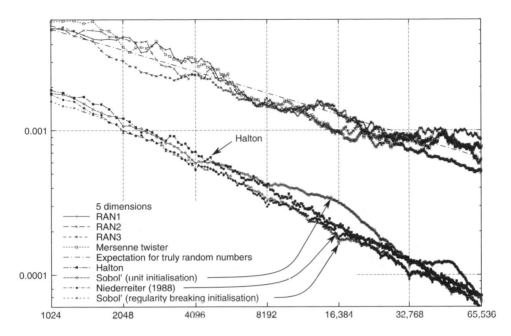

Figure 8.4 $T_N^{(5)}$ as defined in equation (8.4)

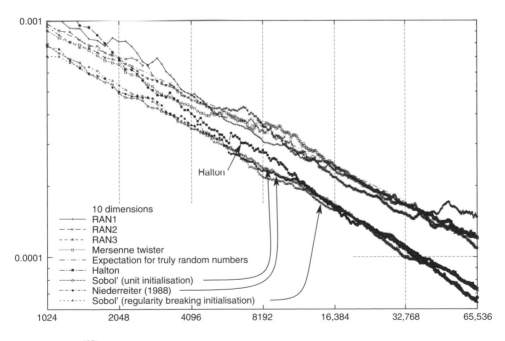

Figure 8.5 $T_N^{(10)}$ as defined in equation (8.4)

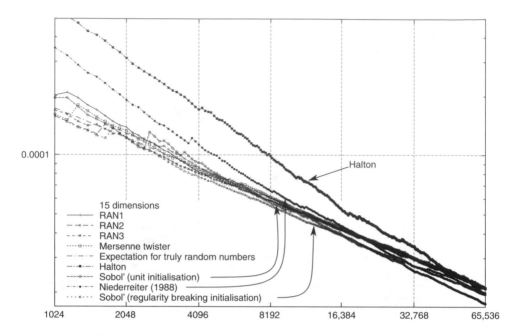

Figure 8.6 $T_N^{(15)}$ as defined in equation (8.4)

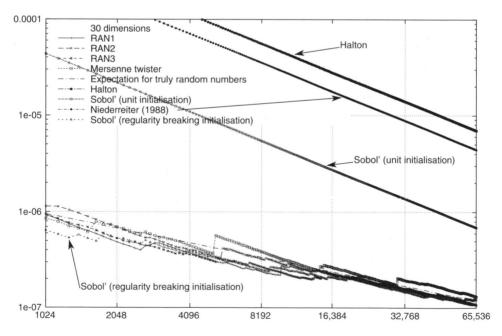

Figure 8.7 $T_N^{(30)}$ as defined in equation (8.4)

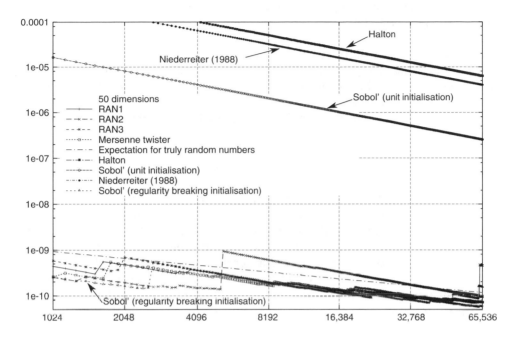

Figure 8.8 $T_N^{(50)}$ as defined in equation (8.4)

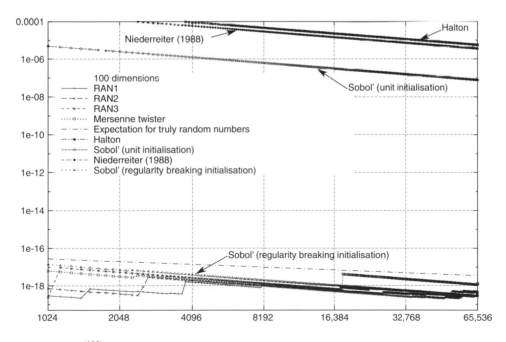

Figure 8.9 $T_N^{(100)}$ as defined in equation (8.4)

motion can be exploited for optimally importance-ranked path construction is discussed in section 10.8, and examples for the good convergence of Sobol' numbers[7] are given in section 10.8.4.

The lesson to learn with respect to well-initialised Sobol' numbers is that they will provide a substantial performance boost in the lower dimensions, and will still work at least as well as pseudo-random number generators in higher dimensions. Thus, we should always try to design the Monte Carlo solution approach such that we can exploit the better convergence in the lower dimensions by assigning them to the problem dimensions of most importance.

8.7   THE NUMBER OF ITERATIONS

As we know, for pseudo-random generators, the number of iterations only affects the expected variance of the result by the central limit theorem, i.e. the more the better. For low-discrepancy numbers, the situation is different. Sobol' numbers, and other number generators based on integer arithmetic modulo two, by construction provide additional equidistribution properties whenever the number of iterations is $N = 2^n - 1$ for some positive integer n. This is easy to see on the unit interval in one dimension, where such a choice of draws always results in a perfectly regular distribution of points, and can also be confirmed in the empirical discrepancy diagrams of section 8.6 up to dimension 5.

8.8   APPENDIX

8.8.1   Explicit Formula for the L_2-norm Discrepancy on the Unit Hypercube

Substituting the formula (8.2) for $n_{S(y)}$ into the squared right-hand side of equation (8.4), we obtain

$$T_N^{(d)\,2} = \frac{1}{N^2} \sum_{i,j=1}^{N} \int_{y \in [0,1]^d} \prod_{k=1}^{d} \mathbf{1}_{\{y_k \geqslant r_{ik}\}} \mathbf{1}_{\{y_k \geqslant r_{jk}\}} \, \mathrm{d}y$$

$$-2\frac{1}{N} \sum_{i=1}^{N} \int_{y \in [0,1]^d} \prod_{k=1}^{d} \mathbf{1}_{\{y_k \geqslant r_{ik}\}} y_k \mathrm{d}y + \int_{y \in [0,1]^d} \prod_{k=1}^{d} y_k^2 \mathrm{d}y \qquad (8.27)$$

$$= \frac{1}{N^2} \sum_{i,j=1}^{N} \prod_{k=1}^{d} \int_{\max(r_{ik}, r_{jk})}^{1} \mathrm{d}y_k - 2\frac{1}{N} \sum_{i=1}^{N} \prod_{k=1}^{d} \int_{r_{ik}}^{1} y_k \mathrm{d}y_k + \prod_{k=1}^{d} \int_{0}^{1} y_k^2 \mathrm{d}y_k \qquad (8.28)$$

$$= \frac{1}{N^2} \sum_{i,j=1}^{N} \prod_{k=1}^{d} (1 - \max(r_{ik}, r_{jk})) - 2\frac{1}{N} \sum_{i=1}^{N} \prod_{k=1}^{d} \frac{1}{2}(1 - r_{ik}^2) + 3^{-d} \qquad (8.29)$$

which is identical to equation (8.7). $\square$

---

[7] Well-initialised ones, of course.

8.8.2   Expected L_2-norm Discrepancy of Truly Random Numbers

In order to derive equation (8.8), the expectation of (8.7) for truly random numbers is calculated below:

$$E\left[T_N^{(d)\,2}\right] = \frac{1}{N^2} \sum_{i,j=1}^{N} E\left[\prod_{k=1}^{d} \left(1 - \max(r_{ik}, r_{jk})\right)\right]$$

$$-\frac{2^{1-d}}{N} \sum_{i=1}^{N} E\left[\prod_{k=1}^{d}\left(1 - r_{ik}^2\right)\right] + 3^{-d}. \qquad (8.30)$$

The expectations over products of terms involving random numbers can be replaced by products over expectations when the random numbers are independent. For this to hold, the first sum has to be split into the terms when $i = j$ and when $i \neq j$. This gives

$$E\left[T_N^{(d)\,2}\right] = \frac{1}{N^2} \left\{ N \prod_{k=1}^{d} E_{\{x_k \in [0,1]\}}[1 - x_k] \right.$$

$$\left. +N(N-1) \prod_{k=1}^{d} E_{\{x_k, y_k \in [0,1]\}}\left[1 - \max\left(x_k, y_k\right)\right] \right\}$$

$$-\frac{2^{1-d}}{N} N \prod_{k=1}^{d} E_{\{x_k \in [0,1]\}}\left[1 - x_k^2\right] + 3^{-d} \qquad (8.31)$$

$$= \frac{1}{N} \left\{ 2^{-d} + (N-1)\left[2 \int_{y=0}^{1} \int_{x=y}^{1} (1-x)\,\mathrm{d}x\mathrm{d}y\right]^{d} \right\}$$

$$-2^{1-d}\left[\int_{x=0}^{1}(1-x)\,\mathrm{d}x\right]^{d} + 3^{-d} \qquad (8.32)$$

$$= \frac{1}{N} \left\{ 2^{-d} + (N-1)\left[1 - \int_{y=0}^{1} 2\left[\frac{x^2}{2}\right]_{x=y}^{1}\mathrm{d}y\right]^{d} \right\}$$

$$-2^{1-d}\left(\frac{2}{3}\right)^{d} + 3^{-d} \qquad (8.33)$$

$$= \frac{1}{N} \left\{ 2^{-d} + (N-1)\left[1 - 1 + \int_{y=0}^{1} y^2\,\mathrm{d}y\right]^{d} \right\} - 3^{-d} \qquad (8.34)$$

$$= \frac{1}{N} \left\{ 2^{-d} + (N-1)3^{-d} \right\} - 3^{-d} \qquad (8.35)$$

$$= \frac{1}{N} \left(2^{-d} - 3^{-d} \right). \qquad (8.36)$$

$\square$

9
Non-uniform Variates

Number generators tend to produce uniform variates on the unit interval. Whenever we wish to carry out a Monte Carlo simulation that requires anything other than a uniform distribution, we have to convert the raw uniform variates to our target distribution, or otherwise ensure that we are meeting our distributional requirements. In this chapter, I discuss some of the known methods available for this purpose.

9.1 INVERSION OF THE CUMULATIVE PROBABILITY FUNCTION

The cumulative probability function of any distribution has the following useful feature: for any variate $x \in \mathbb{R}$ from a given target distribution density $\psi(x)$, the cumulative probability function for x, i.e. $\Psi(x) = \int_{-\infty}^{x} \psi(x') \, dx'$, is a uniform variate on the unit interval. This is because the cumulative probability function is by value just a probability measure, which is uniform by definition. So, if we can invert the cumulative probability function, and take values of the inverse cumulative probability from given uniform variates, we obtain variates of our target distribution!

Example: The Cauchy distribution density and probability were given in equations (2.53) and (2.54) as

$$\psi(x) = \frac{1}{\pi} \frac{1}{1 + x^2},$$

$$\Psi(x) = \frac{1}{\pi} \arctan(x) + \frac{1}{2}.$$

The inverse cumulative density can easily be given as

$$\Psi^{-1}(u) = \tan\left(\pi\left(u - \frac{1}{2}\right)\right). \tag{9.1}$$

As for all distributions that are non-zero for all $x \in \mathbb{R}$, the inverse cumulative probability function of the Cauchy distribution diverges both at $u \to 0$ and at $u \to 1$. It is therefore of paramount importance for numerical applications to ensure that the underlying uniform number generator never returns either of those two limiting values. Unfortunately, almost all uniform number generators that I have come across so far include at least 0 in their range, which must be intercepted in a Monte Carlo implementation (Figure 9.1).

The method of direct inversion of the cumulative probability function is definitely the preferred method for non-uniform variate construction, wherever $\Psi^{-1}(u)$ is readily available and can be computed efficiently. Despite the alternative methods discussed below, for distributions whose inverse cumulative probability function is not so easily computable, such as Student's t whose cumulative is given in equation (2.52) or the

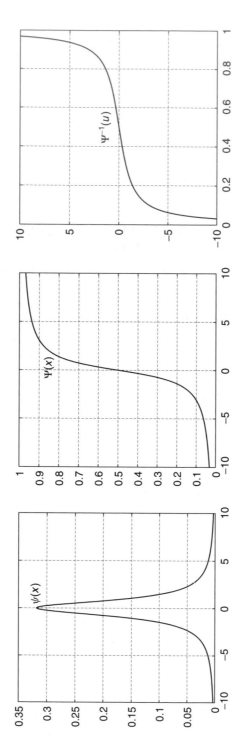

Figure 9.1 Constructing Cauchy variates that are distributed according to $\psi(x)$ as given in equation (2.53) from $\mathcal{U}(0, 1)$ variates is easy by virtue of its inverse cumulative probability $\Psi^{-1}(u)$ in (9.1)

GB2 distribution whose cumulative is (2.62), it may still be advisable to use the inverse cumulative mapping method. However, in those cases, rather than root-search for the inverse cumulative for each new draw, one should set up a (possibly multi-dimensional) interpolation table using cubic splines, monotonicity preserving splines, or your favourite shape-preserving spline method [PTVF92, Hym83, Kva00]. Fortunately, for most known distributions, we have at least the cumulative probability function and can thus readily set up the required interpolation table.

9.2   USING A SAMPLER DENSITY

There may be situations when the inverse cumulative probability function is either not available at all, or would be computationally extremely expensive to evaluate. In this case, we can employ the *sampler density technique* [Mac97]. Instead of drawing directly from the desired target density $\psi(x)$, we choose another, hopefully similar, density $\tilde{\psi}$ from which we can readily draw variates. The simulation is then carried out using variates from the sampler density, and each function evaluation is probability density corrected according to the likelihood ratio of the target density $\psi(x)$ and the sampler density $\tilde{\psi}(x)$. Mathematically, this corresponds to the density transformation

$$\int f(x)\psi(x)\,\mathrm{d}x = \int f(x)\left(\frac{\psi(x)}{\tilde{\psi}(x)}\right)\tilde{\psi}(x)\,\mathrm{d}x \tag{9.2}$$

(Figure 9.2). In other words, the Monte Carlo estimator that was given in equation (2.15) is replaced by the *sampler density Monte Carlo estimator*

$$\hat{v}_N := \frac{1}{N}\sum_{i=1}^{N} f(x_i)\left(\frac{\psi(x_i)}{\tilde{\psi}(x_i)}\right). \tag{9.3}$$

Equation (9.3) gives us an immediate condition on any choice of sampler density: the sampler density $\tilde{\psi}(x)$ must not be zero wherever $f(x)\psi(x)$ is non-zero!

The attentive reader may have noticed that for any finite number N of simulations, the sampler density Monte Carlo estimator for a constant function $f(x) := c$ will, generically, not result in the exact value c, unlike equation (2.15). This can be remedied by renormalisation, which gives us the *normalised sampler density Monte Carlo estimator*

$$\hat{v}_N := \frac{\displaystyle\sum_{i=1}^{N} f(x_i)\left(\frac{\psi(x_i)}{\tilde{\psi}(x_i)}\right)}{\displaystyle\sum_{i=1}^{N}\left(\frac{\psi(x_i)}{\tilde{\psi}(x_i)}\right)}. \tag{9.4}$$

However, by virtue of the continuous mapping theorem, both estimators are valid. In general, the variance of any sampler density estimator will be different from a straight target density estimator, and by virtue of Murphy's law, if we selected the sampler density more or less randomly, we would end up with an increased variance for our Monte Carlo estimator, i.e. a larger Monte Carlo error. What's more, this problem is geometrically compounded as the number of dimensions increases, and this is the reason why drawing

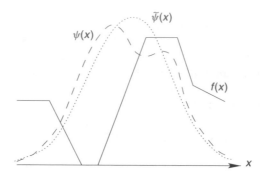

Figure 9.2 The sampler density method uses variates from a different, but preferably similar density, and corrects the average for the misrepresentation of the individual draws by multiplying each function evaluation by the likelihood ratio of the target and the sampler density

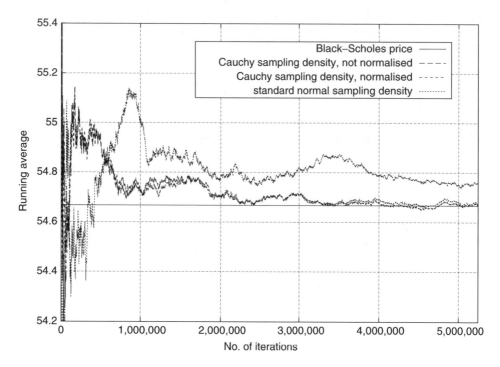

Figure 9.3 Pricing an out-of-the-money call option using a Cauchy sampling density

from the target distribution is to be preferred if it is readily available. For a more mathematical analysis of the problem of increased variance of the sampler density estimator, see [Mac97].

To finish this section, I show in Figure 9.3 the convergence diagram for a standard plain vanilla European call option in the Black–Scholes framework with $S_0 = 123$, $K = 134$, $r = 12\%$, $d = 4\%$, $T = 3.33$ and $\sigma = 67\%$ using the Cauchy density as the sampling distribution in comparison to the direct use of standard normal variates. The first thing to notice is that there is not much between the normalised and the non-normalised versions of the sampling density method in equations (9.4) and (9.3), respectively. There is one surprising feature though: the Cauchy sampler density method appears to converge *faster* for this particular simulation! The explanation is rather simple. In the Black–Scholes framework, the terminal value construction method for S_T given S_0 and a standard normal variate x is

$$S_T = S_0 e^{\left(r-d-\frac{1}{2}\sigma^2\right)T + \sigma\sqrt{T}x}.$$

Solving $S_T = K$ for x, we have

$$x_K = \frac{\ln(K/S_0) - \left(r - d - \frac{1}{2}\sigma^2\right)T}{\sigma\sqrt{T}}.$$

For the parameters given above, the cumulative normal probability for x_K is $\mathrm{N}(x_K) = 67.85\%$. The cumulative Cauchy probability for x_K is, however, only $\Psi_{\mathrm{Cauchy}}(x_K) = 63.82\%$. This means that approximately 4% fewer constructed S_T values end up out-of-the-money when we use the Cauchy sampling density, which gives rise to an improved convergence. What's more, since the Cauchy density has much fatter tails than the normal distribution, the simulations that end up in-the-money tend to have higher values and thus compensate the convexity adjustment, i.e. the Itô term $-\frac{1}{2}\sigma^2 T$, more rapidly. Both effects together amount to the improved convergence behaviour seen in Figure 9.3.

9.2.1 Importance Sampling

Since we have a lot of liberty with respect to the choice of the sampler density, can we take advantage of this freedom in order to reduce the variance of the Monte Carlo estimator? Consider the special choice

$$\tilde{\psi}(x) := \frac{f(x)\psi(x)}{\int f(x)\psi(x)\,dx} \tag{9.5}$$

ignoring for now the fact that we don't actually know the value of the denominator. This particular choice for the sampler density would enable us to calculate (9.2) with any single draw for x since we obtain from equation (9.3)

$$\hat{v}_1 = f(x_1)\left(\frac{\psi(x_1)}{\tilde{\psi}(x_1)}\right)$$

$$= f(x_1)\psi(x_1)\frac{\int f(x)\psi(x)\,dx}{f(x_1)\psi(x_1)}$$

$$= \int f(x)\psi(x)\,dx.$$

Since we don't know the solution of the problem that shows up in the denominator of the right-hand side of equation (9.5), we clearly can't actually do this. However, we can choose a sampler density that takes structural features of the product $f(x)\psi(x)$ into account. A very simple choice that will already provide a significant improvement is to choose a sampler density that is zero wherever $f(x)$ is zero too. An example for an integrand $f(x)$ that has regions of zero value is given by the piecewise affine function in Figure 9.2, and in finance, functions with this feature are everywhere. Specific choices of sampler densities that thus take advantage of the regions of importance of the integrand $f(x)$ are known as *importance sampling methods*. The use of a heavy-tailed distribution for the pricing of an out-of-the-money option as in the example in the previous section is one such application of importance sampling. We will revisit the importance sampling method in sections 10.5 and 11.4.

Incidentally, the example of the ideal sampler density in equation (9.5) highlights that for strongly non-constant functions f, it may be advantageous to carry out the importance sampling technique using the non-normalised estimator given in equation (9.3).

9.2.2   Rejection Sampling

Rejection sampling is the stepsister of importance sampling. For this method, we need to select a sampling density $\tilde{\psi}(x)$ and a scaling constant c such that $c\tilde{\psi}(x) \geqslant \psi(x)$ for all x in the domain of ψ. In order to compute a Monte Carlo estimator over many values for x with $x \sim \psi$, we proceed as follows.

- Draw a variate x from the sampling density $\tilde{\psi}(x)$.
- Compute the value of the sampling density $\tilde{\psi}(x)$ at x, and also the value of the target density $\psi(x)$ at x.
- Draw a uniform variate $u \sim \mathcal{U}(0, 1)$.
- If $u \cdot c\tilde{\psi}(x) > \psi(x)$, reject this attempt to find a suitable variate and start again, otherwise accept x as a variate with $x \sim \psi$ and evaluate the integrand $f(x)$ in the usual manner (Figure 9.4).

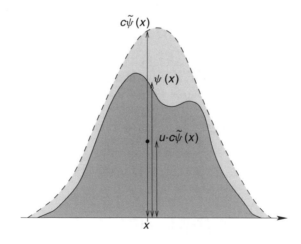

Figure 9.4   For rejection sampling choose a sampling density $\tilde{\psi}$ and establish a scaling constant c such that $c\tilde{\psi}(x) \geqslant \psi(x) \, \forall \, x$. Then, take a draw x from the sampling density $\tilde{\psi}$ and evaluate $\tilde{\psi}(x)$ and $\psi(x)$ at x. Next, draw a uniform $(0, 1)$ variate u. Use the drawn variate x if $u \cdot c\tilde{\psi}(x) \leqslant \psi(x)$, else reject it

There are two main problems with the rejection method. The first one is, again, the geometric implosion of the sampling yield as the number of dimensions increases[1]. The second problem is that they are rather difficult to amend to the efficient application of low-discrepancy numbers. Personally, I don't like rejection methods.

9.3 NORMAL VARIATES

My favourite method for constructing standard normal variates is the highly sophisticated interpolation formula by Peter Acklam [Ack00] for the inverse cumulative normal distribution as discussed in section 2.3. A very crude way to quickly construct (approximately) normally distributed variates is to add up 12 uniform variates and subtract 6, and I have given a diagram that shows the difference from the exact normal distribution in Figure 2.1. For any reasonable application, I would always use either Peter Acklam's method, or Boris Moro's interpolation formula [Mor95].

9.3.1 The Box–Muller Method

There is, however, yet another method for the construction of standard normal variates that is still very popular. It is based on the transformation (u, v) to (x, y) given by

$$\begin{aligned} x &= \sqrt{-2\ln u}\ \sin(2\pi v), \\ y &= \sqrt{-2\ln u}\ \cos(2\pi v). \end{aligned} \tag{9.6}$$

For u and v being independent standard uniform in $(0, 1)^2$, the joint distribution for x and y is given by

$$\psi(x, y) = \left|\frac{\partial(x, y)}{\partial(u, v)}\right| = \left(\frac{\mathrm{e}^{-\frac{1}{2}x^2}}{\sqrt{2\pi}}\right)\left(\frac{\mathrm{e}^{-\frac{1}{2}y^2}}{\sqrt{2\pi}}\right), \tag{9.7}$$

i.e. that of two independent standard normal variates! Techniques for the generation of standard normal variates based on the transformation (9.6) are known as *Box–Muller methods* [BM58, Knu81]. The classical application of the Box–Muller method is to draw two independent uniform variates, and transform them according to equation (9.6), in order to obtain two independent standard normal variates.

Note that the trigonometric terms on the right-hand side of equation (9.6) are the abscissa and ordinate of a point on the perimeter of a unit circle. Another variant of the Box–Muller method is to draw a random point from within a unit circle, and use its cartesian coordinates (s, t) as follows. First, set $u := s^2 + t^2$. Then set

$$\begin{aligned} x &:= s\sqrt{-2\frac{\ln u}{u}}, \\ y &:= t\sqrt{-2\frac{\ln u}{u}}. \end{aligned} \tag{9.8}$$

The advantage of this procedure is that no evaluation of trigonometric functions is required, and it used to be that those trigonometric functions were rather CPU-intensive in

---

[1] This repeated occurrence of high numbers of dimensions causing problems with the evaluation of integrals gave rise to the term *curse of dimensionality*.

their evaluation (in comparison to simpler functions such as the logarithm and the square root)[2]. The only question that remains is: how do we draw a cartesian coordinate pair that describes a point inside a unit circle? The commonly used method for this purpose is a two-dimensional rejection procedure. We simply keep drawing uniform $(-1, 1)$ variate pairs (by drawing standard uniform numbers, multiplying them by two, and subtracting one) until we find one that lies inside the unit circle. Since the area of a unit circle is π, and the area of a 2×2 square is 4, the yield of this rejection method is $\frac{\pi}{4}$.

There are two main problems with the Box–Muller method. The first problem is discussed in the next section. The second problem is that rejection methods are highly dangerous (and should not be used, really) in conjunction with low-discrepancy numbers. An example for this is shown in Figure 9.5. In the top-left diagram of the figure, two-dimensional Gaussian variates constructed from Mersenne twister numbers using equation (9.6) are shown. Next to it, the same transformation method was used with two-dimensional Sobol' numbers. Then, the distribution of two-dimensional Sobol' numbers transformed by the Box–Muller rejection method (9.8) are shown. At the bottom-left, we have the inverse cumulative normal function applied to Mersenne numbers, followed by the same method with two-dimensional Sobol' numbers. The last diagram highlights the danger of combining rejection methods with low-discrepancy numbers: using a one-dimensional sequential generator with the Box–Muller rejection method, as in this example, which is fine for pseudo-random numbers, goes horribly wrong when the number generator is a low-discrepancy algorithm.

9.3.2 The Neave Effect

A problem with highly sophisticated deterministic methods, such as pseudo-random number generators and the Box–Muller algorithm, is that it is often difficult to foresee when their interaction may have undesirable side-effects. In 1973, H. R. Neave discovered one of these hard-to-imagine quirks of undesirable interaction between non-linear systems [Nea73]. When we use simple multiplicative congruential pseudo-random number generators such as Ran0 (also known as GGL[3]) as given in equation (7.6) and discussed in section 7.4 in conjunction with the transformation version of the Box–Muller method given in equation (9.6), there is a nasty surprise in store for us: over the whole period of the number generator of $2^{31} - 1 = 2\,147\,483\,647$ iterations, the smallest pseudo-normal variate that can be drawn for x in equation (9.6) is -4.476239, and the largest we will get is 4.717016 [Tez95]. Strictly speaking, there are two possible ranges for x depending on whether the pairwise transformation starts on the cycle containing the local seed 1, or on the cycle containing the local seed 16,807 in the iteration

$$m_i = a \cdot m_{i-1} \qquad \mathrm{mod}\ M$$

with $a = 16\,807$, $M = 2^{31} - 1$ and m_{i-1} being the local seed for the ith single variate $u_i = m_i/M$. However, the variation in the lower bound and the upper bound between those two possible cycles is beyond the first six decimal digits. According to the cumulative

---

[2]More recently available computing hardware provides substantial improvements for a variety of previously CPU-time expensive functions, see section 14.6.

[3]The only difference between the two is that Ran0 uses a bitwise XOR mask on the seed before and after each iteration mainly to prevent the accidental use of 0 as a seed, which would result in the fixed point 0.

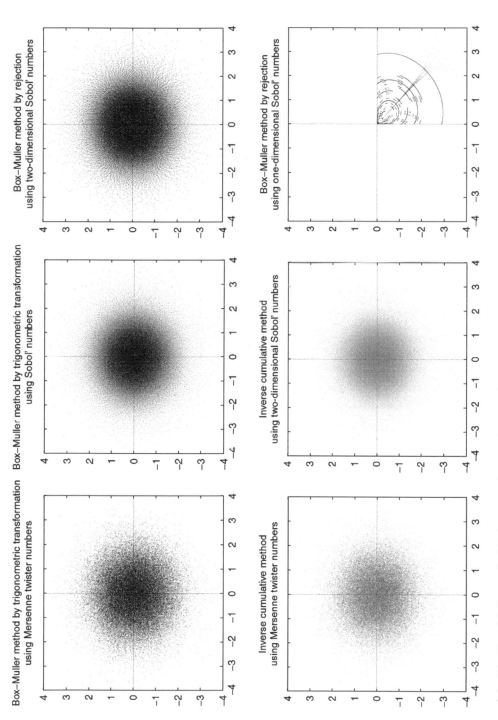

Figure 9.5 The Box–Muller method(s) in comparison to the use of the inverse cumulative normal function. All diagrams were constructed from 65,535 pairs of variates.

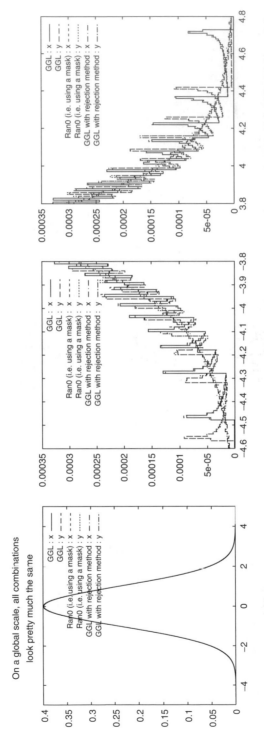

Figure 9.6   The Neave effect is due to an interaction of pseudo-random number generation methods and the trigonometric transformation version of the Box–Muller algorithm (9.6). In this figure, the GGL generator given by equation (7.6) with $a = 16{,}807$, $c = 0$ and $M = 2^{31} - 1$ was used

normal probability function, we would expect to have approximately

$$2^{31} - 1 \cdot N(-4.476239) \approx 8157$$

draws lower than -4.476239, and equally several thousand above 4.717016. So, the range for x isn't too good. The lower bound for y from equation (9.6) is -4.566210, again only showing variation between the two possible cycles beyond the first six decimal digits. The upper bound for y, though, is 6.385757568918 for the cycle beginning with $m_i = 1$, and 6.555541555803 for the cycle beginning with $16,807$. In other words, the upper bound is somewhat better for the y variate, but the lower bound is still no good. What's more, on either side of the distribution resulting from the combination of this number generator with the trigonometric version of the Box–Muller method, there appear to be some kind of wing formations in the tails of the distribution, as shown in Figure 9.6. As you can see, addition of a bitwise XOR mask as is done for the proper Ran0 pseudo-random number method doesn't fix the problem. The Neave effect does fade away, though, when we use the rejection version of the Box–Muller algorithm (9.8). However, there are reports that the rejection method also suffers from problems due to the fact that two (or more) uniform variates are used together for the generation of two normal variates [AW88, Rip87].

Of course, some may say that this is a small effect in the tails of the distribution, which is fair enough. However, in finance we are frequently particularly concerned with the tails since they tend to contain the most feared scenarios. But then, of course, you are probably not using the simple Ran0 aka GGL generator, but one of the much more sophisticated ones that are readily available these days. Unfortunately, number theoreticians have begun to suspect that effects similar to the Neave phenomenon may occur for other number generation classes[4]. The fundamental principle of the problem underlying the Neave effect remains, thus: whenever you use a variate-mixing transformation in order to generate variates from a specific target distribution, you run the risk of some kind of non-linear interaction with the number generation mechanism that may be very hard to foresee, or even very difficult to notice, until something has gone wrong in a very big and unexpected way.

In summary, since there are nowadays highly accurate and efficient interpolation algorithms available for the inverse cumulative normal probability function, it is generally safer to use those rather than to employ the Box–Muller method. It was an invention of great ingenuity and insight at the time, but now it has had its day.

9.4 SIMULATING MULTIVARIATE COPULA DRAWS

The problem of non-uniform variate generation is, of course, not limited to one dimension, or several dimensions of independent variates. The copula approach of creating multi-dimensional variate draws with co-dependence was explained in section 5.2. To conclude this chapter, I give in Figure 9.7 an example for the kind of co-dependence that can be constructed by the use of copulae. The Archimedean copula generating function $\phi(u) = (u^{-1} - 1)^\theta$ as given in equation (5.31) was used with $\theta = \frac{3}{2}$. The Weibull variates were

---

[4]Tezuka states on p. 152 in [Tez95] that the Neave effect '...possibly occurs not only with linear congruential sequences but also with $LS(2)$ sequences'.

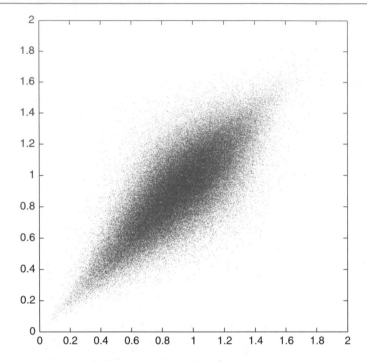

Figure 9.7   131,071 Weibull variates for $\beta = 1$ and $\gamma = 4$ under the Archimedean copula generated by ϕ given in equation (5.31) with $\theta = \frac{3}{2}$

generated from the inverse cumulative Weibull probability function

$$\Psi^{-1}(u) = [-\beta \ln(1 - u)]^{\frac{1}{\gamma}} \tag{9.9}$$

which can be calculated from (2.72), using $\beta = 1$ and $\gamma = 4$. A rather interesting shape, don't you think?

10

Variance Reduction Techniques

As we have seen in Chapter 2, the error estimate for the result of a Monte Carlo simulation is given by the standard deviation of the result (i.e. the average of all samples for a standard Monte Carlo integration), which is known as the standard error and usually estimated as the realised standard deviation of the simulation divided by the square root of the number of iterations. The smaller the variance (and thus the standard deviation) of the calculation, the more accurate will be the result. When I talk about variance here, I don't mean the variance associated with any one individual sample of our Monte Carlo simulation, but the variance associated with repeating the whole simulation many times. A number of techniques have been developed [BBG97] that help to reduce the variance of the result, and thus to reduce the number of simulations required for a given accuracy. Some of these methods can be combined to achieve even higher accuracy, as we will see.

10.1 ANTITHETIC SAMPLING

Whenever we use Gaussian variates to drive a Monte Carlo calculation, or wish to simulate Brownian motion by constructing sample paths of standard Wiener processes, we can make use of the fact that for any one drawn path its mirror image has equal probability. In other words, if a single evaluation driven by a Gaussian variate vector draw z_i is given by $v_i = v(z_i)$, we also use $\tilde{v}_i = v(-z_i)$.

The standard error for antithetic sampling requires some consideration. This is because the central limit theorem underpinning the idea that the standard error can be estimated as the square root of the realised variance divided by the square root of the number of samples requires *independent* draws. However, if instead of viewing both $v_i = v(z_i)$ and $\tilde{v}_i = v(-z_i)$ as individual samples, we only count the pairwise average $\bar{v}_i = \frac{1}{2}(v(z_i) + v(-z_i))$ as an individual sample, all is well again, because the pairwise averages $\bar{v}_i$ are independent, and a standard error can be calculated from them in the ordinary fashion.

Taking into account that each evaluation of $\bar{v}_i$ requires two calculations (albeit only one Gaussian vector draw generation), the antithetic sampling procedure provides a variance reduction if

$$V\left[\tfrac{1}{2}(v_i + \tilde{v}_i)\right] < \tfrac{1}{2}V[v_i] \qquad (10.1)$$

which is equivalent to

$$Cov\left[v_i, \tilde{v}_i\right] < 0. \qquad (10.2)$$

This is always the case if $v(z)$ is monotonic in z. Whenever the first realised moment of the underlying variate draws $\{z_i\}$ has a strong impact on the result of the overall simulation, antithetic sampling is an easy way to improve the accuracy of the calculation, since it corrects the first moment. Of course, if we use Monte Carlo simulation to calculate the value of derivatives contracts that mainly (or only) depend on higher moments, antithetic sampling will not help.

Low-discrepancy numbers, or more specifically, Sobol' numbers, unlike pseudo-random numbers, have the antithetic feature built into them, but only approximately. This is to say, whenever we use a recommended number of draws such as $2^n - 1$ for some n as advocated in section 8.7, the first moment of $\{z\}$ is correct to within the numerical accuracy of the conversion from uniform $(0, 1)$ to Gaussian variates. Also, it is worth remembering that low-discrepancy numbers are very carefully designed, and tinkering with them can result in unexpected and rather undesirable effects. Therefore, even when we are not using $2^n - 1$ draws with low-discrepancy numbers, adding the antithetic method to the use of low-discrepancy numbers is unlikely to improve the accuracy, and instead can lead to erroneous results.

10.2 VARIATE RECYCLING

This method applies when the quantity to be calculated is essentially a re-evaluation of a functional of a (possibly multi-dimensional) discretised stochastic process, or any other re-evaluation using many draws. An example for this is the calculation of the Greeks of options by finite differencing. Let W_i be the discretised representation of our Monte Carlo approximation of a particular standard Wiener process path. Also, let $v(p) = F[p, \{W_i\}_{i=1,\ldots,N}]$ be the approximation of the value of an option by averaging the evaluation functional over the N sampling paths $\{W_i\}_{i=1,\ldots,N}$, depending on the parameter p. The simplest approach to estimate the sensitivity of v with respect to the parameter p is to run a separate Monte Carlo calculation using a slightly larger value for p, namely $p + \Delta p$ to obtain $v(p + \Delta p)$ and set

$$\frac{\partial v}{\partial p} \approx \frac{v(p + \Delta p) - v(p)}{\Delta p}. \tag{10.3}$$

In fact, for specific Greeks such as *Vega*, the dependence with respect to implied volatility, market practitioners may insist that it is mandatory to use forward differencing as in equation (10.3), and use a particular increment Δp (usually one absolute percentage point) for the calculation. Other Greeks where an absolute shift is commonly used are *Rho*, the sensitivity of FX and equity options with respect to domestic interest rates, and also the sensitivity with respect to forecast dividend yields.

Naturally, we are interested in an accurate estimate of the Greeks when using the approach defined by equation (10.3). The standard measure for the accuracy of a Monte Carlo method is the variance of the resulting numerical approximation. The variance of the sensitivity as given by equation (10.3) is thus

$$V\left[\frac{\partial v}{\partial p}\right] \approx \frac{1}{(\Delta p)^2} \cdot \left\{ E\left[(v(p + \Delta p) - v(p))^2\right] - \left(E\left[(v(p + \Delta p) - v(p))\right]\right)^2 \right\} \tag{10.4}$$

$$= \frac{1}{(\Delta p)^2} \cdot \left\{ E\left[v(p + \Delta p)^2\right] - 2E\left[v(p + \Delta p)v(p)\right] + E\left[v(p)^2\right] \right.$$

$$\left. - \left(E\left[v(p + \Delta p)\right]\right)^2 + 2E\left[v(p + \Delta p)\right]E\left[v(p)\right] - \left(E\left[v(p)\right]\right)^2 \right\}$$

$$= \frac{1}{(\Delta p)^2} \cdot \left\{ V\big[v(p + \Delta p)\big] + V\big[v(p)\big] - 2Cov\big[v(p + \Delta p), v(p)\big] \right\}$$

$$= \frac{1}{(\Delta p)^2} \cdot \Bigg\{ V\big[v(p + \Delta p)\big] + V\big[v(p)\big]$$

$$-2\sqrt{V\big[v(p + \Delta p)\big] V\big[v(p)\big]} Corr\big[v(p + \Delta p), v(p)\big] \Bigg\}$$

$$\approx \frac{2}{(\Delta p)^2} \cdot V\big[v(p)\big] \left\{ 1 - Corr\big[v(p + \Delta p), v(p)\big] \right\} \tag{10.5}$$

where I used $V\big[v(p + \Delta p)\big] \approx V\big[v(p)\big]$ in the last step. As equation (10.5) indicates, it is desirable to maximise the correlation of the two separate calculations $v(p + \Delta p)$ and $v(p)$. For monotonic functions $v(p)$, one can show [BBG97] that positive correlation is given if we use the same sample path set $\{W_i\}_{i=1,\dots,N}$ for both calculations, whence one may call this method *variate* or *path recycling*.

The above analysis easily transfers to other calculations of similar nature. Another example is the repeated Monte Carlo evaluation of the same problem with slightly varying parameters in the process of optimisation or within a non-linear solver routine. Naturally, it is advisable to reuse (and wherever possible precalculate all quantities derived from them!) the sample paths, or simply the drawn variates if the problem doesn't involve the concept of discretised stochastic processes.

10.3   CONTROL VARIATES

Many Monte Carlo calculations are carried out for problems that we can almost solve analytically, or that are very similar to other problems for which we have closed form solutions. In this case, the use of *control variates* can be very beneficial indeed. The idea is as follows. Let's assume that we wish to calculate the expectation $E[v]$ of a function $v(u)$ for some underlying vector draw u, and that there is a related function $g(u)$ whose expectation $g^* := E[g]$ we know exactly. Then, we have

$$E\left[\frac{1}{n} \sum_{i=1}^{n} v(u_i) \right] = E\left[\frac{1}{n} \sum_{i=1}^{n} v(u_i) + \beta \left(g^* - \frac{1}{n} \sum_{i=1}^{n} g(u_i) \right) \right] \tag{10.6}$$

for any given $\beta \in \mathbb{R}$ and thus we can replace the ordinary Monte Carlo estimator

$$\hat{v} = \frac{1}{n} \sum_{i=1}^{n} v(u_i) \tag{10.7}$$

by

$$\hat{v}_{CV} = \frac{1}{n} \sum_{i=1}^{n} \left[v(u_i) + \beta \left(g^* - g(u_i) \right) \right]. \tag{10.8}$$

The optimal choice of β is

$$\beta^* = \frac{Cov[v, g]}{V[g]} \tag{10.9}$$

which minimises the variance of $\hat{v}_{CV}$. Note that the function $g(\boldsymbol{u}_i)$ does not have to be the payoff of an analytically known option. It could also be the profit from a self-financing dynamic hedging strategy, i.e. a strategy that starts with zero investment capital. For risk-neutral measures, the expected profit from any such strategy is zero, which means that the control variate is simply the payoff from the dynamic hedging strategy along any one path. An intuitive understanding of the control variate method is to consider the case when v and g are positively correlated. For any draw $v(\boldsymbol{u}_i)$ that overestimates the result, $g(\boldsymbol{u}_i)$ is likely to overestimate g^*. As a result, the term multiplied by β in equation (10.8) is likely to correct the result by subtracting the aberration.

The precise value of β^* is, of course, not known but can be estimated from the same simulation that is used to calculate $\hat{v}_{CV}$. As in all the situations when the parameters determining the result are calculated from the same simulation, this can introduce a bias that is difficult to estimate. In the limit of very large numbers of iterations, this bias vanishes, but the whole point of variance reduction techniques is to require *fewer* simulations and thus a shorter run time. A remedy for the problem of bias due to a correlated estimate of the control parameter β is to use an initial simulation, possibly with fewer iterates than the main run, to estimate β^* in isolation. Fortunately, the control variate technique usually provides such a substantial speed-up in convergence that this initial parameter estimation simulation is affordable. However, for many applications, the magnitude of the bias is negligible. The easiest way to ascertain that there is no bias present that would be relevant for derivatives pricing purposes is to look at a convergence diagram of the simulation method, rather than a single result.

The control variate method can be generalised to take advantage of more than one related closed form solution. However, this necessitates the estimation of more control parameters, and makes the method more susceptible to errors in their estimate. It is generally considered wiser to have one reasonable control variate than several mediocre ones. For instance, an option on a geometric average, which can be priced analytically for geometric Brownian motion, works exceedingly well as a control variate for arithmetic average options, whilst the use of both a standard European option and the underlying asset as joint control variates is only about as effective as the European option used as a control variate by itself [BG97b].

10.4   STRATIFIED SAMPLING

The idea here is to subdivide the sampling domain into smaller areas, for each of which a representative value of the function is selected (Figure 10.1). This can be particularly useful if a good approximation for the average over small subdomains is available. Stratified sampling is conceptually akin to fixed lattice methods. It can also be of advantage when an assessment of the total probability of a small subdomain is difficult, and each evaluation in this domain is rather CPU-time expensive, but it is known that the function which is being sampled varies very little in any one given subdomain. Whenever the probability associated with each segment of the stratification can be well approximated, stratified sampling can be used to evaluate the Monte Carlo integral by simply calculating

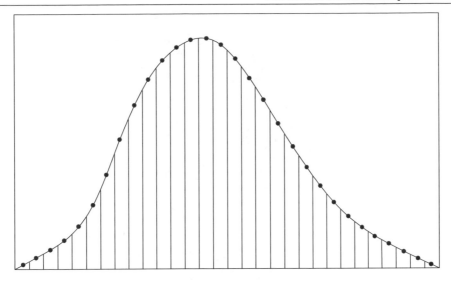

Figure 10.1   An example of stratification with representative values for each segment

the weighted sum over the representative values, which makes it essentially some kind of (possibly irregular) lattice method. The segments into which the subdomain is partitioned don't have to be of equal size. A better choice of stratification is to make the subdomains have approximately equal probability associated with them. However, the biggest problem with stratified sampling is that it is very difficult to obtain any kind of error estimate. Clearly, a statistical error estimate like the conventional standard error for pseudo-random sampling can be very misleading, since the individual function values resulting from each draw are not independent variates in the usual meaning of the word. Also, the accuracy of any one calculation is limited by the stratification, whence taking more and more samples will not make the result eventually converge to the exact answer as it would for a conventional Monte Carlo method following Kolmogorov's strong law. In other words, the very technique that is supposed to increase convergence, i.e. the stratification itself, can introduce a finite bias of unknown sign.

10.5   IMPORTANCE SAMPLING

The concept of *importance sampling* is to focus on those regions which contribute most to the average of a Monte Carlo integration procedure. The most common use of this method in finance is to ensure that all drawn samples are in regions where the function to be evaluated is non-zero. This is the particular difficulty of out-of-the-money option pricing. The standard procedure of generating paths would result in most evaluations resulting in zero payoff, and are thus effectively a waste of CPU time. The main drawback of importance sampling is that it requires additional knowledge of the underlying problem. However, for very specific calculations, it can make a tremendous difference in the convergence speed. Take for instance the function $f(X, Y)$ of two independent standard normal variates X and Y in Figure 10.2. A Monte Carlo integration of such a function will converge substantially faster if we restrict the normal variate draws to be in the subdomain where f is non-zero, in this case $(X, Y) \in [0, 1]^2$. For the specific

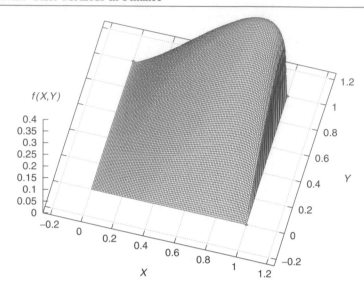

Figure 10.2 The integration of localised functions can be accelerated by the use of importance sampling

example here, this is easily done using our knowledge of the probability p associated with the domain $(X, Y) \in [0, 1]^2$, namely

$$p = (\mathrm{N}(1) - \mathrm{N}(0))^2$$

by which the result of the conditioned Monte Carlo integration simply has to be multiplied. The construction of variates conditioned on the domain of importance is achieved, for the given example, by first drawing a vector of two uniform $(0, 1)$ variates u_X and u_Y, and constructing the importance sampling variates X_{is} and Y_{is} according to

$$X_{\mathrm{is}} = \mathrm{N}^{-1}\left[\mathrm{N}(0) + (\mathrm{N}(1) - \mathrm{N}(0)) \cdot u_X\right]$$

and respectively for Y_{is}. Another, more detailed, example for the potential of the importance sampling method is discussed in section 11.4.

10.6   MOMENT MATCHING

Moment matching used to be a very popular method before efficient and reliable low-discrepancy numbers became available. This method usually gives more accurate results for calculations that use pseudo-random numbers, although it is not guaranteed to do so.

Assume a Monte Carlo simulation is to be carried out using a total of N variate vectors $\boldsymbol{v}$ of dimensionality d of a known joint distribution density $\psi(\boldsymbol{v})$. Then, we can calculate the moments actually realised by the drawn variate vector set $V := \{v_{ij}\}$ with $i = 1, \ldots, N$ and $j = 1, \ldots, d$. The first moment for dimension j is given by

$$\langle \boldsymbol{v} \rangle_j = \frac{1}{N} \sum_{i=1}^{N} v_{ij} \quad j = 1, \ldots, d. \tag{10.10}$$

Using equation (10.10), we can construct a set of first-moment-corrected variates $\tilde{V}$ by subtraction of the average in each dimension, i.e.

$$\tilde{v}_{ij} = v_{ij} - \langle v \rangle_j .\tag{10.11}$$

The realised covariance of the mean-corrected variate set can be represented concisely as

$$\tilde{C} = \tilde{V}^\top \tilde{V}\tag{10.12}$$

if we view $\tilde{V}$ as a matrix whose rows comprise the individual d-dimensional mean-corrected vector draws. Using the same pseudo-square root decomposition approach as discussed in Chapter 6, we can construct a new matrix $\hat{V}$ whose entries will meet the desired covariance C of the target distribution density ψ exactly. Define the elements of the desired covariance matrix C as

$$c_{jk} = \int v_j v_k \psi(v)\, dv_j dv_k.\tag{10.13}$$

Also, define the pseudo-square roots of both C and $\tilde{C}$ by

$$\tilde{C} = \tilde{A} \cdot \tilde{A}^\top \quad \text{and} \quad C = A \cdot A^\top.\tag{10.14}$$

The correction matrix K that transforms $\tilde{V}$ to $\hat{V}$ can be computed by solving the linear system

$$\tilde{A}^\top \cdot K = A^\top,\tag{10.15}$$

i.e.

$$K = \tilde{A}^{\top^{-1}} \cdot A^\top.\tag{10.16}$$

It is easily possible for a covariance matrix not to be of full rank. This is the case whenever there are fewer driving factors than financial assets, for instance. This means that, whilst the original vector draws v are d-dimensional, the target covariance matrix may be $C \in \mathbb{R}^{d' \times d'}$ with $d' > d$, albeit that the rank of C is d. As a consequence, the matrix A will then have d' rows, but only d columns, i.e. $A \in \mathbb{R}^{d' \times d}$. However, $\tilde{A}$ will be of dimensions $d \times d$, and $K \in \mathbb{R}^{d \times d'}$. It is advisable to use a failsafe method for the solution of the linear system (10.15) such as the Moore-Penrose pseudo-inverse explained in section 2.9 in order to avoid problems due to the fact that there may be fewer dimensions in the vector v than there are variates in the target distribution. Another situation that may give rise to problems is when the number N of drawn vector variates is comparatively small, and the resulting realised covariance $\tilde{C}$ of the mean-corrected variate set is nearly singular. Then, the linear system (10.15) is ill-conditioned which can lead to rather unexpected results. In other words, I recommend always to use the Moore-Penrose pseudo-inverse for $\tilde{A}^{\top^{-1}}$ in equation (10.16).

Putting all of the above linear algebra together, we can convince ourselves that the covariance-corrected variate matrix

$$\hat{V} = \tilde{V} \cdot K\tag{10.17}$$

does indeed satisfy

$$\hat{V}^\top \cdot \hat{V} = C.\tag{10.18}$$

Note that when using this method to correct the first and second moments of a set of drawn variates it should be applied to the variates *after* having transformed them from the uniform (0, 1) distribution to whatever distribution is actually used, e.g. a joint normal distribution. This is because the non-linearity in the transformation will have the effect that whilst you may have a set of uniform (0, 1) variates that have exactly the same mean and covariance matrix as in the continuous limit, the normal variates resulting from them after transformation will *not* meet the desired mean and covariance matrix of the joint normal distribution. As a simple example, take the very small set of only two one-dimensional uniform (0, 1) variates $\{u_1, u_2\} = \left\{ \frac{1}{2} - \sqrt{\frac{1}{12}}, \frac{1}{2} + \sqrt{\frac{1}{12}} \right\}$. The first and second moments of this set meet the moments of the continuous uniform (0, 1) distribution $\frac{1}{2}$ and $\frac{1}{3}$ exactly. Transforming (u_1, u_2) to normal variates with the aid of the inverse cumulative normal distribution gives $\{z_1, z_2\} = \{N^{-1}(u_1), N^{-1}(u_2)\} = \{-0.801832717, 0.801832717\}$, which has the desired first moment of exactly zero. However, the second moment of the transformed set is 0.64293571, which is very different from 1 as it should be for a standard normal variate.

The above example of an extremely small set of variates may appear somewhat construed. It does, however, highlight the dangers associated with moment matching. Correcting the first and second moments, or even higher moments for that matter, of a set of drawn variates that are to undergo further transformation does not mean that the final distribution meets those moments equally. This cautioning note applies particularly to the common use of standard normal variates in the construction of geometric Brownian motion. The sheer fact that a discrete set of variates $\{z\}$ has the same first and second moments as the continuous Gaussian distribution does not mean that lognormal variates constructed according to $S_T = S_0 e^{\hat{\sigma}\sqrt{T}z}$ have first and second moments in perfect agreement with the continuous lognormal distribution. What's more, even if we manage to correct the first few moments of the variate set representing the ultimate target distribution, the effects we inflict upon the higher moments are quite unpredictable. Most calculations are affected by more than just the first few moments: even comparatively simple problems such as the pricing of an option with a fairly vanilla payoff depend quite strongly on the third moment, for instance. These considerations bear particular relevance when we actually need to represent a distribution by a very small sample set such as in a stratification method, or in a tree. A discussion of the differences caused by first and second moment matching in the underlying normal variate space or the target lognormal variate space is given in sections 13.7 and 13.6 in the context of non-recombining trees for the pricing of interest rate derivatives in the BGM/J framework.

As for the standard error estimate when we use pseudo-random numbers in conjunction with moment matching, this is somewhat problematic since the variates can no longer be considered independent. This directly affects another nice feature of Monte Carlo simulations: with ordinary Monte Carlo simulations, it is possible to continue drawing variates and monitor the running error estimate until the latter has dropped below a specified level of required accuracy. Not only is it no longer justified to use the running standard error as a statistical error measure, since any new draw is no longer strictly independent (as we would have to rematch the moments), but since this would also involve recomputing the correction matrix K from equation (10.16) in each step, it would clearly become computationally prohibitively expensive. As a matter of fact, the one-off calculation of the realised covariance matrix (10.12) can easily be extremely CPU-intensive since it grows like the square of the total dimensionality of the problem, and linearly in the number of vector draws (i.e. paths for option pricing) that are used. Should you ever use the moment matching method, you would be well advised to monitor the CPU time that is actually being spent in total in the correction step, in comparison to the time spent in the main Monte Carlo simulation. For example, for multi-asset options of Asian style, the total dimensionality (which is the product of the number of time steps and the number of underlyings) can easily be moderately large. Since the computing effort grows as the square of d, it is not uncommon for such calculations to spend 90% or more of the total calculation time just in the moment matching part of the simulation, in particular since those multi-asset calculations frequently involve the evaluation of a very simple payoff function. In comparison to the use of low-discrepancy numbers, the moment matching method with pseudo-random numbers rarely provides a substantial speed-up in convergence as a function of the number of simulations, which means that the same accuracy could be achieved by slightly increasing the number of iterations using, for example, Sobol' numbers. It is important to remember that any user's perception of Monte Carlo simulation convergence is mainly a function of the time spent waiting for the result. Therefore, the moment matching method can easily make the Monte Carlo method appear slower for multi-asset, multi-time-stepped simulations.

Finally, I ought to mention that moment matching *should not* be combined with the use of low-discrepancy methods. This is because their careful construction from number-theoretical principles already tries to match all the moments in a well-balanced way, and interfering with them can have unexpected effects. A simple way to ensure that the first moment is exactly met when using Sobol' numbers, for instance, is to use $N = 2^n - 1$ vector draws for some positive integer n, as explained in section 8.7. You will also find that the second moment is almost exactly met, especially when compared to pseudo-random numbers. Since Sobol' numbers are particularly fast to construct, I never found a situation when just using a few more draws with straightforward Sobol' numbers did not outperform the use of moment matching with pseudo-random numbers, even for very low-dimensional problems. For high-dimensional, i.e. multi-asset simulation problems, importance-aware path construction as outlined in section 10.8 in order to achieve an effective dimensionality reduction ensures that Sobol' numbers still give a convergence improvement over pseudo-random numbers when measured just in terms of the number of iterations required until a certain accuracy is met. As discussed above, though, when measured in terms of CPU time (which is a much better measure), moment matching becomes prohibitively CPU-time expensive for high-dimensional problems. Just in case the message is still not clear: *use the moment matching method at your peril.*

10.7 LATIN HYPERCUBE SAMPLING

Latin hypercube sampling isn't actually a Monte Carlo method. Latin hypercube sampling is a way to crash cars. Seriously. This technique used when probing the sampling space is (quite literally) extremely expensive. Basically, a Latin hypercube sampling scheme is an attempt to place sampling points in a multi-dimensional stratification with as little overlap in all one-dimensional projections as possible. Imagine that you wish to evaluate the effect of four control parameters on the safety of the driver of a car measured by the impact forces experienced in a frontal collision. The control parameters could be, for instance, the angle of the steering wheel column, the elasticity of the back rest of the driver's seat, the rigidity of the front of the vehicle's chassis, and the amount of leg space in front of the driver's seat. For each of those parameters, you have chosen seven possible settings, which represents a four-dimensional stratification. Clearly, it is desirable not to have to crash $7^4 = 2401$ cars to get an idea what the optimal combination of settings would be. The Latin hypercube scheme is a systematic method to sample the stratified layer in each control parameter (at least) once. An example for such an arrangement is shown in Figure 10.3, in all of the possible two-dimensional projections of the four-dimensional domain. Incidentally, the points shown in Figure 10.3 were taken as the first seven points of a four-dimensional Sobol' sequence, which highlights another advantage of that particular number generation method: Sobol' numbers have the Latin hypercube property built-in.

10.8 PATH CONSTRUCTION

In many applications, we need to construct a simulated discretised path of a standard Wiener process over a set $\{t_i\}$, $i = 1, \dots, n$, points in time. We can view the values $w_i := W(t_i)$ of the Wiener process at those points in time as a vector of random variates. Since we are talking about a standard Wiener process starting at $W(0) = 0$, the global expectation of all the w_i as averaged over many simulated paths must be zero. The elements of their covariance matrix C, however, are given by

$$c_{ij} = \mathsf{Cov}\big[W(t_i), W(t_j)\big] = \min(t_i, t_j). \tag{10.19}$$

Given a vector z of independent Gaussian variates, we can transform them into a vector w representing a single simulated Wiener process path according to

$$w = A \cdot z \tag{10.20}$$

provided that the matrix A satisfies

$$A \cdot A^\top = C \tag{10.21}$$

with the elements c_{ij} of C given by (10.19). The decomposition of C as in equation (10.21) is not unique, and for Monte Carlo simulations driven by pseudo-random numbers it is also completely irrelevant which method is used. The specific path construction technique employed does not have a direct impact on the variance of the result of any Monte Carlo simulation. However, as I will elaborate below, a fortunate choice of the path construction method can aid in the reduction of what is called the *effective dimensionality*, which is the key to unleashing the full potential of Sobol' numbers, and can lead to a significantly improved convergence behaviour when compared with ordinary pseudo-random numbers. It is because of the effect that the choice of the path construction method has on the convergence behaviour of simulations using Sobol' numbers that I discuss them in this chapter.

10.8.1 Incremental

Probably the simplest way to construct a Wiener process path is the *incremental path construction*. It can be seen as a direct application of the Markov property of a Wiener process. The construction is carried out by simply adding a new increment that is scaled according to the time step

$$w_{i+1} = w_i + \sqrt{\Delta t_{i+1}} \cdot z_i \quad \text{with} \quad z_i \sim \mathcal{N}(0, 1). \tag{10.22}$$

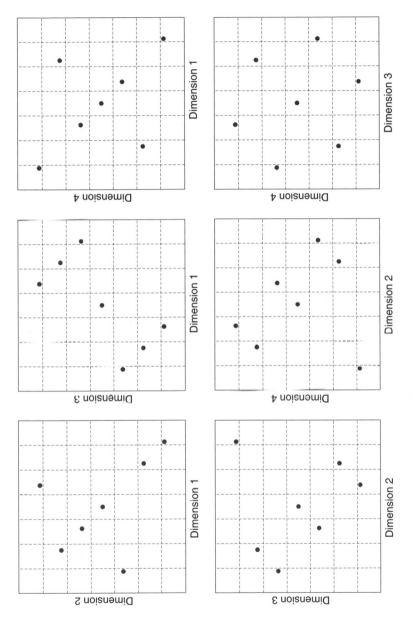

Figure 10.3 The Latin hypercube arrangement of sampling points

The construction matrix of the incremental method is given by the Cholesky decomposition of the covariance matrix

$$
A_{\text{incremental}} = \begin{pmatrix}
\sqrt{\Delta t_1} & 0 & 0 & 0 & \cdots & 0 \\
\sqrt{\Delta t_1} & \sqrt{\Delta t_2} & 0 & 0 & \cdots & 0 \\
\sqrt{\Delta t_1} & \sqrt{\Delta t_2} & \sqrt{\Delta t_3} & 0 & \cdots & 0 \\
\vdots & \vdots & \vdots & \ddots & \cdots & \vdots \\
\vdots & \vdots & \vdots & \vdots & \ddots & \vdots \\
\sqrt{\Delta t_1} & \sqrt{\Delta t_2} & \sqrt{\Delta t_3} & \cdots & \cdots & \sqrt{\Delta t_n}
\end{pmatrix} .
\tag{10.23}
$$

As you can see from equation (10.22), the incremental construction is an extremely fast way to convert a vector of n Gaussian variates into a standard Wiener path over n steps in time. Since all of the square roots can be precalculated, all that is involved for each path is a total of n multiplications, and $n - 1$ additions. It is because of this speed advantage that incremental path construction is the method of choice when pseudo-random numbers are used.

10.8.2   Spectral

In section 6.2, I explained how any symmetric positive definite matrix can be split into its spectral pseudo-square root. The same method can be used here to compute a spectral path construction matrix A_{spectral} that satisfies (10.21).

It is also possible to use an approximation for the spectral discrete path construction matrix. This approximation is given by the spectral decomposition of a continuous Wiener path over the time interval $[0, T]$ into an orthogonal Hilbert basis. In order to construct a fully continuous Wiener path over any time interval, we would need an infinite number of driving Gaussian variates. The Gaussian variates are the coefficients $\{z_k\}$ of the decomposition of $W(t)$ in

$$
W(t) = \sqrt{\frac{2}{T}} \sum_{k=1}^{\infty} z_k \frac{\sin \omega_k t}{\omega_k} \quad \text{with} \quad \omega_k = \left(\frac{2k-1}{2} \right) \frac{\pi}{T} .
\tag{10.24}
$$

The approximation of the element a_{kl} of the spectral construction matrix A_{spectral} is to be calculated as follows. First, populate an initial stage approximation that is simply given by the continuous counterpart for the path from $t_0 = 0$ to $t_n = T$:

$$
a'_{ik} = \sqrt{\frac{2}{T}} \frac{\sin \omega_k t_i}{\omega_k} .
\tag{10.25}
$$

Now, the most important part of the path construction is that the variance of $w_i = W(t_i)$ must be equal to t_i, i.e.

$$
V[w_i] = t_i .
\tag{10.26}
$$

The initial stage approximation A' does not satisfy this. This deficit can be rectified by defining τ_i as the sum of the squares of all the entries of the ith row of A':

$$
\tau_i := \sum_{k=1}^{n} \left(a'_{ik} \right)^2 .
\tag{10.27}
$$

The elements $\tilde{a}_{ik}$ of the approximation for the discrete spectral path construction matrix $\tilde{A}$ are then given by

$$\tilde{a}_{ik} = \sqrt{\frac{t_i}{\tau_i}}\, a'_{ik} = \sqrt{t_i}\,\frac{\sin \omega_k t_i/2k - 1}{\sqrt{\sum_{l=1}^{n}(\sin \omega_l t_i/2l - 1)^2}}. \tag{10.28}$$

The approximate spectral split calculated in this way for a 12-step discretisation of a Wiener process path from $t = 0$ to $t = 3$ is shown below:

$$\tilde{A}_{\text{spectral}} = \begin{pmatrix} 0.2142 & 0.2094 & 0.1998 & 0.1860 & 0.1685 & 0.1479 & 0.1252 & 0.1011 & 0.0766 & 0.0526 & 0.0299 & 0.0093 \\ 0.4141 & 0.3771 & 0.3091 & 0.2208 & 0.1257 & 0.0376 & -0.0319 & -0.0754 & -0.0909 & -0.0813 & -0.0539 & -0.0180 \\ 0.6070 & 0.4885 & 0.2931 & 0.0867 & -0.0674 & -0.1332 & -0.1127 & -0.0405 & 0.0357 & 0.0771 & 0.0698 & 0.0264 \\ 0.7897 & 0.5265 & 0.1579 & -0.1128 & -0.1755 & -0.0718 & 0.0607 & 0.1053 & 0.0465 & -0.0416 & -0.0752 & -0.0343 \\ 0.9591 & 0.4852 & -0.0411 & -0.2231 & -0.0670 & 0.1136 & 0.0961 & -0.0402 & -0.0919 & -0.0108 & 0.0693 & 0.0417 \\ 1.1121 & 0.3707 & -0.2224 & -0.1589 & 0.1236 & 0.1011 & -0.0855 & -0.0741 & 0.0654 & 0.0585 & -0.0530 & -0.0484 \\ 1.2462 & 0.2004 & -0.3115 & 0.0293 & 0.1612 & -0.0869 & -0.0736 & 0.0967 & 0.0121 & -0.0820 & 0.0286 & 0.0542 \\ 1.3591 & 0.0000 & -0.2718 & 0.1942 & 0.0000 & -0.1236 & 0.1045 & 0.0000 & -0.0799 & 0.0715 & 0.0000 & -0.0591 \\ 1.4489 & -0.2001 & -0.1200 & 0.2070 & -0.1610 & 0.0546 & 0.0462 & -0.0966 & 0.0852 & -0.0316 & -0.0286 & 0.0630 \\ 1.5140 & -0.3694 & 0.0811 & 0.0580 & -0.1231 & 0.1376 & -0.1165 & 0.0739 & -0.0239 & -0.0214 & 0.0528 & -0.0658 \\ 1.5535 & -0.4825 & 0.2486 & -0.1363 & 0.0666 & -0.0186 & -0.0157 & 0.0400 & -0.0561 & 0.0654 & -0.0689 & 0.0675 \\ 1.5727 & -0.5242 & 0.3145 & -0.2247 & 0.1747 & -0.1430 & 0.1210 & -0.1048 & 0.0925 & -0.0828 & 0.0749 & -0.0684 \end{pmatrix} \tag{10.29}$$

This is to be compared with an exact spectral split:

$$A_{\text{spectral}} = \begin{pmatrix} 0.1996 & 0.1965 & 0.1902 & 0.1810 & 0.1689 & 0.1541 & 0.1369 & 0.1176 & 0.0964 & 0.0736 & 0.0497 & 0.0251 \\ 0.3961 & 0.3653 & 0.3078 & 0.2307 & 0.1438 & 0.0578 & -0.0172 & -0.0727 & -0.1033 & -0.1073 & -0.0872 & -0.0486 \\ 0.5863 & 0.4829 & 0.3078 & 0.1131 & -0.0464 & -0.1325 & -0.1348 & -0.0727 & 0.0143 & 0.0829 & 0.1030 & 0.0690 \\ 0.7672 & 0.5326 & 0.1902 & -0.0865 & -0.1833 & -0.1074 & 0.0341 & 0.1176 & 0.0879 & -0.0135 & -0.0934 & -0.0851 \\ 0.9361 & 0.5076 & 0.0000 & -0.2234 & -0.1097 & 0.0922 & 0.1305 & 0.0000 & -0.1085 & -0.0632 & 0.0607 & 0.0959 \\ 1.0902 & 0.4112 & -0.1902 & -0.1983 & 0.0899 & 0.1420 & -0.0505 & -0.1176 & 0.0284 & 0.1056 & -0.0129 & -0.1006 \\ 1.2271 & 0.2571 & -0.3078 & -0.0294 & 0.1863 & -0.0390 & -0.1241 & 0.0727 & 0.0781 & -0.0908 & -0.0380 & 0.0990 \\ 1.3447 & 0.0669 & -0.3078 & 0.1608 & 0.0687 & -0.1566 & 0.0661 & 0.0727 & -0.1121 & 0.0267 & 0.0796 & -0.0912 \\ 1.4410 & -0.1327 & -0.1902 & 0.2344 & -0.0197 & 0.1158 & 0.1176 & 0.0420 & 0.0518 & -0.1014 & 0.0777 \\ 1.5146 & -0.3137 & 0.0000 & 0.1380 & -0.1775 & 0.1492 & -0.0806 & 0.0000 & 0.0671 & -0.1023 & 0.0982 & -0.0592 \\ 1.5644 & -0.4506 & 0.1902 & -0.0584 & -0.0234 & 0.0756 & -0.1057 & 0.1176 & -0.1139 & 0.0973 & -0.0707 & 0.0371 \\ 1.5895 & -0.5242 & 0.3078 & -0.2125 & 0.1576 & -0.1209 & 0.0939 & -0.0727 & 0.0550 & -0.0396 & 0.0257 & -0.0126 \end{pmatrix} \tag{10.30}$$

The effective covariance of the approximate spectral construction matrix (10.29) is

$$\tilde{A}_{\text{spectral}} \cdot \tilde{A}_{\text{spectral}}^{\top} = \begin{pmatrix} 0.2500 & 0.2726 & 0.2669 & 0.2668 & 0.2656 & 0.2655 & 0.2650 & 0.2648 & 0.2646 & 0.2645 & 0.2644 & 0.2654 \\ 0.2726 & 0.5000 & 0.5247 & 0.5187 & 0.5187 & 0.5172 & 0.5169 & 0.5162 & 0.5160 & 0.5156 & 0.5155 & 0.5173 \\ 0.2669 & 0.5247 & 0.7500 & 0.7757 & 0.7698 & 0.7699 & 0.7682 & 0.7680 & 0.7672 & 0.7670 & 0.7665 & 0.7695 \\ 0.2668 & 0.5187 & 0.7757 & 1.0000 & 1.0263 & 1.0205 & 1.0208 & 1.0191 & 1.0188 & 1.0180 & 1.0179 & 1.0214 \\ 0.2656 & 0.5187 & 0.7698 & 1.0263 & 1.2500 & 1.2710 & 1.2714 & 1.2697 & 1.2696 & 1.2688 & 1.2738 \\ 0.2655 & 0.5172 & 0.7699 & 1.0205 & 1.2766 & 1.5000 & 1.5269 & 1.5214 & 1.5220 & 1.5203 & 1.5204 & 1.5255 \\ 0.2650 & 0.5169 & 0.7682 & 1.0208 & 1.2710 & 1.5269 & 1.7500 & 1.7771 & 1.7718 & 1.7725 & 1.7709 & 1.7782 \\ 0.2648 & 0.5162 & 0.7680 & 1.0191 & 1.2714 & 1.5214 & 1.7771 & 2.0000 & 2.0273 & 2.0220 & 2.0232 & 2.0294 \\ 0.2646 & 0.5160 & 0.7672 & 1.0188 & 1.2697 & 1.5220 & 1.7718 & 2.0273 & 2.2500 & 2.2777 & 2.2724 & 2.2832 \\ 0.2645 & 0.5156 & 0.7670 & 1.0180 & 1.2696 & 1.5203 & 1.7725 & 2.0220 & 2.2777 & 2.5000 & 2.5285 & 2.5323 \\ 0.2644 & 0.5155 & 0.7665 & 1.0179 & 1.2688 & 1.5204 & 1.7709 & 2.0232 & 2.2724 & 2.5285 & 2.7500 & 2.7928 \\ 0.2654 & 0.5173 & 0.7695 & 1.0214 & 1.2738 & 1.5255 & 1.7782 & 2.0294 & 2.2832 & 2.5323 & 2.7928 & 3.0000 \end{pmatrix} \tag{10.31}$$

As you can see, the diagonal elements meet the requirements exactly. The off-diagonal elements, however, indicate that a simulation based on this approximate spectral split would effectively simulate the realisations of the standard Wiener process to have a somewhat exaggerated correlation. Considering that we spend significant effort elsewhere to ensure that the realised variances and covariances of all our random variates meet the specifications given by any financial model as closely as possible, the approximate spectral path construction may seem a little bit too inaccurate.

There is, however, another important lesson we can learn from the approximate spectral decomposition. The eigenvalues of the spectral decomposition are given by

$$\lambda_k = \frac{1}{\omega_k^2} \tag{10.32}$$

and thus decay as $\mathcal{O}\left(k^{-2}\right)$. Since the eigenvalues of a discrete path covariance matrix are well approximated by those of the continuous counterpart, we can conclude that these, too, decay very quickly. As a matter of fact, for a completely uniform spacing of monitoring times such as the one used above with $\Delta t = \frac{1}{4}$, both eigenvalues and eigenvectors can be derived analytically, as shown in appendix section 10.9.1.

The importance of the eigenvalues is given by the fact that they directly represent the amount of variance that can be reproduced by using only a smaller subset of the orthogonal eigenvectors and thus attempt to mimic an effectively n-dimensional variate draw (namely the standard Wiener process path over n points) by using only m Gaussian variates, with $m < n$. In statistics, there is the notion of the *variability explained* by using just the first m column vectors in a complete path construction matrix. It is given by the sum of all the squares of the elements of the vectors used. For the spectral decomposition, this is just the sum of the eigenvalues as given in (10.32). In this sense, the spectral decomposition (given that the eigenvectors are sorted by decreasing size of their associated eigenvalues) is the optimal way to assign most importance to the first Gaussian variates in any given vector draw z. As it happens, this kind of *effective dimensionality reduction* is precisely what makes low-discrepancy numbers converge the fastest, so this might be the best path construction method of choice in conjunction with Sobol' numbers. If only there wasn't always some catch. In this case the problem is as follows. The spectral path construction method may provide the fastest convergence in conjunction with Sobol' numbers as a function of the number of iterations that are carried out. However, more important is the amount of time spent in the simulation. Apart from the fact that the calculation of the (accurate) spectral path construction matrix is effectively a task involving $\mathcal{O}\left(n^{3}\right)$ mathematical operations, the actual use of the matrix A_{spectral} during the simulation involves n^2 multiplications and $n(n-1)$ additions for the construction of each and every path. When n is in the hundreds, this means that for a simulation involving possibly several tens of thousands of iterations we end up spending most of our time just in the transformation from standard normal variates to Wiener path coordinates. In the next section, I discuss my favourite path construction method which gives almost the same effective dimensionality reduction as the spectral method, but at the expense of only about $3n$ multiplications and $2n$ additions for each constructed path!

10.8.3 The Brownian Bridge

Similar to the spectral path construction method, the *Brownian bridge* is a way to construct a discretised Wiener process path by using the first Gaussian variates in a vector draw z to shape the overall features of the path, and then adding more and more of the fine structure. The very first variate z_1 is used to determine the realisation of the Wiener path at the final time t_n of our n-point discretisation of the path by setting $W_{t_n} = \sqrt{t_n}z_1$. The next variate is then used to determine the value of the Wiener process as it was realised at an intermediate time step t_j conditional on the realisation at t_n (and at $t_0 = 0$ which is, of course, zero). The procedure is then repeated to gradually fill in all of the realisations of the Wiener process at all intermediate points, in an ever refining algorithm. In each step of the refinement procedure to determine W_{t_j}, given that we have already established W_{t_i} and W_{t_k} with $t_i < t_j < t_k$, we make use of the fact that the conditional distribution of W_{t_j} is Gaussian with mean

$$E[W_{t_j}] = \left(\frac{t_k - t_j}{t_k - t_i}\right) W_{t_i} + \left(\frac{t_j - t_i}{t_k - t_i}\right) W_{t_k} \qquad (10.33)$$

and variance

$$V[W_{t_j}] = \frac{\left(t_j - t_i\right)\left(t_k - t_j\right)}{\left(t_k - t_i\right)}. \qquad (10.34)$$

A proof of equations (10.33) and (10.34) is sketched in appendix section 10.9.2.

Since all of the weighting coefficients can be precalculated, we only need to carry out three multiplications and two additions for each point in the Brownian bridge. Exceptions are, of course, the terminal point for which only a multiplication is required, and all those whose left-hand side conditioning point is the beginning of the path at zero.

The Brownian bridge is particularly easy to construct if the number of steps is a power of two, because then each interval divides into two intervals containing the same number of steps. In general, we can construct the Brownian bridge by always subdividing the interval from the last point that was set to the next one that is already set, and halve this interval into two parts containing approximately the same number of points. An example for this procedure is illustrated in Figure 10.4. The algorithm for the construction of a Brownian bridge over an arbitrary number of steps can be separated into two parts. The first part is the calculation of the indices determining the order of the point construction, the weighting coefficients, and the conditional variances, or their square roots, respectively. The second part is the mapping of a vector of standard Gaussian variates to a single Wiener path at run time of the Monte Carlo simulation. I give in Code Example 10.1 a concrete implementation of a C++ class providing these two stages. The constructor of the class carries out all the initial calculations. The build-Path method is then to be called in the main loop of the Monte Carlo simulation. Each time the procedure buildPath is executed, it transforms a vector of uncorrelated standard normal variates given by the input vector normalVariates into a standard Wiener path with equal time steps of size $\Delta t = 1$ and stores it in the output vector path.

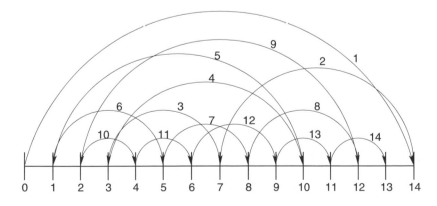

Figure 10.4 The construction of a Brownian bridge over 14 steps

When we wish to construct paths that represent Brownian motions over points in time t_i for $i = 1..m$, and the realisation of the Brownian path at each time horizon t_i is to be consistent with an implied volatility coefficient $\hat{\sigma}_i$, we need to take into account the resulting term structure of instantaneous volatility and variance. Given that we have a Brownian process B that is generated from a standard Wiener process W by the multiplication with a deterministic volatility function $\sigma(t)$ according to

$$dB = \sigma(t)dW, \tag{10.35}$$

the conditional mean and variance for the realisation of $B(t_j)$ given that we have knowledge of $B(t_i)$ and $B(t_k)$ with $t_i < t_j < t_k$ is

$$E[B_{t_j}] = \left(\frac{v_k - v_j}{v_k - v_j}\right) B_{t_i} + \left(\frac{v_j - v_i}{v_k - v_i}\right) B_{t_k} \tag{10.36}$$

and

$$v[B_{t_j}] = \frac{(v_j - v_i)(v_k - v_j)}{(v_k - v_i)} \tag{10.37}$$

with

$$v_q = \int_{s=0}^{t_q} \sigma(s)^2 ds. \tag{10.38}$$

Of course, the relationship between the variances v_i and the implied volatilities $\hat{\sigma}_i$ is $v_i = \hat{\sigma}_i^2 t_i$. In other words, it is easy to write another constructor for the class BrownianBridge in code example 10.1 that takes into account a given implied volatility vector and a vector whose elements are the associated time horizons, and precomputes the necessary weighting and scaling coefficients leftWeight rightWeight, and stddev. In fact, once we have added a temporary vector v in the body of the constructor and populated it such that $v[j] = \hat{\sigma}_j^2 t_j$, all that needs to be done is to replace the corresponding statements with:

```
stddev[0]       = sqrt (v[numberOfSteps-1]);
...
leftweight[i]   = (v[k]-v[1])/(v[k]-v[j-1]);
rightweight[i]  = (v[1]-v[j-1])/(v[k]-v[j-1]);
stddev[i]       = sqrt((v[1]-v[j-1])*(v[k]-v[1])/v[k]-v[j-1]));
```

Another application of the normalised path vector as constructed directly by build-Path in code example 10.1 may actually require individual increments, for instance in order to carry out an Euler or Milstein integration of a stochastic differential equation driven by an underlying Wiener process. In this case, one would take the constructed normalised path stored in the vector path, and back out the path increments by taking the differences $\Delta W_i = \text{path}[i] - \text{path}[i-1]$ (apart from the first entry stored in path[0], of course, which is directly equal to ΔW_0). Each of the so constructed ΔW_i is then a standard normal variate (with unit variance). In order to transform the so resulting standard Wiener increments of variance 1 to a desired time step Δt, we

```cpp
#include <vector>
#include <assert.h>
class BrownianBridge {      //    Builds Wiener process paths of equal time steps of delta t = 1.
public:
  BrownianBridge( unsigned long numberOfSteps );
  void buildPath( vector <double> &theWienerProcessPath, const vector <double> &gaussianVariates );
private:
  unsigned long numberOfSteps;
  vector <unsigned long> leftIndex, rightIndex, bridgeIndex;
  vector <double> leftWeight, rightWeight, stddev;
};

BrownianBridge::BrownianBridge( unsigned long numberOfSteps_ ) : numberOfSteps(numberOfSteps_),
  leftIndex(numberOfSteps), rightIndex(numberOfSteps), bridgeIndex(numberOfSteps),
  leftWeight(numberOfSteps), rightWeight(numberOfSteps), stddev(numberOfSteps)
{
  assert(numberOfSteps);                     //  There must be at least one step.
  vector <unsigned long> map(numberOfSteps);
  // map is used to indicate which points are already constructed. If map[i] is zero, path point i
  // is yet unconstructed.  map[i]-1 is the index of the variate that constructs the path point # i.
  unsigned long i,j,k,l;
  map[numberOfSteps-1] = 1;                  //  The first point in the construction is the global step.
  bridgeIndex[0] = numberOfSteps-1;          //  The global step is constructed from the first variate.
  stddev[0] = sqrt(numberOfSteps);           //   The variance of the global step is numberOfSteps*1.0.
  leftWeight[0] = rightWeight[0] = 0.;       //  The global step to the last point in time is special.
  for (j=0,i=1;i<numberOfSteps;++i){
    while (map[j]) ++j;                       //  Find the next unpopulated entry in the map.
    k=j;
    while ((!map[k])) ++k;                    //  Find the next populated entry in the map from there.
    l=j+((k-1-j)>>1);                         //  l is now the index of the point to be constructed next.
    map[l]=i;
    bridgeIndex[i] = l;                       //  The i-th Gaussian variate will be used to set point l.
    leftIndex[i]   = j;                       //  Point j-1 is the left strut of the bridge for point l.
    rightIndex[i]  = k;                       //  Point  k is the right strut of the bridge for point l.
    leftWeight[i]  = (k-l)/(k+1.-j);
    rightWeight[i] = (l+1.-j)/(k+1.-j);
    stddev[i]      = sqrt(((l+1.-j)*(k-l))/(k+1.-j));
    j=k+1;
    if (j>=numberOfSteps) j=0; // Wrap around.
  }
}

void BrownianBridge::buildPath( vector <double> &path, const vector <double> &normalVariates ){
  assert( normalVariates.size() == numberOfSteps && path.size() == numberOfSteps );
  unsigned long i,j,k,l;
  path[numberOfSteps-1] = stddev[0]*normalVariates[0];       //  The global step.
  for (i=1;i<numberOfSteps;i++){
    j = leftIndex[i];
    k = rightIndex[i];
    l = bridgeIndex[i];
    if (j) path[l] = leftWeight[i]*path[j-1] + rightWeight[i]*path[k] + stddev[i]*normalVariates[i];
    else   path[l] = rightWeight[i]*path[k] + stddev[i]*normalVariates[i];
  }
}
```

Code Example 10.1   The Brownian bridge algorithm in a C++ class

simply multiply them with $\sqrt{\Delta t}$. The reader might wonder why one would want to jump through all these hoops only to arrive at another set of standard normal variates. Empirically, I found that the use of Wiener increments backed out of a path constructed with the Brownian bridge method driven by Sobol' sequences shows better convergence properties for the numerical integration of stochastic differential equations. In particular, so constructed increments typically perform better than standard normal variates computed directly from pseudo-random numbers, or Sobol' numbers for that matter, for most financial applications where the overall path skeleton structure has the biggest impact on the convergence of the calculation. Also, this apparently somewhat convoluted method of constructing standard increments from a given Sobol' vector draw is still faster than the calculation of standard normal variates by the aid of most pseudo-random number generators of high grade since the construction of a single Sobol' vector is so exceptionally fast.

10.8.4 A Comparison of Path Construction Methods

As was already mentioned, the Brownian bridge requires approximately three multiplications and two additions per dimension for each constructed path. For most Monte Carlo simulations based on the construction of Wiener paths, the CPU time required for the evaluation of the function(al) dependent on the constructed sample path grows at least linearly with the dimensionality of the problem. Thus, the *relative* run time requirement of the path construction at worst levels out to a constant ratio with increasing dimensionality when the Brownian bridge is used, and usually actually decreases for higher dimensions. This is in stark contrast to the CPU time used by the spectral path construction which increases as the square of the dimensionality. On the other hand, when compared with the incremental path construction, the Brownian bridge manages to explain a much higher percentage of the total variability when only the first few variates are taken into account. In fact, as shown in Table 10.1, the first four dimensions, if ordered using the Brownian bridge path construction method, suffice to explain over 93% of the total variability for the previous example of a 12-step construction from $t = 0$ to $t = 3$. This is to be compared with 95.6% from the spectral method, but only 53.9% when we construct paths incrementally. Of course, if we actually carry out a factor truncation at, say, the level of four driving Gaussian draws for any one path, the spectral method will still be superior to the Brownian bridge. However, if there is an advantage in ordering the dimensions according to their importance, as there is for low-discrepancy numbers, the Brownian bridge method offers the benefit of almost optimal ordering (in the sense of maximal variability explained) whilst only requiring three multiplications per dimension. In order to give a more visual argument to the similarity of the spectral path construction and the Brownian bridge, I give the first four column vectors of the constructing matrix A for the three methods discussed in figure 10.5 for a path constructed over 64 equal steps in time. As we can see, the coefficients of the Brownian bridge path construction matrix appear almost like a piecewise affine mimic of the sinusoidal waves of the spectral path construction vectors. In the continuous description of the decomposition of Brownian

Table 10.1 The cumulative variability explained by an increasing number of dimensions for three path construction methods

Ordered dimension #	1	2	3	4	5	6	7	8	9	10	11	12
Incremental	15.4%	29.5%	42.3%	53.9%	64.1%	73.1%	80.8%	87.2%	92.3%	96.2%	98.7%	100%
Spectral	81.3%	90.4%	93.8%	95.6%	96.7%	97.5%	98.1%	98.5%	99.0%	99.3%	99.7%	100%
Brownian bridge	69.4%	85.0%	89.1%	93.2%	94.2%	95.3%	96.4%	97.4%	98.1%	98.7%	99.4%	100%

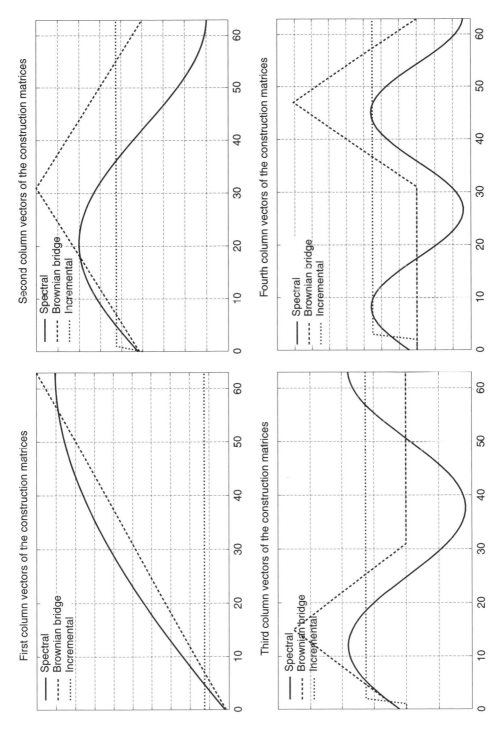

Figure 10.5 The first four column vectors of the path construction matrices

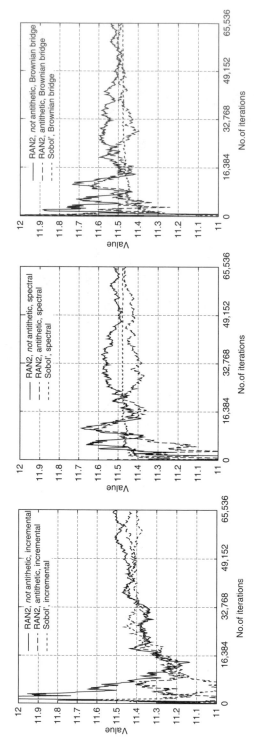

Figure 10.6   Convergence diagrams over the number of iterations for the pricing simulation of an Asian call option

motion into basis functions, there are many more possibilities to choose a set of basis functions than the spectral analysis given by equation (10.24). The basis functions that produce the continuous time equivalent of the Brownian bridge are known as *Schauder* functions, which in turn are the primitives of *Haar* functions [ABG97]. Looking at the diagrams in Figure 10.5, we can intuitively understand the similar performance of the spectral method and the Brownian bridge. In contrast, the incremental method has no similarity with the other two methods at all.

The right path construction method can make a substantial difference to the performance of Monte Carlo implementation for many applications. In Figure 10.6, I show the convergence of the Monte Carlo simulation for the pricing of a standard at-the-money Asian call option. The maturity of the option was one year with 252 monitoring days over that period. The weights were all equal. Both spot and strike were set at 100, and neither interest rates nor yields on the underlying asset were taken into account. The number of iterations taken is shown along the abscissa in Figure 10.6. Compare this to the convergence behaviour as a function of the CPU time taken[1] by the simulation, which is shown in Figure 10.7.

When we compare the spectral method with the Brownian bridge as a function of the number of iterations, there doesn't appear to be much between them. However, when viewed as a function of the CPU time needed for the simulation, we will probably prefer the Brownian bridge since it appears to converge within a few seconds for this problem.

10.8.5 Multivariate path construction

When we need to construct paths of correlated Wiener processes, we can combine different techniques in order to tailor the right method for the particular problem at hand. For instance, if we wish to carry out Monte Carlo simulations for a pricing problem that is most significantly influenced by the joint distribution of a set of strongly correlated underlying Wiener processes at the first time horizon along a discretised path, we might want to use incremental path construction, but at each time horizon use the spectral decomposition in order to incorporate the correlation. Given the dimension d of the Wiener process, and the number of time horizons m over which the correlated path ought to be constructed, we need to draw standard normal variate vectors of dimension $d \cdot m$. Each of those vector draws is then used to construct all of the realisations of all of the d Wiener processes over all of the relevant m time horizons for one iteration in the Monte Carlo simulation. Let us define the covariance matrix $C(t)$ whose elements are given by

$$c_{kl}(t) = \int_0^t \sigma_k(s)\sigma_l(s)\rho_{kl}(s)\mathrm{d}s. \qquad (10.39)$$

For incremental path construction with spectral decomposition of the correlation information, one would take the first d elements of a given standard normal variate vector draw $z \in \mathbb{R}^{d \cdot m}$. These first d elements would then be multiplied with the spectral split, i.e. the spectral pseudo-square root of $C(t_1)$ in order to construct the vector x_1 of realisations of correlated Wiener processes at time t_1. The realisations at time horizon t_2 are then obtained by taking x_1 and adding to it the product of the second set of d variates (out of the vector draw z) with a pseudo-square root of the stepwise covariance matrix from time

---

[1]The CPU time shown was measured on an AMD K6-III processor running at 400 MHz.

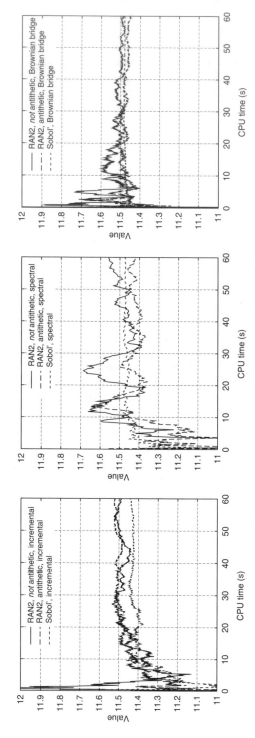

Figure 10.7 Convergence diagrams over the CPU time taken for the pricing simulation of an Asian call option

t_1 to t_2 which I denote by $\sqrt{C(t_2) - C(t_1)}$. This gives us x_2, and all of the realisations at the subsequent time horizons are computed accordingly. Of course, if you have reason to believe that the decomposition of any of the stepwise covariances is better exploited by the use of the Cholesky algorithm, you can just use that instead (albeit that I couldn't think of an example when the Cholesky method for the stepwise covariance split would be more appropriate).

For most Monte Carlo simulations in finance that involve multidimensional correlated Wiener processes, I use the Brownian bridge in conjunction with stepwise spectral decomposition, though. The reason is that we rarely have hundreds and thousands of correlated Wiener processes, the most I have encountered is a few dozen, not more than five dozen or so. In contrast, however, it is well possible to have hundreds or even thousands of monitoring times of relevance, and the spectral path construction becomes very expensive indeed when we are dealing with thousands of time steps. The construction of multivariate correlated Wiener processes by the aid of the Brownian bridge and spectral decomposition at each time horizon in order to incoporate the correlation information can thus be done as follows. First, we construct d uncorrelated normalised Wiener process paths $\boldsymbol{W}(t) \in \mathbb{R}^d$ from the given vector draw $z \in \mathbb{R}^{d \cdot m}$ using the Brownian bridge. For this, we take the first d entries in z in order to construct the realisations of all of the uncorrelated Wiener processes at the final time horizon t_m. Next, we take the second set of d variates from z in order to construct the realisations of all of the uncorrelated Wiener processes at an intermediate time step t_k With $k \simeq m/2$, and so forth, following the Brownian bridge algorithm outlined in section 10.8.3 (see code example 10.1). From this set of d uncorrelated Wiener process path realisations over the m time horizons of interest, one then obtains Wiener process increments in the obvious fashion. Next, each set of uncorrelated increments is transformed to a set of correlated and volatility-scaled Wiener increments by setting

$$\Delta \boldsymbol{B}_k = A_k \cdot \wedge \boldsymbol{W}_k. \tag{10.40}$$

with A_k being the spectral pseudo square root of the covariance matrix increment $C(t_k) - C(t_{k-1})$ whose elements are defined in equation (10.39). Note that A_k contains both the scaling for the actual size of the time step (all of the uncorrelated increments $\boldsymbol{W}_k$ were constructed assuming that all time steps are of size $\Delta t = 1$) and the volatility scaling. And finally, the correlated Wiener process path increments are added up again, as if we had constructed the correlated paths in an incremental fashion right from the start.

Whenever the correlation between the Wiener processes is constant for all time steps and each of the processes has constant volatility, it is possible to simplify this procedure somewhat. In this case, one can avoid the construction from stepwise covariance increments. Let us denote the volatility of the j-th process as σ_j, and let R be the time-constant correlation matrix. Now, set Q to be the spectral pseudo-square root of R such that

$$R = Q Q^\top. \tag{10.41}$$

In other words, we have the following relationship amongst the elements of R and Q:

$$r_{kl} = \sum_j q_{kj} q_{lj} \tag{10.42}$$

The procedure to construct correlated Wiener processes using a Brownian bridge when volatilities and correlations are constant is thus as follows. First, construct uncorrelated standard Wiener processes for the correct monitoring times as outlined in section 10.8.3 by setting $v_j = t_j$ for all $j = 1 \ldots m$ and assuming unit volatility (i.e. 100%). Thus, we will have constructed paths such that the variance of W_{jk}, i.e. the variance of the realisation of the j-th Wiener process at time k, is t_k, and the covariance of any pair of w_{jk} and w_{ih} is

$$\text{Cov}\big[w_{jk}, w_{ih}\big] = \delta_{ij} \min(t_k, t_h). \tag{10.43}$$

Then, set

$$b_{jk} = \sigma_j \sum_l q_{jl} w_{lk}. \tag{10.44}$$

Due to the property (10.43), it is straightforward to show that

$$\text{Cov}\big[b_{jk}, b_{ih}\big] = \sigma_i \sigma_j r_{ij} \min(t_k, t_h) \tag{10.45}$$

as it should be for correlated Wiener processes with constant volatility and correlation.

10.9   APPENDIX

10.9.1   Eigenvalues and Eigenvectors of a Discrete-time Covariance Matrix

The covariance matrix of the realisations W_i at a set of discrete times chosen to be homogeneously stepped such that $t_i = i$ for $i = 1, \ldots, n$ is given by

$$C_n = \begin{pmatrix} 1 & 1 & 1 & \cdots & 1 \\ 1 & 2 & 2 & \cdots & 2 \\ 1 & 2 & 3 & \cdots & 3 \\ \vdots & \vdots & \vdots & \ddots & \vdots \\ 1 & 2 & 3 & \cdots & n \end{pmatrix}. \tag{10.46}$$

The eigenvalues are given by

$$D_n(\lambda) = 0 \tag{10.47}$$

with

$$D_n(\lambda) = \begin{vmatrix} 1-\lambda & 1 & 1 & \cdots & 1 \\ 1 & 2-\lambda & 2 & \cdots & 2 \\ 1 & 2 & 3-\lambda & \cdots & 3 \\ \vdots & \vdots & \vdots & \ddots & \vdots \\ 1 & 2 & 3 & \cdots & n-\lambda \end{vmatrix}. \tag{10.48}$$

Subtracting the first row of the matrix inside the determinant operator $| \cdot |$ from all subsequent ones gives

$$D_n(\lambda) = \begin{vmatrix} 1-\lambda & 1 & 1 & \cdots & 1 \\ \lambda & 1-\lambda & 1 & \cdots & 1 \\ \lambda & 1 & 2-\lambda & \cdots & 2 \\ \vdots & \vdots & \vdots & \ddots & \vdots \\ \lambda & 1 & 2 & \cdots & n-1-\lambda \end{vmatrix} \tag{10.49}$$

and then subtracting the second row from the first, we obtain

$$D_n(\lambda) = \begin{vmatrix} 1-2\lambda & \lambda & 0 & \cdots & 0 \\ \lambda & 1-\lambda & 1 & \cdots & 1 \\ \lambda & 1 & 2-\lambda & \cdots & 2 \\ \vdots & \vdots & \vdots & \ddots & \vdots \\ \lambda & 1 & 2 & \cdots & n-1-\lambda \end{vmatrix}. \tag{10.50}$$

An expansion by the first row yields

$$D_n(\lambda) = (1-2\lambda)D_{n-1}(\lambda) - \lambda \begin{vmatrix} \lambda & 1 & 1 & \cdots & 0 \\ \lambda & 2-\lambda & 2 & \cdots & 2 \\ \lambda & 2 & 3-\lambda & \cdots & 3 \\ \vdots & \vdots & \vdots & \ddots & \vdots \\ \lambda & 2 & 3 & \cdots & n-1-\lambda \end{vmatrix}. \tag{10.51}$$

Factorising λ out of the column of the explicit determinant on the right-hand side, and repeating the procedure of subtracting the first row from all subsequent ones, followed by a subtraction of the second row from the first, we get

$$D_n(\lambda) = (1-2\lambda)D_{n-1}(\lambda) - \lambda^2 \begin{vmatrix} 1 & \lambda & 0 & \cdots & 0 \\ 0 & 1-\lambda & 1 & \cdots & 1 \\ 0 & 1 & 2-\lambda & \cdots & 2 \\ \vdots & \vdots & \vdots & \ddots & \vdots \\ 0 & 1 & 2 & \cdots & n-2-\lambda \end{vmatrix}. \tag{10.52}$$

An expansion of the explicit determinant on the right-hand side now gives us the recursion formula

$$D_n(\lambda) = (1-2\lambda)D_{n-1}(\lambda) - \lambda^2 D_{n-2}(\lambda) \tag{10.53}$$

with the initial conditions

$$\begin{aligned} D_0(\lambda) &= 1, \\ D_1(\lambda) &= 1-\lambda. \end{aligned} \tag{10.54}$$

Using the Ansatz

$$D_n(\lambda) \propto [\alpha(\lambda)]^n \tag{10.55}$$

we obtain

$$\alpha^2 - (1-2\lambda)\alpha + \lambda^2 = 0 \tag{10.56}$$

and thus

$$\alpha_\pm = \tfrac{1}{2}\left(1 - 2\lambda \pm \sqrt{1-4\lambda}\right). \tag{10.57}$$

Since the determinants D_n, D_{n-1} and D_{n-2} all appear linearly in equation (10.53), we substitute the linear combination

$$D_n(\lambda) = \varkappa_+\alpha_+^n + \varkappa_-\alpha_-^n \tag{10.58}$$

into (10.54), solve for $\varkappa_+$ and $\varkappa_-$ and obtain

$$D_n(\lambda) = \left(\frac{1 - \lambda - \alpha_-}{\alpha_+ - \alpha_-}\right)\alpha_+^n - \left(\frac{1 - \lambda - \alpha_+}{\alpha_+ - \alpha_-}\right)\alpha_-^{-n}. \tag{10.59}$$

Making use of the fact that $\alpha_+\alpha_- = \lambda^2$, which can be seen from equation (10.56), we now get

$$D_n(\lambda) = \frac{\lambda^n}{2\sqrt{1 - 4\lambda}}\left[\left(1 + \sqrt{1 - 4\lambda}\right)\left(\frac{\alpha_+}{\lambda}\right)^n - \left(1 - \sqrt{1 - 4\lambda}\right)\left(\frac{\alpha_+}{\lambda}\right)^{-n}\right]. \tag{10.60}$$

Let us now define

$$u := \frac{\alpha_+(\lambda)}{\lambda} \tag{10.61}$$

which means

$$\lambda = \frac{u}{(u + 1)^2}. \tag{10.62}$$

The eigenvalues of C_n are given by $D_n(\lambda) = 0$ which, together with the above definitions, reduces to

$$u^{2n+1} = 1 \tag{10.63}$$

whence

$$u = e^{i\pi \frac{2m}{2n+1}} \quad \text{for } m = 1, \ldots, n. \tag{10.64}$$

This, in conjunction with (10.62), finally simplifies to

$$\lambda = \frac{1}{4\cos^2\left(\frac{m\pi}{2n+1}\right)}. \tag{10.65}$$

A simple analysis of equation (10.65) shows that as n increases, the smallest eigenvalue of D_n converges to $\frac{1}{4}$ from above, whilst the largest eigenvalue grows as n^2. Thus, the importance of the smaller eigenvalues decreases like $1/n^2$.

Given the definition

$$\omega_{nj} := \left(\frac{2j - 1}{2n + 1}\right) \cdot \frac{\pi}{2} \tag{10.66}$$

we can re-express (10.65) as

$$\lambda_{nj} := \frac{1}{4\sin^2 \omega_{nj}}. \tag{10.67}$$

The ordering is now such that λ_{n1} is the largest eigenvalue of C_n, and λ_{nn} is the smallest eigenvalue. As for the eigenvectors, which are the column vectors of the matrix S in the decomposition

$$C_n = S_n \cdot \Lambda_n \cdot S_N^\top \tag{10.68}$$

with Λ_n being diagonal, we have for the elements s_{nkl} of S_n:

$$s_{nkl} = \frac{\sin(2k\omega_{nl})}{\sqrt{\sum_{j=1}^{n} \sin^2(2j\omega_{nl})}}. \tag{10.69}$$

Since

$$\sin^2 x = \frac{1}{2} - \frac{1}{2}\cos(2x) \tag{10.70}$$

and

$$\sum_{j=1}^{n} \cos\left[2\pi\left(\frac{2j-1}{2n+1}\right)\right] = -\frac{1}{2} \tag{10.71}$$

equation (10.69) simplifies to

$$s_{nkl} = \frac{2}{\sqrt{2n+1}}\sin(2k\omega_{nl}). \tag{10.72}$$

This means that the elements a_{nkl} of the spectral pseudo-square root A_n of C_n satisfying

$$C_n = A_n \cdot A_n^\top$$

are given by

$$a_{nkl} = \frac{1}{\sqrt{2n+1}} \cdot \frac{\sin\left(k\pi \frac{2l-1}{2n+1}\right)}{\sin\left(\frac{2l-1}{2n+1}\frac{\pi}{2}\right)}. \tag{10.73}$$

For a homogeneous time-discretisation over time steps of an arbitrary Δt instead of 1, the elements of the covariance matrix C_n simply need to be multiplied by Δt, and the elements of the spectral pseudo-square root are given as in (10.73), only that they require multiplication with $\sqrt{\Delta t}$. Sadly, for inhomogeneous time steps, the best approximation available is the one from the continuous case as in equation (10.28).

10.9.2   The Conditional Distribution of the Brownian Bridge

Let us start off by assuming that the Wiener path from t_i to t_j, and then to t_k, has been constructed incrementally from two independent standard Gaussian variates x and y:

$$W_{t_j} = W_{t_i} + \sqrt{t_j - t_i}\, x, \tag{10.74}$$

$$W_{t_k} = W_{t_j} + \sqrt{t_k - t_j}\, y = W_{t_i} + \sqrt{t_j - t_i}\, x + \sqrt{t_k - t_j}\, y. \tag{10.75}$$

The joint probability density of a vector draw (x, y) is the product of the densities of the variates x and y, i.e. $\varphi(x) \cdot \varphi(y)$. As we know, the density of a weighted sum of Gaussians is also a Gaussian, and thus we can rewrite (10.75) as

$$W_{t_k} = W_{t_j} + \sqrt{t_k - t_i}\, z. \tag{10.76}$$

The variate

$$z := \frac{\sqrt{t_j - t_i}\, x + \sqrt{t_k - t_j}\, y}{\sqrt{t_k - t_i}} = \frac{1}{\sqrt{t_k - t_i}} \left(W_{t_k} - W_{t_i} \right) \tag{10.77}$$

is, of course, *not* independent of x and y, but its probability density is again that of a standard normal variate.

The *conditional density* of a vector draw (x, y) that satisfies (10.77) is given by its unconditional density divided by the probability density of (10.77) holding, which is $\varphi(z)$. In other words, if we view

$$y(x, z) = \frac{\sqrt{t_k - t_i}\, z - \sqrt{t_j - t_i}\, x}{\sqrt{t_k - t_i}} \tag{10.78}$$

as a dependent variate in the path construction conditional on x and z, we obtain the conditional Brownian bridge density

$$
\begin{aligned}
\psi_{\text{Brownian bridge}}(x|z) &= \frac{\varphi(x)\varphi(y(x, z))}{\varphi(z)} \\
&= \frac{1}{\sqrt{2\pi}} e^{-\frac{1}{2}(x^2 + y(x,z)^2 - z^2)} \\
&= \frac{1}{\sqrt{2\pi}} e^{-\frac{1}{2}\left(\frac{x - \sqrt{\frac{t_j - t_i}{t_k - t_i}}\, z}{\sqrt{\frac{t_k - t_j}{t_k - t_i}}} \right)^2}.
\end{aligned} \tag{10.79}
$$

In other words, x is a normal variate with mean

$$E[x] = \sqrt{\frac{t_j - t_i}{t_k - t_i}}\, z = \frac{\sqrt{t_j - t_i}}{t_k - t_i} \left(W_{t_k} - W_{t_i} \right) \tag{10.80}$$

and variance

$$V[x] = \frac{t_k - t_j}{t_k - t_i}. \tag{10.81}$$

Substituting this into equation (10.74), we obtain

$$W_{t_j} = W_{t_i} + \frac{t_j - t_i}{t_k - t_i} \left(W_{t_k} - W_{t_i} \right) + \sqrt{\frac{(t_j - t_i)(t_k - t_j)}{(t_k - t_i)}}\, v \tag{10.82}$$

$$= \left(\frac{t_k - t_j}{t_k - t_i} \right) W_{t_i} + \left(\frac{t_j - t_i}{t_k - t_i} \right) W_{t_k} + \sqrt{\frac{(t_j - t_i)(t_k - t_j)}{(t_k - t_i)}}\, v \tag{10.83}$$

with $v \sim \mathcal{N}(0, 1)$, which completes the proof for equations (10.33) and (10.34).

11

Greeks

11.1 IMPORTANCE OF GREEKS

The fundamental key to option pricing is to calculate the cost of replication of the sold derivative contract. For some options, we can construct a static replication strategy. The price that we need to charge is then simply given by the cost of setting up the initial hedge. Having done that, *we may forget about this position*[1], since we are hedged, whence some people call this strategy *hedge-and-forget*. For most options, though, there is no static replication, and we need to use the strategy of dynamic hedging in order to protect us from the market risk posed by our short position in the option. The choice of a model process for the underlying securities, establishing the risk-neutral measure, and solving the mathematics and numerics of the numéraire-denominated[2] expectation then gives us the value of the deal. In some sense, for the quantitative analyst, the job finishes there, whilst for the trader who has to manage the position, the fun only just starts. The position now has to be rehedged dynamically, which requires knowledge of the various hedge parameters known as the *Greeks*, owing to the market practice of using the names of Greek letters (real and invented) to represent these risk parameters. This means we not only need to be able to value the option, but also to calculate how its value depends on changes in model parameters and the traded price of the underlying asset. In the following sections, I will outline some Monte Carlo methods that are available for this purpose and discuss their respective benefits and disadvantages. In doing so, we will focus on the calculation of *Delta*, i.e. the first derivative with respect to the underlying security, and *Gamma*, i.e. the second derivative with respect to the underlying asset. *Mutatis mutandis*, the methods presented here transfer readily to other Greeks such as *Vega*, the volatility sensitivity, cross-Gammas for multi-asset options, etc.

11.2 AN UP-OUT-CALL OPTION

Before starting the discussion of different techniques to calculate Greeks with Monte Carlo, let me briefly define the test scenario that I have chosen as an illustrative example for the performance of the individual methods. We are looking at an option of the type that is actually quite common in the equity derivatives world, although in its accurate analysis highly untractable: a discretely monitored Up-Out-Call option. The option is of European type and has the same payoff as a plain vanilla call option, provided that the underlying

---

[1] Strictly speaking, only about the market risk presented by this option. There may still be settlement risk and credit risk since the source of our hedging contracts will be a different counterparty than the client to whom we sold the option.

[2] We know, by virtue of the path-breaking theorem by Harrison and Pliska [HP81], that we may use any traded asset as a numéraire. For the calculation of the value of many equity and FX options we use a zero-coupon bond as numéraire, which means that we have to calculate an expectation and then discount it by the chosen discount factor. In general, though, the numéraire can be a very different asset such as a cash annuity when we calculate swaptions, or even another equity asset as in the case of max-options, as shown by Margrabe [Mar78].

asset is never on or above the predefined knock-out level on any of the monitoring dates (which usually includes maturity), else the payoff is zero. This product can be priced approximately using the continuous barrier formula with an adjusted knock-out level according to the approximation by Broadie *et al.* [BGK99] given in equation (1.3). However, when the monitoring frequency is comparatively low, or when the spot value is near the actual barrier level, the error of the approximation can be considerable. I won't even start the discussion on how to handle the smile properly, but instead assume a standard Black–Scholes process of geometric Brownian motion with a constant volatility of $\sigma = 30\%$. Since neither a deterministic interest rate nor a continuous dividend yield alter the fundamentals of the discussion[3], we simply set them to zero which corresponds to the assumption that the contract is actually written with the forward value as the underlying quantity. The value of the underlying asset is modelled to evolve lognormally as in

$$S(t) = S(0)e^{-\frac{1}{2}\sigma^2 t + \sigma W(t)} \tag{11.1}$$

with W_t being a standard Wiener process. Since we only need to monitor the spot at the n monitoring times, we can view one path of the evolution of the underlying asset from inception to maturity as a vector of n values S_1 to S_n, i.e.

$$\boldsymbol{S} = (S_1, S_2, \dots, S_n).$$

Any one path can thus be constructed from a set of n standard normal variates $z_1, z_2, \dots, z_n$ with $z_i \sim \mathcal{N}(0, 1)$. The reader is most certainly aware that the equation coupling them is

$$S_i = S_{i-1}e^{-\frac{1}{2}\sigma^2 \Delta t_i + \sigma \sqrt{\Delta t_i} z_i} = S_0 e^{-\frac{1}{2}\sigma^2 t_i + \sigma \sum_{k=1}^{i} \sqrt{\Delta t_k} z_k}. \tag{11.2}$$

Naturally, in order to price this option, we generate a set of, say, m paths $\boldsymbol{S}^1, \boldsymbol{S}^2, \dots, \boldsymbol{S}^m$, and each of those paths in S is actually constructed by an n-dimensional vector of standard normal variates $\boldsymbol{z}^j$, i.e. we can express it as an n-valued function of the drawn vector $\boldsymbol{z}$ and the given parameters

$$\boldsymbol{S}^j = \boldsymbol{S}(\boldsymbol{z}^j; S_0, H, K, \sigma, T, n). \tag{11.3}$$

For each of those path vectors $\boldsymbol{S}^j$, we then evaluate the simulated payoff $\pi(\boldsymbol{S}^j)$ conditional on no knock-out occurring for the path, and average to obtain an m-sample Monte Carlo approximation. In a general sense, we can express the Monte Carlo price $\hat{v}$ as

$$\hat{v}(S_0, H, K, \sigma, T, n) = \frac{1}{m} \sum_{j=1}^{m} \pi(\boldsymbol{S}^j). \tag{11.4}$$

11.3   FINITE DIFFERENCING WITH PATH RECYCLING

Like with other option valuation methods, there is one fallback technique for the calculation of the Greeks. We can always redo the entire valuation with varied inputs reflecting the potential change in the underlying asset, and use an explicit finite differencing approach

---

[3]The examples in the Excel workbook GreeksWithMonteCarlo.xls on the accompanying CD do not make this assumption and allow for the specification of a non-zero risk-free interest and dividend rate.

to compute the Greek we are after. For Delta, we can just recalculate once with an upshift in the underlying asset, $S_0 \rightarrow S_0 + \Delta S_0$, resulting in a new value $v(S_0 + \Delta S_0)$, and take

$$\text{Delta} = \frac{\partial v}{\partial S_0} \approx \frac{v(S_0 + \Delta S_0) - v(S_0)}{\Delta S_0}. \tag{11.5}$$

Alternatively to the forward differencing approach above, we can recalculate twice, once for an upshift and once for a downshift, and approximate the desired Delta to

$$\text{Delta} = \frac{\partial v}{\partial S_0} \approx \frac{v(S_0 + \Delta S_0) - v(S_0 - \Delta S_0)}{2\Delta S_0}. \tag{11.6}$$

Using the centre differencing approach in equation (11.6) has the added advantage that we can then approximate Gamma directly as

$$\text{Gamma} = \frac{\partial^2 v}{\partial S_0^2} \approx \frac{v(S_0 + \Delta S_0) - 2v(S_0) + v(S_0 - \Delta S_0)}{\Delta S_0^2}. \tag{11.7}$$

Whilst this is in itself all self-explanatory and straightforward, one important question is often not addressed in textbooks outlining the above procedure. The question is: how do we choose ΔS_0? In order to answer it, let us consider the consequences of using a ΔS_0 that is either far too large or far too small. The centre differencing approach is accurate up to (and including) second-order terms in the Taylor expansion, i.e. Gamma has no effect on the estimate (11.6) for Delta. However, when we choose a ΔS_0 that is far too large, we may start to see the effect of the third order in the Taylor expansion, and our approximation for Delta will be inaccurate. Also, since we should reuse the same variates for the path construction in each of the calculations for $v(S_0)$, $v(S_0 + \Delta S_0)$ and $v(S_0 - \Delta S_0)$, as explained in section 10.2, the variance of our estimate will increase because the correlation of the individual calculations decreases the larger ΔS_0 is, see equation (10.5). On the other hand, if we choose ΔS_0 too small, the fact that most derivative contracts have a final payoff function that is at best continuous but rarely differentiable everywhere comes into play. If we choose a very small ΔS_0, say the smallest that can be handled on our computer, even for a contract as benign as a plain vanilla call option, we are essentially averaging over a sequence of zeros and ones[4]. For a far-out-of-the-money option, the convergence diagram of the Monte Carlo Delta then looks like a hyperbolic decay over the number of paths used with an occasional up jump whenever a single path pair terminates in-the-money and thus contributes to the sensitivity calculation. For Gamma, the situation is even worse. In this case, we are essentially averaging over a sequence of zeros and terms of magnitude $\mathcal{O}(\Delta S_0^{-1})$, only this time they do not result from the path pair or trio terminating in-the-money or out-of-the-money (i.e. as if we sampled a Heaviside function), but instead a non-zero value is only returned if the terminating spot levels of the path trio straddle the strike of the option. In other words, the calculation of Gamma by explicit finite differencing for options with payoff functions that exhibit a kink anywhere is equivalent to carrying out a Monte Carlo sampling computation over a Dirac spike, i.e. a non-zero value is only ever obtained if the spot value at maturity is right at the strike. The situation becomes even worse if the payoff function is not even continuous, as one can imagine. What's more, and this is the starting point for the following analysis, for very small ΔS_0, the inevitable numerical roundoff error will taint the result. In order to obtain

---

[4]The precise value is actually the Delta of the forward contract, which is e^{-dT}.

a reasonable rule of thumb for the numerical magnitude of ΔS_0 one should use, let us recall that for finite differencing approximations of the derivative of a numerically defined function one should optimally use a number determined by an equation balancing the error due to numerical roundoff in the calculation of the function itself, and the error due to the higher order Taylor expansion. For the approximate Gamma to be by expectation as close to the exact value as possible, one should ideally use a finite differencing width of

$$\Delta S_0 = \sqrt[4]{12 \frac{v}{v''''} \cdot \varepsilon} \qquad (11.8)$$

with ε being a suitable representation of the machine precision[5]. To see this, we start from a Taylor expansion of the value v, taking into account that any numerical representation suffers a roundoff error

$$v(S_0 + \Delta S_0) \approx v + v'\Delta S_0 + \frac{1}{2}v''\Delta S_0^2 + \frac{1}{6}v'''\Delta S_0^3 + \frac{1}{24}v''''\Delta S_0^4 + \mathcal{O}(\Delta S_0^5) + \varepsilon v. \qquad (11.9)$$

The last term represents the numerically inevitable inaccuracy which is of the same order of magnitude as the left-hand side. Using equation (11.7) to obtain an estimate $\hat{\Gamma}(S_0; \Delta S_0, \varepsilon)$ for Gamma, which will clearly depend on both the chosen finite differencing width and the machine precision, we again have to take into account that all numerical operations are subject to roundoff errors

$$\hat{\Gamma}(S_0; \Delta S_0, \varepsilon) = v'' + \frac{1}{12}v''''\Delta S_0^2 + \frac{\varepsilon v}{\Delta S_0^2} + \varepsilon_2 v''. \qquad (11.10)$$

Herein, the last term represents the newly introduced roundoff error incurred when carrying out the operations given by equation (11.7). It is now evident in equation (11.10) that for very large ΔS_0, the term $\frac{1}{12}v''''\Delta S_0^2$ will give rise to an error in our estimate of Gamma, and for very small ΔS_0, the numerical roundoff error due to $\varepsilon v/\Delta S_0^2$ will dominate. Thus, ideally, these two terms should be balanced, which leads to equation (11.8).

Clearly, in practice, we don't have enough information to evaluate expression (11.8). Without prejudice, we can only make assumptions. An arguably sensible assumption is that all terms in the Taylor expansion are of equal magnitude, i.e. $\mathcal{O}(v) \approx \mathcal{O}(v''''S_0^4)$, which leads to

$$\Delta S_0 \approx \sqrt[4]{\varepsilon} \cdot S_0. \qquad (11.11)$$

Using the above value for ΔS_0, we can now calculate the Monte Carlo finite differencing approximations for Delta and Gamma:

$$\widehat{\text{Delta}} = \frac{\hat{v}(S_0 + \Delta S_0) - \hat{v}(S_0 - \Delta S_0)}{2\Delta S_0}$$

$$= \frac{1}{2m\Delta S_0}\sum_{j=1}^{m}\left[\pi\left(S(z^j; S_0 + \Delta S_0)\right) - \pi\left(S(z^j; S_0 - \Delta S_0)\right)\right] \qquad (11.12)$$

---

[5]One commonly used proxy for the abstract concept of *machine precision* is the smallest positive number ε such that 1 and $1 + \varepsilon$ are still distinct numbers in the machine's representation. In C/C++, the preprocessor directive #include <float.h> provides the macro DBL_EPSILON which is defined in this way for floating point numbers of type double.

and analogously

$$\widehat{\text{Gamma}} = \frac{\hat{v}(S_0 + \Delta S_0) - 2\hat{v}(S_0) + \hat{v}(S_0 - \Delta S_0)}{\Delta S_0^2}$$

$$= \frac{1}{m\Delta S_0^2} \sum_{j=1}^{m} \left[\pi\left(S(z^j; S_0 + \Delta S_0)\right) - 2 \cdot \pi\left(S(z^j; S_0)\right) + \pi\left(S(z^j; S_0 - \Delta S_0)\right) \right].$$

$$(11.13)$$

Of course, the assumptions made above are utterly unjustifiable when we know that we are trying to calculate the Gamma of derivatives such as Up-Out-Call options that have a particularly nasty double Gamma singularity at the barrier level. In practice, the explicit finite differencing method, even when we recycle the used variates as in the above equations (11.12) and (11.13) for reasons explained in section 10.2, for any options of sufficient complexity that we might want to use a Monte Carlo technique, performs so badly that it is virtually unusable. I will demonstrate this in some of the figures towards the end of this chapter. First, though, we will explain alternatives to the straightforward explicit finite differencing approach.

11.4 FINITE DIFFERENCING WITH IMPORTANCE SAMPLING

It was explained in section 11.3 how the calculation of Delta and other Greeks is hindered by the discontinuity of the payoff profile or its slope. In mathematical terms, the calculation of Gamma using Monte Carlo methods is so difficult because the payoff function is not an element of the class C^2 of all functions that are twice differentiable in all of their variables. In fact, for an Up-Out-Call option, the payoff profile is not even continuous in all of its variables, i.e. $\pi(S) \notin C^0$.

Sometimes, though, life is good to us. For the chosen test case, we can restrict our Monte Carlo sampling domain to just the region where the payoff function is in C^∞. The way to do this is to construct only paths that *do not knock-out and end up in-the-money*. In more general terms, we only sample the domain where the function to be evaluated is non-zero. This method belongs to the general class of *importance sampling* techniques. How we do this is explained below.

First, let us recall that we generate the required standard normal variates by drawing uniform $(0, 1)$ variates and map them into Gaussians with the aid of an inverse cumulative normal function, i.e.

$$z_i = N^{-1}(u_i) \quad \text{and} \quad u_i = N(z_i). \quad (11.14)$$

Now, let us assume that we have constructed a single path up to S_{i-1} and wish to construct the next monitoring variable S_i from equation (11.2), but ensure that the path is not knocked-out. Using

$$h_i := N\left(\frac{\ln \frac{H}{S_{i-1}} + \frac{1}{2}\sigma^2 \Delta t_i}{\sigma \sqrt{\Delta t_i}} \right) \quad (11.15)$$

we can do this by constructing z_i to be applied in equation (11.2) not as usual, simply from the underlying uniform variate u_i as in equation (11.14), but instead as

$$z_i = N^{-1}(u_i \cdot h_i). \quad (11.16)$$

Furthermore, we have to ensure that the path ends up in-the-money at maturity. This means that the last normal variate z_n for this path has to be constructed as in

$$z_n = N^{-1}\left(u_n \cdot (h_n - k) + k\right) \tag{11.17}$$

where

$$k := N\left(\frac{\ln\frac{K}{S_{n-1}} + \frac{1}{2}\sigma^2 \Delta t_n}{\sigma\sqrt{\Delta t_n}}\right). \tag{11.18}$$

In addition to the careful path construction outlined above, we also need to take into account that we are sampling only from a subdomain of the space of all possible path evolutions. Fortunately, we did calculate the corrective factor needed on the fly as we built the importance sampled path S_{is}. We simply need to multiply the payoff associated with the constructed path by the product of all the limiting factors $p := (h_n - k) \cdot \prod_{i=1}^{n-1} h_i$:

$$\hat{v}_{is} = \frac{1}{m}\sum_{j=1}^{m} p(S_{is}^j) \cdot \pi\left(S_{is}^j\right). \tag{11.19}$$

The importance sampling Monte Carlo technique is very useful in its own right to calculate expectations for the purpose of option pricing, in particular for far-out-of-the-money options. Furthermore, it can be a very powerful enhancement technique to the finite differencing method for the calculation of Greeks. Of course, it can also be used in conjunction with variate recycling and/or pathwise differentiation. How well this works will be demonstrated in various figures further on, but first I want to explain the two remaining methods to be presented in this chapter.

11.5   PATHWISE DIFFERENTIATION

Let's have a closer look at what we are really trying to calculate for the example of Delta in equation (11.6). All occurrences of the true price v in that equation are numerically evaluated as a Monte Carlo approximation. Thus

$$\widehat{Delta} = \frac{\partial \hat{v}}{\partial S_0} = \frac{\partial}{\partial S_0}\left[\frac{1}{m}\sum_{j=1}^{m}\pi\left(S(z^j; S_0)\right)\right]. \tag{11.20}$$

In the true sense of the partial derivative in the above equation, an infinitesimal change of the initial spot level S_0 can only give rise to infinitesimal changes of the spot level at any of the monitoring dates. It can be shown that for Lipschitz-continuous payoff functions, i.e. those that are continuous[6] in all of the elements of the vector S and have a finite partial derivative $|\partial\pi/\partial S_i| < \infty$, the order of differentiation and expectation can be interchanged. For such payoff functions, it is perfectly consistent to assign a Delta of zero to all paths that terminate out-of-the-money, and a Delta equal to $\partial S_T/\partial S_0$ with S_T as constructed by equation (11.2).

This method is called *pathwise differentiation* or *infinitesimal perturbation analysis* and can easily be transferred to other Greeks such as Vega [BG96, Cur98]. However, for

---

[6]This is a handwaving definition of Lipschitz-continuous, but sufficient for the discussion here.

the calculation of Gamma, we still have to implement a finite differencing scheme for two individually calculated Deltas for an upshift and a downshift, and both of these can individually be computed using pathwise differentiation.

Alas, for the chosen example of a discretely monitored Up-Out-Call option, this method cannot be readily applied since the payoff function is not even continuous, let alone Lipschitz-continuous, due to the knock-out feature. However, it is possible to apply the pathwise differentiation technique to paths constructed using the importance sampling method presented in the previous section. This is because the construction of paths using equations (11.15) to (11.18) represents a transformation of variables into an integral over the unit hypercube $(0, 1)^n$ such that the integrand is actually Lipschitz-continuous everywhere. In other words, equation (11.19) is to be seen as

$$
v_{is} = \int_{(0,1)^n} p(\boldsymbol{S}_{is}(\boldsymbol{u})) \cdot \pi(\boldsymbol{S}_{is}(\boldsymbol{u})) \, \mathrm{d}u^n .
\tag{11.21}
$$

When we calculate $\partial v_{is}/\partial S_0$ from this equation, we can readily change the order of differentiation and integration. However, we then have to observe carefully the precise dependencies of the individual terms with respect to the parameter that corresponds to the Greek we wish to calculate. As a consequence, we end up with a sum of terms representing the possibility of knock-out on each of the monitoring dates, which makes this approach somewhat cumbersome. In the next section, I present another method that also utilises the idea of transformation. Conversely to pathwise differentiation, though, it does not require any kind of continuity of the payoff function, and even results in surprisingly simple equations.

11.6   THE LIKELIHOOD RATIO METHOD

The option pricing problem by Monte Carlo is a numerical approximation to an integration

$$
v = \int \pi(S) \, \psi(S) \, \mathrm{d}S .
\tag{11.22}
$$

Numerically, we construct evolutions of the underlying assets represented by S given a risk-neutral distribution density $\psi(S)$. As in equation (11.2), we hereby typically construct the paths with the aid of a set of standard normal variates, which corresponds to

$$
v = \int \pi(S(z; \alpha)) \, \varphi(z) \, \mathrm{d}z
\tag{11.23}
$$

and all dependence on further pricing parameters (herein represented by α) such as the spot level at inception, volatility, time to maturity, etc. is absorbed into the path construction $S(z; \alpha)$. Any derivative with respect to any of the parameters will thus suffer from any discontinuities of π in S:

$$
\frac{\partial v}{\partial \alpha} = \int \frac{\partial}{\partial \alpha} \pi(S(z; \alpha)) \, \varphi(z) \, \mathrm{d}z .
\tag{11.24}
$$

The key insight behind the *likelihood ratio* method [BG96] is to shift the dependence on any of the parameters over into the density function. In other words, a transformation of the density is required to look at the pricing problem in the form of equation (11.22). In this way, the Greek evaluation problem becomes

$$\frac{\partial v}{\partial \alpha} = \int \pi(S) \, \frac{\partial}{\partial \alpha} \psi(S; \alpha) \, \mathrm{d}S = \int \pi(S) \, \frac{\partial \psi(S; \alpha)/\partial \alpha}{\psi(S; \alpha)} \, \psi(S; \alpha) \, \mathrm{d}S. \qquad (11.25)$$

The calculation of the desired Greek now looks exactly like the original pricing problem, only with a new payoff function

$$\chi(S; \alpha) := \pi(S) \cdot \omega(S; \alpha) \qquad (11.26)$$

with

$$\omega(S; \alpha) := \frac{\partial \psi(S; \alpha)/\partial \alpha}{\psi(S; \alpha)}. \qquad (11.27)$$

The term $\omega(S; \alpha)$ may be interpreted as a *likelihood ratio* since it is the quotient of two density functions, whence the name of the method. Using this definition, the Greek calculation becomes

$$\frac{\partial v}{\partial \alpha} = \int \chi(S; \alpha) \, \psi(S; \alpha) \, \mathrm{d}S. \qquad (11.28)$$

The beauty of this idea is that for the probability density functions that we typically use, such as the one corresponding to geometric Brownian motion, the function $\chi(S; \alpha)$ is an element of C^∞ in the parameter α and thus doesn't cause the trouble that we have when approaching the Greek calculation problem in the form of equation (11.23). The application is now straightforward. Alongside the calculation of the option price, for each constructed path, apart from calculating the payoff $\pi(S)$, also calculate the likelihood ratio $\omega(S; \alpha)$. The approximation for Delta, for instance, thus becomes

$$\widehat{\mathrm{Delta}} = \frac{1}{m} \sum_{j=1}^{m} \left[\pi\left(\mathbf{S}^j; S_0\right) \cdot \omega_{\widehat{\mathrm{Delta}}}\left(\mathbf{S}^j; S_0\right) \right]. \qquad (11.29)$$

The likelihood ratio method can actually be viewed as a special case of a more general class of applications of *Malliavin calculus* to the problem of the calculation of Greeks using Monte Carlo methods [FLL+99, FLLL01]. In the framework of Malliavin calculus, the transformation of integrals containing derivatives such as equation (11.24) to the form given in equation (11.25) is seen as a partial integration of an integral involving stochastic processes. It can be shown that there is usually more than one way to choose a weighting function ω for the payoff in order to calculate any one given parametric derivative, i.e. Greek. However, and this is in general the biggest problem of Malliavin calculus, not all of them provide a faster convergence than, say, plain finite differencing. For geometric Brownian motion, the choice of ω that provides the least variance of the result is the one that can be derived directly as a likelihood ratio calculation, as is done here. For other processes, this may be different, and the full-blown Malliavin calculus may then lead to superior weighting functions ω. However, the stochastic calculus involved can be quite daunting and the highly complicated analytical computations required make this method somewhat error prone when applied to more sophisticated process assumptions and more complex derivatives contracts. For our test case of a discretely monitored Up-Out-Call option, though, the calculation is straightforward and, leaving it up to the reader to go through the involved calculus and algebra in his own time, I just present the results here. Starting from the path construction description (11.2), we arrive at

$$\omega_{\widehat{\text{Delta}}} = \frac{z_1}{S_0 \sigma \sqrt{\Delta t_1}} \tag{11.30}$$

$$\omega_{\widehat{\text{Gamma}}} = \frac{z_1^2 - z_1 \sigma \sqrt{\Delta t_1} - 1}{S_0^2 \sigma^2 \Delta t_1} \tag{11.31}$$

which may look surprisingly simple considering all of the above discussion. It is worth noting that only the variate z_1 responsible for the very first step enters. Also, if a piecewise constant term structure of instantaneous volatility is used, it is the volatility coefficient for the first time step that applies. A similar formula can be derived for Vega, i.e. the price sensitivity with respect to the volatility coefficient, which is done in appendix section 11.9.1, and also for the sensitivities with respect to interest rates and dividend yields (see appendix section 11.9.2). As for the limitations of the method, I should mention that since the likelihood ratios $\omega_{\widehat{\text{Delta}}}$ and $\omega_{\widehat{\text{Gamma}}}$ in equations (11.30) and (11.31) are inversely proportional to $\sigma \sqrt{\Delta t_1}$ and $\sigma^2 \Delta t_1$ respectively, the variance incurred by this calculation of Delta and Gamma may increase dramatically for low volatilities or very short time intervals in between monitoring dates.

As a side note, I would like to point out that the method presented in this section did not specifically depend on the payoff being an Up-Out-Call option. In fact, the resulting decomposition into payoff π times likelihood ratio ω remains the same for any payoff, be it a discretely monitored lookback, hindsight, Asian, or whichever option. It can also be extended to more challenging model processes, such as the BGM/J framework for interest rates, which involve stochastic drift coefficients [GZ99].

11.7   COMPARATIVE FIGURES

In order to demonstrate the usefulness of the methods discussed in the previous sections, I selected two test scenarios. Both are on the same Up-Out-Call option. Scenario A represents the case that there is exactly $T = 1$ year to maturity, the current spot level is 100, the strike is at 100 and the barrier at 150. The underlying asset evolves lognormally with constant volatility of $\sigma = 30\%$ and monitoring happens at the end of each month. In scenario B, there is only $T = 0.52$ left until expiry, the spot has risen to a level of 160, and we are 5 trading days (out of 250 per year) away from an end-of-month monitoring date. Since the different methods involve varying amounts of computational effort, all convergence diagrams are with respect to CPU time required on an AMD K6-III processor running at 400 MHz. It should be mentioned, though, that all of the presented calculations were carried out using the Sobol' low-discrepancy sequence in conjunction with a Brownian bridge which provides a major convergence enhancement.

The purpose of Figure 11.1 is thus to demonstrate that the calculation of both Delta and Gamma, along with the actual price, does not impose a prohibitive burden for any of the methods. The reader may notice that the line for the analytical approximation is missing from the graph for scenario B in this and the following figures. This is because the analytical approximation, by virtue of using an adjusted barrier level in a continuous barrier option formula, results in a value that is identically zero since the spot level of 160 is outside the adjusted barrier level of 157.8. Also, it is worth noticing that in

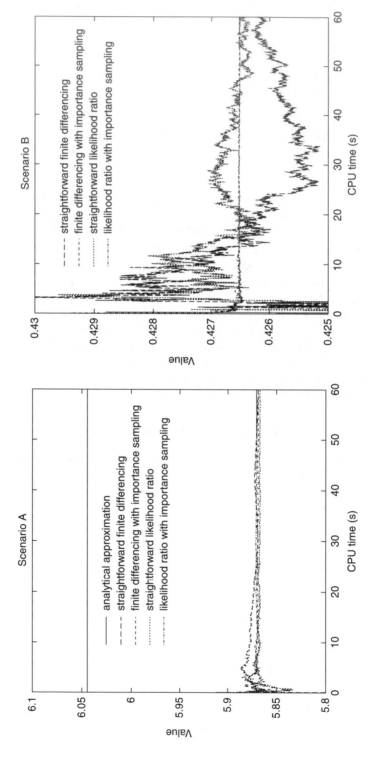

Figure 11.1 The value of the Up-Out-Call option for scenarios A and B

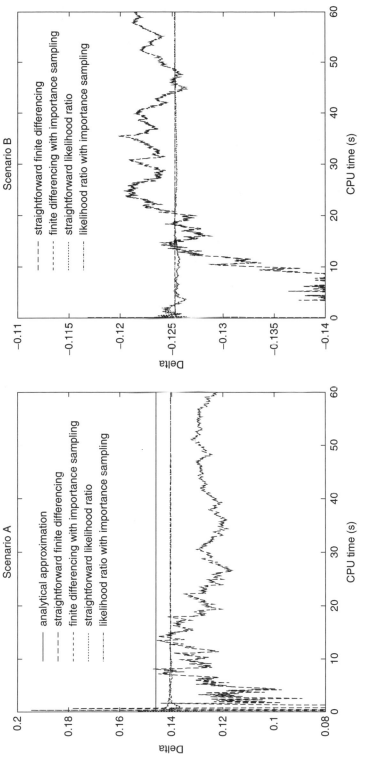

Figure 11.2 Delta of the Up-Out-Call option for scenarios A and B

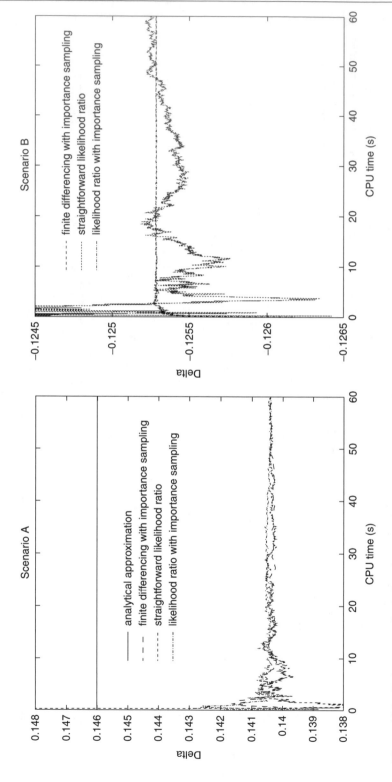

Figure 11.3 Enlargement for Delta of the Up-Out-Call option for scenarios A and B

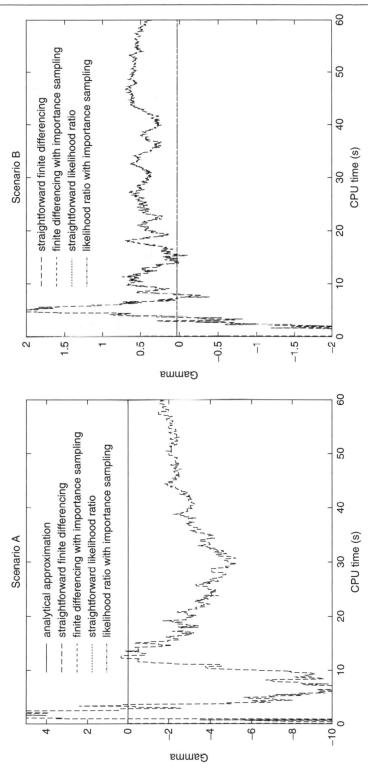

Figure 11.4 Gamma of the Up-Out-Call option for scenarios A and B

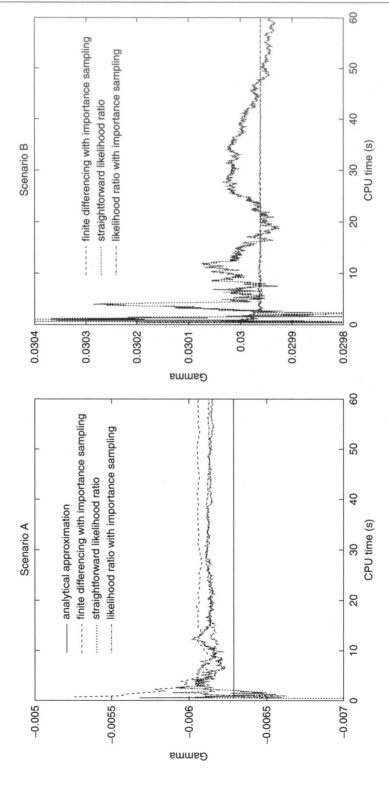

Figure 11.5 Enlargements for Gamma of the Up-Out-Call option for scenarios A and B

scenario B, similarly to a far-out-of-the-money option, the importance sampling method very significantly enhances the convergence behaviour for the value itself.

Next, in Figure 11.2, the convergence behaviour for Delta is shown. Since the differences in performance are difficult to show on one scale, I also show an enlargement in Figure 11.3. Finally, the convergence diagrams for Gamma are given in Figures 11.4 and 11.5.

Overall, it is probably fair to say that, whilst straightforward finite differencing is virtually useless for the calculation of Gamma (we estimate that several CPU months would be required before satisfactory convergence could be achieved), both the importance sampling and the likelihood ratio enhancement work remarkably well, and can also be combined.

11.8   SUMMARY

Combine et impera! There are various methods out there, and you can pick and choose. Also, the methods outlined in this chapter can readily be adapted to some of the process descriptions that generate a skew and/or smile introduced in Chapter 3. In many cases, we can combine two or more of the presented techniques for even greater convergence speed. As I have demonstrated, nothing stops you from using finite differencing in conjunction with importance sampling. Also, one can combine the likelihood ratio method with importance sampling. *The world is your oyster.*

11.9   APPENDIX

11.9.1   The Likelihood Ratio Formula for Vega

In a Black–Scholes setting with constant volatility, etc., and a single time horizon of interest, i.e. the maturity T itself, the likelihood ratio for the calculation of Vega is[7]

$$\omega_{\widehat{\text{Vega}}} = \frac{z^2 - 1}{\sigma} - z\sqrt{T}. \tag{11.32}$$

The variate z is hereby the standard normal variate used for the construction of the terminal spot value draw

$$S_T = S_0 \cdot e^{\left(r - d - \frac{1}{2}\sigma^2\right)T + \sigma\sqrt{T}z}. \tag{11.33}$$

Of more interest is the case when we have a payoff function that depends not only on the value of an underlying asset at the final maturity, but also on the realisations at intermediate times t_i for $i = 1, \ldots, n$ with $t_n := T$ and $t_0 := 0$. In the standard Black–Scholes framework fashion I assume that paths can be seen as being constructed incrementally[8] by

$$S_i \equiv S(t_i) = S_0 \cdot e^{\sum_{k=1}^{i}\left[\left(\mu_k - \frac{1}{2}\sigma_k^2\right)\Delta t_k + \sigma\sqrt{\Delta t_k}\, z_k\right]} \tag{11.34}$$

---

[7]The formula for the Vega likelihood ratio given in [FLLL01], unfortunately, is slightly in error. However, the same formula is correct in the preceding article by the same authors (third equation on p. 405) in [FLL+99].

[8]This means that if you actually use a different method for the path construction such as the Brownian bridge (see section 10.8.3), you need to back out the set of z variables such that you can identify with equation (11.34).

with $\Delta t_i := t_i - t_{i-1}$. The cost-of-carry coefficients μ_i are given by $\mu_i := r_i - d_i$ with r_i representing a continuously compounded risk-free (funding/lending) forward interest rate for the time interval from t_{i-1} to t_i, and similarly d_i denoting a continuously compounded dividend yield. In (11.34), I have also allowed for a piecewise constant term structure of instantaneous (or forward implied) volatility. In a trading environment, we are usually most interested in hedge parameters with respect to market quoted implied volatilities, i.e. implied volatility coefficients that apply to a time interval from today to a certain time horizon. I will now first derive the likelihood ratio that enables us to compute the sensitivity of a given payoff function with respect to all of the individual forward volatility coefficients in equation (11.34), and then transform them to the conventional format of implied volatilities 'out of today'.

Forward Volatility Exposure for Multiple Time Steps

The joint distribution density ϕ of a vector of n independent standard normal variates is given by

$$\phi(z) = \prod_{k=1}^{n} \varphi(z_k). \tag{11.35}$$

This density can be transformed to the density of the vector S of realisations of the underlying asset along the path with the aid of the Jacobian determinant of the transformation $z \to S$, i.e.

$$\psi(S) = \phi(z) \cdot \left| \frac{\partial(z)}{\partial(S)} \right|. \tag{11.36}$$

Solving (11.34) for the dependence of z on S, we obtain

$$z_j = \frac{1}{\sigma_j \sqrt{\Delta t_j}} \left(\ln S_j - \ln S_{j-1} - \left(\mu_j - \tfrac{1}{2}\sigma_j^2 \right) \Delta t_j \right) \tag{11.37}$$

and consequently

$$\frac{\partial z_j}{\partial S_k} = \frac{1}{\sigma_j \sqrt{\Delta t_j}} \left(\delta_{jk} \frac{1}{S_j} - \delta_{j-1,k} \frac{1}{S_{j-1}} \right). \tag{11.38}$$

This means that the Jacobian matrix $(\partial(z)/\partial(S))$ is triangular[9] and we obtain the following expression for the density:

$$\psi(S) = \prod_{j=1}^{n} \frac{\varphi(z_j)}{S_j \sigma_j \sqrt{\Delta t_j}} \tag{11.39}$$

wherein z_j is to be seen as an explicit function of S_j, S_{j-1}, and the parameters according to (11.37). The likelihood ratio for the sensitivity with respect to any of the σ_j is given by

$$\omega_{\sigma_k} = \frac{\partial \psi(S)/\partial \sigma_k}{\psi(S)}. \tag{11.40}$$

---

[9]Actually, it is just the diagonal and the upper off-diagonal.

Combining this with (11.39), we can calculate

$$\omega_{\sigma_k} = \sum_{j=1}^{n} \left[\left(\frac{\partial \varphi(z_j)/\partial z_j}{\varphi(z_j)} \right) \frac{\partial z_j}{\partial \sigma_k} \right] - \frac{1}{\sigma_k}. \tag{11.41}$$

Recall that $\varphi(z)$ is the standard normal distribution density given in (2.23) and thus

$$\frac{\partial \varphi(z_j)}{\partial z_j} = -z_j \varphi(z_j). \tag{11.42}$$

From (11.37), we can compute

$$\frac{\partial z_j}{\partial \sigma_k} = \delta_{jk} \left(-\frac{z_j}{\sigma_k} + \sqrt{\Delta t_j} \right). \tag{11.43}$$

Putting all of this together, we arrive at

$$\omega_{\sigma_k} = \frac{z_k^2 - 1}{\sigma_k} - z_k \sqrt{\Delta t_k}. \tag{11.44}$$

The likelihood ratio Monte Carlo estimator for the sensitivity of a derivative contract with value v with respect to the forward volatility coefficient σ_k from a simulation with m paths is thus

$$\frac{\partial v}{\partial \sigma_k} \simeq \frac{1}{m} \sum_{j=1}^{m} \left[\pi \left(\mathbf{S}^j ; S_0, \boldsymbol{\sigma} \right) \cdot \omega_{\sigma_k} \right] \tag{11.45}$$

with ω_{σ_k} as given above.

Implied Volatility Exposure for Multiple Time Steps

Given a vector of volatility coefficients $\boldsymbol{\sigma}$ representing a piecewise constant term structure of instantaneous volatility, we can calculate the equivalent Black–Scholes implied volatility $\hat{\sigma}_k$ from $t_0 = 0$ to t_k according to

$$\hat{\sigma}_k^2 t_k = \int_{t=0}^{t_k} \sigma(t)^2 \, dt = \sum_{j=1}^{k} \sigma_j^2 \Delta t_j. \tag{11.46}$$

Thus

$$\frac{\partial \hat{\sigma}_k}{\partial \sigma_j} = \frac{\sigma_j \Delta t_j}{\hat{\sigma}_k t_k} \cdot \mathbf{1}_{\{j \leqslant k\}}. \tag{11.47}$$

Now,

$$\frac{\partial v}{\partial \sigma_j} = \sum_{k=1}^{n} \frac{\partial v}{\partial \hat{\sigma}_k} \frac{\partial \hat{\sigma}_k}{\partial \sigma_j}$$

$$= \sum_{k=1}^{n} \frac{\partial v}{\partial \hat{\sigma}_k} \frac{\sigma_j \Delta t_j}{\hat{\sigma}_k t_k} \mathbf{1}_{\{j \leqslant k\}}$$

$$= \sum_{k=j}^{n} \frac{\partial v}{\partial \hat{\sigma}_k} \frac{\sigma_j \Delta t_j}{\hat{\sigma}_k t_k} \tag{11.48}$$

which gives us

$$\frac{1}{\sigma_j \Delta t_j} \frac{\partial v}{\partial \sigma_j} - \mathbf{1}_{\{j<n\}} \frac{1}{\sigma_{j+1} \Delta t_{j+1}} \frac{\partial v}{\partial \sigma_{j+1}} = \frac{1}{\hat{\sigma}_j t_j} \frac{\partial v}{\partial \hat{\sigma}_j} \tag{11.49}$$

and thus

$$\frac{\partial v}{\partial \hat{\sigma}_j} = \frac{\hat{\sigma}_j t_j}{\sigma_j \Delta t_j} \frac{\partial v}{\partial \sigma_j} - \mathbf{1}_{\{j<n\}} \frac{\hat{\sigma}_j t_j}{\sigma_{j+1} \Delta t_{j+1}} \frac{\partial v}{\partial \sigma_{j+1}}. \tag{11.50}$$

The likelihood ratio Monte Carlo estimator for the sensitivity with respect to the implied volatility $\hat{\sigma}_k$ from a simulation with m paths is therefore

$$\frac{\partial v}{\partial \hat{\sigma}_k} \simeq \frac{1}{m} \sum_{j=1}^{m} \left[\pi\left(S^j; S_0, \sigma\right) \cdot \omega_{\hat{\sigma}_k} \right] \tag{11.51}$$

with

$$\omega_{\hat{\sigma}_k} = \left(\frac{\hat{\sigma}_k t_k}{\sigma_k \Delta t_k}\right) \omega_{\sigma_k} - \mathbf{1}_{\{k<n\}} \left(\frac{\hat{\sigma}_k t_k}{\sigma_{k+1} \Delta t_{k+1}}\right) \omega_{\sigma_{k+1}}. \tag{11.52}$$

11.9.2   The Likelihood Ratio Formula for Rho

Given the same setting as in the previous section

$$S_i \equiv S(t_i) = S_0 \cdot e^{\sum_{k=1}^{i} \left[\left((r_k - d_k) - \frac{1}{2}\sigma_k^2\right)\Delta t_k + \sigma \sqrt{\Delta t_k}\, z_k\right]} \tag{11.53}$$

with r_i denoting the continuously compounded forward interest that is assumed to be constant from t_{i-1} to t_i, we can calculate the likelihood ratio for the calculation of the sensitivity with respect to the forward interest rates. We have to be careful though: the interest rate appears not only in the path construction but also in the discount factor that has to be applied to each payoff. In the following, I assume that the only cashflow constituting the payoff of the (path-dependent) derivative contract whose value is v is paid at the final maturity $T = t_n$. Taking this into account, we arrive at

$$\omega_{r_k} = \left(\frac{z_k}{\sigma_k \sqrt{\Delta t_k}} - 1\right) \Delta t_k. \tag{11.54}$$

Just as for Vega, for real hedging purposes the exposure with respect to zero-coupon rates out of today is more relevant. Denoting the spot rate associated with today's discount factor for a cashflow that is payable at time t_k as $\hat{r}_k$ we can equate

$$e^{-\hat{r}_k t_k} = e^{-\sum_{j=1}^{k} r_j \Delta t_j}. \tag{11.55}$$

Then, following a transformation analysis similar to the one for Vega, we obtain

$$\omega_{\hat{r}_k} = \left(\frac{z_k}{\sigma_k \sqrt{\Delta t_k}} - 1 \right) t_k - \mathbf{1}_{\{k<n\}} \left(\frac{z_{k+1}}{\sigma_{k+1} \sqrt{\Delta t_{k+1}}} - 1 \right) t_k. \tag{11.56}$$

At this point, I am sure you believe me without further ado that the equivalent sensitivities with respect to the respective dividend yield coefficients can be calculated by virtue of the following likelihood ratios:

$$\omega_{d_k} = -\frac{z_k \sqrt{\Delta t_k}}{\sigma_k}, \tag{11.57}$$

$$\omega_{\hat{d}_k} = -\frac{z_k t_k}{\sigma_k \sqrt{\Delta t_k}} + \mathbf{1}_{\{k<n\}} \frac{z_{k+1} t_k}{\sigma_{k+1} \sqrt{\Delta t_{k+1}}}. \tag{11.58}$$

12

Monte Carlo in the
BGM/J Framework

12.1 THE BRACE–GATAREK–MUSIELA/JAMSHIDIAN
MARKET MODEL

The pricing of options in the interest rate market has been the subject of many publications in the financial literature. Whilst most of the earlier models allowed short rates to evolve according to a normal distribution [Vas77, HL86, HW90], later developments avoided the possibility of (in principle unlimited) negative interest rates by modelling the short rate lognormally [BDT90, BK91]. With the arrival of the general no-arbitrage conditions linking the drift of short or forward rates to the term structure of their instantaneous volatility function [HJM92b], practitioners now had a general framework for the calibration of interest rate models to the implied volatilities of options that are liquid enough in the market to serve as hedging instruments. When options on a discrete forward rate or a swap rate are used to hedge the volatility exposure of exotic interest rate derivatives, it is intuitively appealing to view the same discrete rates as the fundamental stochastic quantity underlying the contract. Rather than modelling the behaviour of an instantaneous short rate, Brace–Gatarek–Musiela and Jamshidian (BGM/J) and several other authors [MSS97, BGM97, Jam97, MR97] described the evolution of the forward rates themselves to be given by a lognormal stochastic differential equation. This formulation, however, leads to fully state-dependent drift terms for the individual forward rates and thus makes it impossible to build recombining tree lattices [Hul97, Reb98, Reb99]. As long as the exotic interest rate derivative contract that is to be priced is of European style, i.e. involves no exercise decision by the holder of the option, Monte Carlo methods can readily be applied since they are not affected by the high dimensionality of the problem[1].

Unfortunately, though, one of the most important derivatives in the interest rate market is the contract known as a *Bermudan swaption* which gives the holder the right to enter into a swap of a fixed terminal maturity date on a set of prespecified exercise opportunity dates. Even though several articles on the issue of early exercise opportunities in the context of Monte Carlo simulations for the pricing of derivatives have been published in the past (see, e.g., [BG97a] for an excellent overview), all of them are only approximate and one has little certainty about the error actually incurred when applying any of the general-purpose American Monte Carlo methods to a specific problem. The nature of the Bermudan swaption contract makes it possible though to devise bespoke Monte Carlo techniques that exploit the specifics of this derivative contract particularly well, as demonstrated recently by Longstaff and Schwarz [LS98] and Andersen [And00]. Whilst the new method presented here is structurally somewhat similar to the latter, which is in turn superior to the former, it does not require approximative evaluations of option values

---

[1]This is to say that Monte Carlo methods do not suffer from 'the curse of dimensionality' whereby the number of evaluations explodes exponentially with the number of time steps or exercise opportunities. At worst, the computational effort grows linearly with the dimensionality and number of time steps for Monte Carlo techniques.

during the simulation itself. Instead, an exercise decision strategy is based on a parametric exercise decision function chosen to match observed heuristics in two carefully selected coordinates. The free parameters are then optimised for each individual pricing calculation.

In theory, one can always use a non-recombining tree method such as the one explained in Chapter 13 to price Bermudan swaptions. In practice, however, this technique can only be applied to contracts of rather limited duration, or more precisely, of rather limited number of cashflows and exercise opportunities. In this chapter, I present a Monte Carlo method that overcomes this limitation and yet manages to produce prices remarkably close to those given by a non-recombining tree wherever the latter can be applied. The new technique is based on the functional parametrisation of the exercise boundary in a suitable coordinate system carefully selected by the aid of a non-recombining tree.

It is well known by interest rate derivatives practitioners that the main benefits of using the BGM/J framework are not so important when it comes to products such as European or even Bermudan swaptions, since these types of contracts are most sensitive to changes in the yield curve that are well represented by the lowest principal vectors of the decomposition of the yield curve's covariance matrix. Derivatives that are accurately priced by adequately modelling the changes in level, and possibly slope, of the yield curve can usually be safely priced using a one- or two-factor short rate model. However, for other interest rate derivatives such as trigger swaps, ratchets, and flexicaps, the story is very different. For trigger swaps, for instance, it is inherently difficult to model appropriately the correlation behaviour of any one forward rate (being the index rate determining whether the swap is triggered in) to the forward swap rate starting with the very same forward rate simultaneously for all forward rate/forward swap rate pairs unless a full factorisation is allowed, i.e. there is one model factor for each forward rate comprising the yield curve of interest. For those products whose price depends strongly on the effective correlation between adjacent forward rates and forward swap rates, the BGM/J framework not only provides a way of more adequately allowing for all possible evolutions of the yield curve that could affect the value of the derivative, but in doing so also enables the practitioner to obtain a better understanding of the financial mechanisms behind the value of the optionality with greater ease. In this light, we can say that the BGM/J framework is particularly useful and beneficial where path dependence plays an important role, or where the value depends strongly on the high-frequency components of the changes in yield curve, i.e. the eigenvectors of the yield curve's covariance matrix associated with the higher modes and thus lower eigenvalues. Despite this, I have chosen to explain the intricacies of the BGM/J Monte Carlo simulation approach with the example of Bermudan swaptions for the following two reasons. Firstly, it is one of the (if not *the*) most important interest rate derivatives around and any new approach must provide ways of pricing this contract. Secondly, pricing Bermudan swaptions in the BGM/J setup immediately forces the practitioner to tackle the most difficult problem in the market model world, namely the existence of early exercise opportunities. The generic description of the Monte Carlo BGM/J model in this chapter is easily applied to all path-dependent products, and thus any product serves equally well as an example. The approach I take here for the design of a Monte Carlo method in order to price an early exercise strategy-dependent contract such as the Bermudan swaption is, however, general enough to be transferred readily to other derivatives such as flexicaps and others involving early exercise opportunities.

In this chapter, I outline how Monte Carlo simulations can be used for the pricing of interest rate derivatives in the Libor market model. The nature of the so-called market model is that any set of rates that completely determines the present value of a single certain cashflow at all of the points of interest on the yield curve can be used as the basic set of modelled quantities. The driving stochastic process for those state variables of the yield curve can then be chosen at will, and the drifts follow by virtue of the martingale conditions resulting from the choice of numéraire. The most common ways of building the yield curve are to use a complete set of co-terminal or co-initial swap rates, or a complete set of spanning FRAs. In this chapter, I use the latter approach whereby the modelled state variables are forward Libor rates. The reason that I don't even touch on the swap rate-based approach is that in my practical experience the available approximations for discrete time step drift terms and approximate prices of options on composites of the state variables[2] are all unsatisfactory. In contrast, there are highly accurate approximations for European swaptions in the FRA-based BGM/J framework, and very reliable drift stepping techniques.

This chapter is structured as follows. In section 12.2, I give a brief introduction to the BGM/J Libor market model framework and explain how the number of driving factors can be reduced should one wish to do so in order to compare with short rate models of a lower factorisation. In section 12.3, I briefly state the Bermudan swaption pricing problem in my notation and in section 12.4, a formula is given that provides a remarkably accurate price for European swaptions for most major interest rate markets at the time of writing, without the need for simulations. The handling of the state-dependent drift term arising in the BGM/J framework is then addressed in section 12.5. Then, I demonstrate the *real* exercise boundary of the Bermudan swaption for a specific example in section 12.6. A suitable parametrisation for this boundary is suggested in section 12.7. In the following two sections, I explain the actual Monte Carlo algorithm and present numerical results for various examples. At the end of the chapter, a summary is given.

12.2 FACTORISATION

In the BGM/J Libor market model, it is assumed that each of n spanning forward rates f_i evolves lognormally according to the stochastic differential equation

$$\frac{\mathrm{d}f_i}{f_i} = \mu_i(f, t)\mathrm{d}t + \sigma_i(t)\mathrm{d}\widetilde{W}_i. \tag{12.1}$$

Correlation is incorporated by the fact that the n standard Wiener processes in equation (12.1) satisfy

$$E\left[\mathrm{d}\widetilde{W}_i \mathrm{d}\widetilde{W}_j\right] = \varrho_{ij}\mathrm{d}t. \tag{12.2}$$

The elements of the instantaneous covariance matrix $C(t)$ of the n forward rates are thus

$$c_{ij}(t) = \sigma_i(t)\sigma_j(t)\varrho_{ij}. \tag{12.3}$$

Using a decomposition of $C(t)$ into a pseudo-square root[3] $\tilde{A}$ such that

$$C = \tilde{A} \cdot \tilde{A}^\top \tag{12.4}$$

---

[2] Recall that if the yield curve is fully described by a set of either co-terminal or co-initial swap rates, all bar one caplet actually become options on a payoff function that involves more than one of the basic state variables, i.e. the swap rates.

[3] Convenient procedures are the Cholesky method or spectral decomposition. A description of the latter is given in section 6.2.

we can transform equation (12.1) to

$$\frac{\mathrm{d}f_i}{f_i} = \mu_i \mathrm{d}t + \sum_j \tilde{a}_{ij} \mathrm{d}W_j \tag{12.5}$$

with $\mathrm{d}W_j$ being n independent standard Wiener processes, where dependence on time has been omitted for clarity.

It is also possible to drive the evolution of the n forward rates with fewer underlying independent standard Wiener processes than there are forward rates, say only m of them. In this case, the coefficient matrix $\tilde{A} \in \mathbb{R}^{n \times n}$ is to be replaced by $A \in \mathbb{R}^{n \times m}$ which must satisfy

$$\sum_{j=1}^{m} a_{ij}^2 = c_{ii} \tag{12.6}$$

in order to retain the calibration of the options on the FRAs, i.e. the caplets. In practice, this can be done very easily by calculating the decomposition as in equation (12.4) as before and rescaling according to

$$a_{ij} = \tilde{a}_{ij} \sqrt{\frac{c_{ii}}{\sum\limits_{k=1}^{m} \tilde{a}_{ik}^2}}. \tag{12.7}$$

The effect of this procedure is that the individual variances of each of the rates are still correct, even if we have reduced the number of driving factors to one, but the effective covariances will differ. For instance, for a single factor model, all of the correlation coefficients will be unity and the covariances just the products of the pairs of associated volatilities. The procedure described above is to ensure consistent calibration to caplet prices. There are many other choices one can make, such as to calibrate against European swaptions, etc. The subject of calibration is a very delicate one indeed, and I will explain how one can calibrate to European swaptions without the need for Monte Carlo simulations in the next section. Here, I only meant to indicate one of the simplest calibration approaches preserving the desired calibration independent on the number of factors used in the evolution of the yield curve.

If the forward yield curve is given by n spanning forward rates f_i, whereby the payoff of forward rate agreement i is $f_i \tau_i$ paid at time t_{i+1}, and a zero-coupon bond that pays one currency unit at t_N is used as numéraire, as illustrated schematically in Figure 12.1, then the drifts μ_i in equations (12.1) and (12.5) can be calculated with the aid of Itô's lemma to be:

$$\mu_i(\boldsymbol{f}(t), t) = \begin{cases} -\sigma_i \sum\limits_{k=i+1}^{N-1} \dfrac{f_k(t)\tau_k}{1 + f_k(t)\tau_k} \sigma_k \varrho_{ik} & \text{for} \quad i < N-1, \\[2ex] 0 & \text{for} \quad i = N-1, \\[2ex] \sigma_i \sum\limits_{k=N}^{i} \dfrac{f_k(t)\tau_k}{1 + f_k(t)\tau_k} \sigma_k \varrho_{ik} & \text{for} \quad i \geqslant N. \end{cases} \tag{12.8}$$

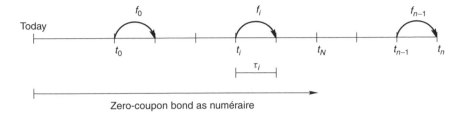

Figure 12.1   The yield curve is specified by a set of spanning forward rates

12.3   BERMUDAN SWAPTIONS

A Bermudan swaption contract denoted by 'X-non-call-Y' gives the holder the right to enter into a swap at a prespecified strike rate K on a number of exercise opportunities. The first exercise opportunity in this case would be Y years after inception. The swap that can be entered into always has the same terminal maturity date, namely X, independent of when exercise takes place. A Bermudan swaption that entitles the holder to enter into a swap in which he pays the fixed rate is known as *payer's*, otherwise as *receiver's*.

For the owner of a payer's Bermudan swaption, the present value of exercising at time t_j is given by the intrinsic value $I(t_j)$ of the swap to be entered into at that time:

$$I(t_j) = \sum_{k=j}^{n-1} \left[P_{k+1}(t_j) \cdot \left(f_k(t_j) - K \right) \tau_k \right] = \sum_{k=j}^{n-1} \left[\left(\prod_{l=j}^{k} [1 + f_l(t_j)\tau_l]^{-1} \right) \cdot \left(f_k(t_j) - K \right) \tau_k \right]. \tag{12.9}$$

Hereby and in the following, I assume a constant notional of 1 and that the contract is a payer's Bermudan swaption to simplify the notation. $P_{k+1}(t_j)$ indicates the t_j-present value of a zero-coupon bond paying 1 at t_{k+1} or, in other words, the t_j-realised discount factor from t_j to t_{k+1}.

In order to decide optimally about early exercise at time t_j, the holder compares the present intrinsic value with the expected profit to be made by not exercising at that time. Thus, the t_j-value of the Bermudan swaption $V(t_j)$ is given by

$$V(t_j) = \begin{cases} \max \left\{ I(t_j), E(t_j) \left[V(t_{j+1}) \right] \right\} & \text{for} \quad j = 1, \dots, n-2, \\ \max \left\{ I(t_j), 0 \right\} & \text{for} \quad j = n-1. \end{cases} \tag{12.10}$$

It should be mentioned that the above specifications describe fairly plain vanilla Bermudan swaptions. In the marketplace, many variations are common such as differing payment frequencies between fixed and floating leg, margins on top of the floating payment, varying notionals (*rollercoaster* or *amortising* swaptions are not uncommon), time-varying strike of the swap to enter into, cross-currency payoff (quanto), and many more. The method presented below, however, is general enough to be amenable to almost all of these special cases.

12.4   CALIBRATION TO EUROPEAN SWAPTIONS

Alternatively to the definition of the yield curve by a set of spanning forward rates, it is also possible to choose a set of *co-terminal forward swap rates* as depicted in

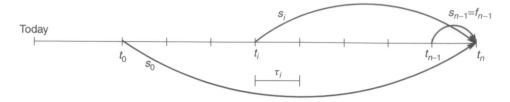

Figure 12.2   The yield curve can also be defined by a set of co-terminal forward swap rates

Figure 12.2. Jamshidian used this set of yield curve coordinates for a swap-based market model [Jam97]. Using the annuity associated with a specific forward swap as the numéraire asset for the evolution out to the reset time of the same swap, we can model the swap rates as perfectly lognormal and thus obtain the calibration to European swaptions by construction. However, there are a number of drawbacks to this approach. Firstly, it is not particularly easy to come up with a parametrisation of the swap rates' instantaneous volatilities that allows for some degree of time homogeneity. Essentially, one needs a functional form that amongst all other parameters also caters for the intrinsic differences between the different forward swap rates. This is because whilst forward rates are all equally associated with a single cash payment of the same order of magnitude, the annuities associated with all the forward swap rates vary considerably with the residual maturity or duration of the individual forward swap rate. Secondly, it is not easy to conjure up a parametrisation of the swap rates' correlation that is equally satisfactory and simple, which is also due to the intrinsic differences between the natural assets associated with the forward swap rates, i.e. the annuities. Thirdly, the drift terms resulting from the no-arbitrage martingale conditions are much more cumbersome than for an FRA-based market model.

Today's exotic interest rate derivatives are rarely based purely on only forward rates *or* forward swap rates just by themselves. A classic example of this are trigger swaps where the fixing value of a specific forward rate determines whether a swap starting there and then comes to life. Even for Bermudan swaptions, the exercise decision depends not only on the next resetting swap rate, but also on the shape (and primarily the slope) of the yield curve, as best seen by looking at the variations between all forward rates. Thus, when we value Bermudan swaptions, we may wish to represent the overall stochastic dynamics of the forward rates reasonably well, and in particular account for their correlation in an econometrically sound fashion, but also to calibrate such that we reproduce the market-given prices of European swaptions.

I will now outline one possible approach to calibrate an FRA-based BGM/J model to European swaptions. First, we have to decide on a suitable instantaneous volatility function for the forward rate, and I use the one suggested by Rebonato [Reb99]:

$$\sigma_i(t) = k_i[(a + b(t_i - t))e^{-c(t_i - t)} + d] \cdot \mathbf{1}_{\{t \leqslant t_i\}}. \qquad (12.11)$$

The common parameters a, b, c and d determine the overall shape of the term structure of instantaneous volatility. The FRA-specific parameter k_i allows us to scale the volatility curve for each forward rate to match the market given implied volatility for the associated caplet. This functional form appears to give good fits to the main volatility structure for most major markets, for which there is an example in Figure 12.3. The next function to

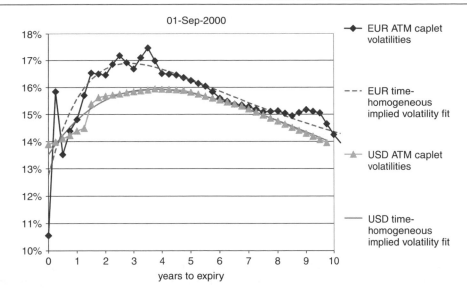

Figure 12.3 Market given implied volatilities for caplets and the best fit using equation (12.11) with all $k_i \equiv 1$

choose is the FRA/FRA correlation. One suitable choice is

$$\varrho_{ij}(t) = \mathrm{e}^{-\beta\left|(t_i-t)^\gamma-(t_j-t)^\gamma\right|} \cdot \mathbf{1}_{\{t \leqslant \min(t_i,t_j)\}} \tag{12.12}$$

with $\beta = 0.35$ and $\gamma = 0.5$. However, choosing $\gamma = 1$ and $\beta = 0.1$ (which results in very similar initial values for the correlation elements and makes no noticeable difference to the price of Bermudan swaptions), we can evaluate the pairwise covariance integrals $c_{ij}(t,T) = \int_t^T \sigma_i(u)\sigma_j(u)\varrho_{ij}(u)\,\mathrm{d}u$ with $t \leqslant T \leqslant \min(t_i, t_j)$ analytically, since we can take the correlation term out of the integral. The primitive, i.e. the indefinite integral, of $\sigma_i(t)\sigma_j(t)\varrho_{ij}$ then becomes

$$\int \varrho_{ij}\sigma_i(t)\sigma_j(t)\mathrm{d}t = \mathrm{e}^{-\beta|t_i-t_j|} \cdot k_i k_j \cdot \frac{1}{4c^3}$$

$$\cdot \left(4ac^2 d \left[\mathrm{e}^{c(t-t_j)} + \mathrm{e}^{c(t-t_i)} \right] + 4c^3 d^2 t \right.$$

$$-4bcd\mathrm{e}^{c(t-t_i)}\left[c(t-t_i)-1\right] - 4bcd\mathrm{e}^{c(t-t_j)}\left[c(t-t_j)-1\right]$$

$$+\mathrm{e}^{c(2t-t_i-t_j)}\left(2a^2c^2 + 2abc[1+c(t_i+t_j-2t)]\right.$$

$$\left.\left. + b^2\left[1+2c^2(t-t_i)(t-t_j)+c(t_i+t_j-2t)\right]\right)\right). \tag{12.13}$$

Clearly, we can always use formula (12.13) to calculate the implied volatility $\hat{\sigma}_i(t_i) = \int_0^{t_i}\sigma_i^2(t)\,\mathrm{d}t/t_i$ of any one caplet consistent with the parametrisation (12.11). In practice, one can use this formula to calculate the k_i such that $\hat{\sigma}_i(t_i)$ equals a market given Black volatility.

In order to establish a link between forward rate and forward swap rate volatilities for the purpose of calibration to European swaptions, we remind ourselves that a forward swap rate SR_i (starting with the reset time of the forward rate f_i) can be written as the ratio

$$SR_i = \frac{A_i}{B_i} \tag{12.14}$$

of the floating leg value

$$A_i = \sum_{j=i}^{n-1} P_{j+1} f_j \tau_j N_j \quad \text{for } i = 0, \ldots, n-1 \tag{12.15}$$

and the annuity

$$B_i = \sum_{j=i}^{n-1} P_{j+1} \tau_j N_j \quad \text{for } i = 0, \ldots, n-1. \tag{12.16}$$

N_j is the notional associated with accrual period τ_j. Since the market convention of price quotation for European swaptions uses the concept of implied Black volatilities for the forward swap rate, it seems appropriate to think of the swap rates' covariance matrix in relative terms just as much as for the forward rates themselves. The elements of the swap rate covariance matrix C^{SR} can therefore be written as

$$
\begin{aligned}
C_{ij}^{SR} &= \left\langle \frac{\mathrm{d}SR_i}{SR_i} \cdot \frac{\mathrm{d}SR_j}{SR_j} \right\rangle \\
&= \sum_{\substack{k=0 \\ l=0}}^{n-1} \frac{\partial SR_i/\partial f_k \cdot \partial SR_j/\partial f_l}{SR_i \cdot SR_j} \cdot f_k f_l \cdot \left\langle \frac{\mathrm{d}f_k}{f_k} \frac{\mathrm{d}f_l}{f_l} \right\rangle \\
&= \sum_{\substack{k=0 \\ l=0}}^{n-1} \frac{\partial SR_i}{\partial f_k} \frac{f_k}{SR_i} \cdot C_{kl}^{FRA} \cdot \frac{f_l}{SR_j} \frac{\partial SR_j}{\partial f_l}.
\end{aligned}
\tag{12.17}
$$

Defining the elements of the matrix $Z^{FRA \to SR}$ by

$$Z_{ik}^{FRA \to SR} = \frac{\partial SR_i}{\partial f_k} \frac{f_k}{SR_i} \tag{12.18}$$

the mapping from the FRA covariance matrix C^{FRA} to the swap rate covariance matrix C^{SR} can be seen as a matrix multiplication

$$C^{SR} = Z^{FRA \to SR} \cdot C^{FRA} \cdot Z^{FRA \to SR\,\top}. \tag{12.19}$$

Using

$$\frac{\partial}{\partial f_k} \left(\frac{P_{i+1}}{P_n} \right) = \left(\frac{P_{i+1}}{P_n} \right) \frac{\tau_k}{1 + f_k \tau_k} \cdot \mathbf{1}_{\{k \geqslant i\}} \quad \text{for } i, k < n \tag{12.20}$$

where $\mathbf{1}_{\{k \geqslant i\}}$ is one if $k \geqslant i$ and zero otherwise, and equations (12.15), (12.16) and (12.14), we have

$$\frac{\partial SR_i}{\partial f_k} = \left\{ \frac{P_{k+1} \tau_k N_k}{B_i} - \frac{\tau_k}{1 + f_k \tau_k} \cdot \frac{A_k}{B_i} + \frac{\tau_k}{1 + f_k \tau_k} \cdot \frac{A_i B_k}{B_i^2} \right\} \cdot \mathbf{1}_{\{k \geqslant i\}}. \qquad (12.21)$$

This enables us to calculate the elements of the forward rate to swap rate covariance transformation matrix $Z^{FRA \to SR}$ to obtain the expression

$$Z_{ik}^{FRA \to SR} = \left[\underbrace{\frac{P_{k+1} N_k f_k \tau_k}{A_i}}_{\text{constant weights approximation}} + \underbrace{\frac{(A_i B_k - A_k B_i) f_k \tau_k}{A_i B_i (1 + f_k \tau_k)}}_{\text{shape correction}} \right] \cdot \mathbf{1}_{\{k \geqslant i\}}. \quad (12.22)$$

The second term inside the square brackets of equation (12.22) is called the *shape correction*. Rewriting it as

$$\frac{(A_i B_k - A_k B_i) f_k \tau_k}{A_i B_i (1 + f_k \tau_k)} = \frac{f_k \tau_k}{A_i B_i (1 + f_k \tau_k)} \cdot \sum_{l-i}^{k-1} \sum_{m=k}^{n-1} P_{l+1} P_{m+1} N_l N_m \tau_l \tau_m (f_l - f_m)$$

$$(12.23)$$

highlights that it is a weighted average over inhomogencities of the yield curve. In fact, for a flat yield curve, all of the terms $(f_l - f_m)$ are identically zero and the mapping matrix $Z^{FRA \to SR}$ is equivalent to the constant weights approximation (11.7) in [Reb99]. As things stand at this point, we have a map between the instantaneous FRA/FRA covariance matrix and the instantaneous swap/swap covariance matrix. Unfortunately, though, the map involves the state of the yield curve at any one given point in time via the matrix Z. The price of a European swaption, however, does not just depend on one single realised state or even path of instantaneous volatility. It is much more appropriate to think about some kind of *path integral average volatility*. Using arguments of factor decomposition and equal probability of up and down moves (in log space), Rebonato shows in [JR00] that the specific structure of the map allows us to approximate the effective implied swaption volatilities by simply using today's state of the yield curve for the calculation of the mapping matrix Z:

$$\hat{\sigma}_{SR_i}(t, T) = \sqrt{\sum_{k=i,l=i}^{n-1} Z_{ik}^{FRA \to SR}(0) \cdot \frac{\int_t^T \sigma_k(t') \sigma_l(t') \rho_{kl} dt'}{T - t} \cdot Z_{il}^{FRA \to SR}(0)} \qquad (12.24)$$

This approximate equivalent implied volatility can now be substituted into the Black swaption formula to produce a price *without the need for a single simulation!* In practice, the formula (12.24) works remarkably well. This is demonstrated for a whole sequence of co-terminal European swaptions in figure 12.4. An explanation for the remarkable accuracy of approximation (12.24) is beyond the scope of this section, but can be found in [JR00].

Using the above preliminaries, I now outline the calibration procedure in detail. For a given time step from t to T, populate a time-unscaled FRA/FRA covariance matrix

$$C_{kl}^{FRA} = \frac{\int_t^T \sigma_k(t') \sigma_l(t') \varrho_{kl}(t') dt'}{(T - t)}. \qquad (12.25)$$

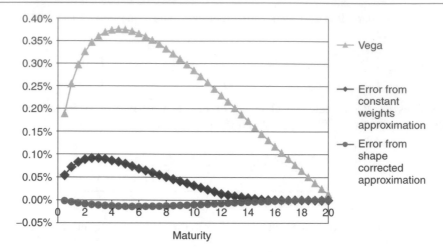

Figure 12.4 The pricing error from equation (12.24) using only the constant weights approximation in the formula (12.22) or when including the shape correction for a GBP yield curve for August 10th, 2000

Next, map this matrix into a time-unscaled swap/swap covariance matrix using the Z matrix calculated from the initial state of the yield curve

$$C^{SR} = Z \cdot C^{FRA} \cdot Z^\top \tag{12.26}$$

and calculate from it the swap/swap correlation matrix R^{SR} given by

$$R_{ij}^{SR} = \frac{C_{ij}^{SR}}{\sqrt{C_{ii}^{SR} C_{jj}^{SR}}}. \tag{12.27}$$

Now, we compute the spectral pseudo-square root B of R^{SR} which satisfies

$$R^{SR} = B^{SR} \cdot B^{SR\ \top}. \tag{12.28}$$

At this point, we take into account the market given swaption prices. Denote the market implied volatility of the swaption expiring at time t_h by $\sigma_{SR_h}^{\text{market}}$ and define the diagonal matrix Ξ by

$$\Xi_{gh} = \hat{\sigma}_{SR_h}^{\text{market}} \cdot \frac{\hat{\sigma}_{SR_h}(t, T)}{\hat{\sigma}_{SR_h}(0, t_h)} \cdot \delta_{gh} \tag{12.29}$$

with δ_{gh} being the Kronecker symbol (which is zero unless $g = h$ when it is one) and both $\hat{\sigma}_{SR_h}(t, T)$ and $\hat{\sigma}_{SR_h}(0, t_h)$ calculated from the FRA instantaneous volatility parametrisation through equation (12.24). The final step is now to construct the FRA driver[4] matrix A^{FRA} by scaling up the swap/swap correlation driver matrix B^{SR} and mapping back to FRA coordinates:

$$A^{FRA} = Z^{-1} \cdot \Xi \cdot B^{SR}. \tag{12.30}$$

---

[4] Karatzas and Shreve call this matrix the *dispersion matrix* [KS91] (p. 284).

The effective (time-unscaled) FRA/FRA covariance matrix is finally

$$C^{FRA}_{\text{effective}} = A^{FRA} \cdot A^{FRA^\top}. \tag{12.31}$$

In order to use the matrices $C^{FRA}_{\text{effective}}$ and A^{FRA} for the evolution over the time step $t \to T$ from a set of standard normal variates, we still need to multiply them by $(T - t)$ and $\sqrt{(T - t)}$, respectively. Within the limits of the approximation (12.24), using these matrices wherever we have expressions involving a_{ij} and c_{ii} in the following sections will provide calibration to European swaption prices whilst retaining as much calibration to the caplets as possible without violating the overall FRA/FRA correlation structure too much, which is typically exactly what a practitioner wants for the pricing of Bermudan swaptions. As a side note, it should be mentioned that various other combinations of carrying out the split into $C^{FRA}_{\text{effective}}$ and A^{FRA} are possible, whilst still preserving calibration to European swaptions. In my experience, however, the above approach represents the best method to preserve as much of the overall FRA/FRA correlation structure in the calibration as possible.

12.5   THE PREDICTOR–CORRECTOR SCHEME

In order to price a Bermudan swaption in a Monte Carlo framework, we need to evolve the set of forward rates f from its present values into the future according to the stochastic differential equation

$$\mathrm{d}f_i(t) = f_i(t) \cdot \mu_i(\boldsymbol{f}(t), t)\mathrm{d}t + f_i(t) \cdot \sum_{j=1}^{m} a_{ij}\mathrm{d}W_j \tag{12.32}$$

driven by an m-dimensional standard Wiener process $\boldsymbol{W}$. The drift terms given by equation (12.8) are clearly state-dependent and thus indirectly stochastic, which forces us to use a numerical scheme to solve equation (12.32) along any one path. Ideally, we would want to evolve the forward yield curve f only over the points in time which we actually need to monitor, i.e. the possible exercise dates. The simplest numerical scheme for the integration of stochastic differential equations[5] is the Euler method

$$f_i^{\text{Euler}}(\boldsymbol{f}(t), t + \Delta t) = f_i(t) + f_i(t) \cdot \mu_i(\boldsymbol{f}(t), t)\Delta t + f_i(t) \cdot \sum_{j=1}^{m} a_{ij}(t)z_j\sqrt{\Delta t} \tag{12.33}$$

with z_j being m independent normal variates. This would imply that we approximate the drift as constant over the time step $t \to t + \Delta t$. Moreover, this scheme effectively means that we are using a normal distribution for the evolution of the forward rates over this time step. Whilst we may agree to the approximation of a piecewise constant (in time) drift coefficient μ_i, the normal distribution may be undesirable, especially if we envisage using large time steps Δt for reasons of computational efficiency. However, when we assume piecewise constant drift, we might as well carry out the integration over the time step Δt analytically and use the scheme

$$f_i^{\text{constant drift}}(\boldsymbol{f}(t), t + \Delta t) = f_i(t) \cdot \mathrm{e}^{\mu_i(\boldsymbol{f}(t), t)\Delta t - \frac{1}{2}c_{ii} + \sum_{j=1}^{m} a_{ij}z_j} \tag{12.34}$$

---

[5]See [KP99] for a whole variety of methods for the integration of stochastic differential equations.

whereby the time step scaling by $\sqrt{\Delta t}$ for A and by Δt for C has been absorbed into the respective matrices. In other words, I have set $A' := A \cdot \sqrt{\Delta t}$ and $C' := C \cdot \Delta t$ and dropped the primes. Equation (12.34) can also be viewed as the Euler scheme in logarithmic coordinates.

The above procedure works very well as long as the time steps Δt are not too long, and is widely used and also referred to in publications [And00, GZ99]. Since the drift term appearing in the exponential function in equation (12.34) is in some sense a stochastic quantity itself, we begin to notice that we are ignoring Jensen's inequality when the term $\mu_i \Delta t$ becomes large enough. This happens when we choose a big step Δt, or the forward rates themselves or their volatility are large. Therefore, we should use a predictor–corrector method which models the drift as indirectly stochastic [HJJ01]. In the notation of Kloeden and Platen [KP99], depending on the time dependence of the instantaneous volatility function, this is an explicit order 2.0 weak scheme or order 1.0 weak predictor–corrector method[6]. This combination of the Euler scheme in logarithmic space with the predictor-corrector method for the drift results in a remarkable accuracy and is used throughout all of the calculations reported in this chapter. The method is as follows. First, given a current evolution of the yield curve denoted by $f(t)$, we calculate the predicted solution $f^{\text{constant drift}}(f(t), t + \Delta t)$ using one m-dimensional normal variate draw z following equation (12.34). Next, we recalculate the drift using this evolved yield curve. The predictor-corrector approximation $\tilde{\mu}_i$ for the drift is then given by the average of these two calculated drifts, i.e.

$$\tilde{\mu}_i(f(t), t \to t + \Delta t) = \frac{1}{2} \left\{ \mu_i(f(t), t) + \mu_i(f^{\text{constant drift}}(f(t), t + \Delta t), t) \right\}. \quad (12.35)$$

Finally, the predictor–corrector evolution is given by

$$f_i^{\text{predictor–corrector}}(f(t), t + \Delta t) = f_i(t) \cdot e^{\tilde{\mu}_i(f(t), t \to t + \Delta t)\Delta t - \frac{1}{2}c_{ii} + \sum_{j=1}^{m} a_{ij}z_j} \quad (12.36)$$

wherein we reuse the same normal variate draw z, i.e. we only correct the drift of the predicted solution.

A handwaving reasoning for the above approximation goes as follows. If we had to choose, for the calculation of a constant drift approximation, for any one time step, whether we use the initial forward rates $f(t)$, or those at the end of the time step $f(t + \Delta t)$, neither of them appears to be superior over the other for the job. This is equivalent to the considerations about explicit and implicit methods for the numerical solution of both ordinary and partial differential equations. We don't actually know the drift at the end of a desired time step, and solving for it as we would in an implicit method would require solving a high-dimensional non-linear system *each and every time*. However, we can approximate the drift term at the end of the time step, and then take the average of the two individual drift approximations, in analogy to the predictor–corrector method used in other areas of numerical analysis.

---

[6]To be precise, a hybrid method is used here. In the approach presented, I integrate in equation (12.25) the volatility functions independently over the time step to obtain an equivalent discrete time step covariance matrix, and then treat these covariance matrices as if they had been given by a process of volatility functions that are constant in time. Therefore, neither is the explicit order 2.0 weak scheme given by eqn (15.1.4) in [KP99] used, nor the order 1.0 weak predictor–corrector method as in eqn (15.5.4) [KP99]. In the case of constant, i.e. time-independent volatility, however, these two schemes are identical. Thus, following the general notion that it is always beneficial to use as many explicit analytical solutions as possible in any numerical scheme, one can say that we are using a predictor–corrector scheme *only for the drift term*, not for the entire stochastic differential equation driving the evolution.

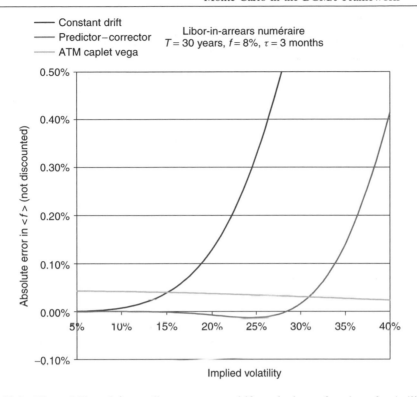

Figure 12.5 The stability of the predictor–corrector drift method as a function of volatility level

A number of numerical experiments confirm that this method is very robust and works very well (the error is never more than a fraction of the bid–offer spread which is typically around one vega of the option) for the prevailing interest rates and volatility levels for all of the major markets, even for very long dated (tens of years) options when only a single step to maturity is used. In order to demonstrate this, it is shown in Figures 12.5 and 12.6 how the predictor–corrector drift approach performs for a Libor-in-arrears scenario in comparison to the piecewise constant drift approach where the drift term over any one time step is given by the state of the yield curve at the beginning of the step. In both figures, the error in the expectation of the Libor-in-arrears contract for both stepping methods for *a single step to maturity* is compared with a measure for the bid-offer spread, namely the price difference resulting from a 1% move in implied volatility. As you can see, the method is remarkably accurate, even for very long time steps. When we price Bermudan swaptions, however, we never have such long individual steps since we need to model the evolution at each exercise date. This means that the predictor–corrector drift approximation is highly accurate in the context of Bermudan swaption modelling.

12.6 HEURISTICS OF THE EXERCISE BOUNDARY

At any reset time t_i as sketched in Figure 12.1, the residual yield curve of interest is fully described by the vector $f(t_i)$ whose elements are the $n - i$ remaining forward rates in the yield curve out to the last payment time of the Bermudan swaption. Amongst many

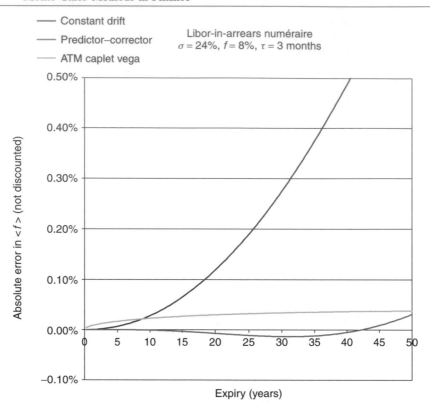

Figure 12.6   The stability of the predictor–corrector drift method as a function of time to expiry

other possible ways to describe the yield curve at time t_i out to t_n are the vector $\boldsymbol{P}(t_i)$, whose elements are the t_i-present values of zero-coupon bonds maturing on $t_{i+1}, \ldots, t_n$, and the vector $\boldsymbol{s}(t_i)$ consisting of the swap rates of all co-terminal swaps out to t_n. All of these determine the yield curve unambiguously. Since it is in general a good idea to exploit the specific structure of the particular problem one wishes to solve using simulation techniques, it is conducive to first of all look at the geometry of the exercise domain of the Bermudan swaption problem. Strictly speaking, the exercise boundary at time t_i is an $(n - i - 1)$-dimensional hypersurface in an $(n - i)$-dimensional space. Using the non-recombining tree procedure explained in Chapter 13, we can produce diagrams of two-dimensional projections of exercise decisions. If we find a coordinate pair in whose projection the domain of exercise decision events appears to be reasonably separated from the domain where exercise was not optimal, we may be able to reduce the early exercise decision to the evaluation of a parametric function in those two coordinates. To demonstrate that this is possible, the exercise decisions were evaluated using a four-factor non-recombining tree for a 6-non-call-2 annual Bermudan swaption. The tree was constructed with five branches out of each node representing five different possible evolutions of the yield curve, and both the *alternating simplex direction* and *optimal simplex alignment* technique presented in section 13.3 were applied to improve homogeneity of the distribution of the evolved yield curve and enhance convergence. All discrete forward rates were set to 10% annually compounded, volatilities were assumed to be 30%, and the correlation ϱ_{ij} between forward rates f_i and f_j was modelled as before by

$$\varrho_{ij} = e^{-\beta|t_i - t_j|} \tag{12.37}$$

with $\beta = 0.1$. The strike was set to be at-the-money, i.e. at 10%. The tree was constructed with 10 steps to the first exercise decision at $t = 1$, and then one in between each subsequent exercise opportunity[7].

In Figure 12.7, the t_i-evolved yield curve is represented by the first two forward rates f_i and f_{i+1}. Next, in Figure 12.8, the evolved yield curve is projected onto the first two of the set of residual co-terminal swap rates s_i and s_{i+1}. The diagram in Figure 12.7 illustrates that using the first two forward rates to project onto will make the domain of exercise appear to overlap with the domain where not exercising is optimal. Using the projection onto the first two residual co-terminal swap rates results in a projection where all points are very near the diagonal, which will make it numerically difficult to determine the exercise boundary. Also, the very nature of the swap rate is that both an upward and a downward sloping yield curve can result in the very same value for the swap rate, but

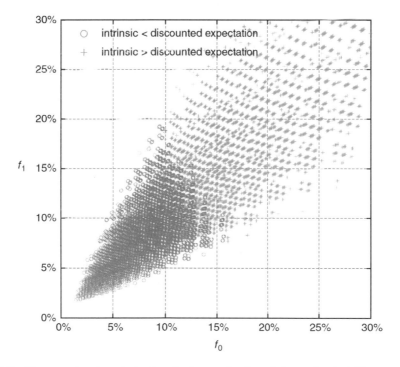

Figure 12.7   The exercise domain in the f_i–f_{i+1} projection of the evolved yield curve at $t_i = 2$

---

[7]Many other calculations with different distributions of the steps between the relevant monitoring times were conducted and all lead to the same shape of the exercise boundary. This particular one was chosen for the generation of the diagrams since it best highlights the location of the boundary and the overlapping versus non-overlapping feature in the different projections. The total number of $5^{10} = 9\,765\,625$ points resulting from this calculation was reduced by sorting along the abscissa and retaining only every seventh point in order to make the volume of data somewhat manageable.

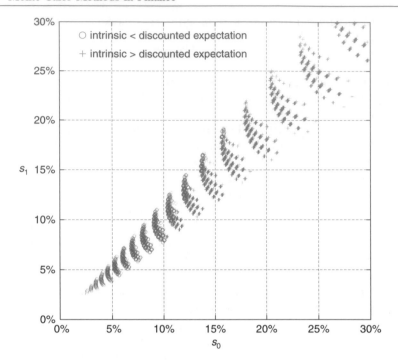

Figure 12.8   The exercise domain in the s_i–s_{i+1} projection of the evolved yield curve at $t_i = 2$

it is much more likely to be optimal to exercise a payer's Bermudan early in a downward sloping than in an upward sloping yield curve environment.

Another choice of coordinates could include the annuity of the residual swaps B_i and B_{i+1} respectively, making the new variables the values $(s_i B_i)$ and $(s_{i+1} B_{i+1})$ of the respective floating legs. This does not appear to improve on the above selection of projections though, as can be seen in Figure 12.9. However, using the projection onto the first forward rate f_i and the forward swap rate s_{i+1} starting from the reset time of f_{i+1} going out to the terminal maturity results in a reasonable separation of exercise and non-exercise decisions with very little overlap, as can be seen in Figure 12.10. Ideally, we could use a principal component decomposition of the dynamics of the yield curve and project onto the first two modes. In order to retain a direct financial intuition as to the meaning of the coordinate system, the method was developed using the f_i–s_{i+1} projection, in particular since the short rate and the long swap rate are in practice very good proxies for the first two fundamental modes of the yield curve.

12.7   EXERCISE BOUNDARY PARAMETRISATION

Taking into account all the heuristic observations about the shape of the exercise boundary in various projections for many different shapes of the yield curve and volatility structures, the following function was chosen as the basis for the subsequent exercise decision

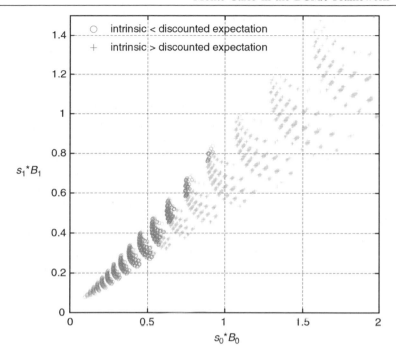

Figure 12.9 The exercise domain in the $(s_i B_i)$–$(s_{i+1} B_{i+1})$ projection of the evolved yield curve at $t_i = 2$

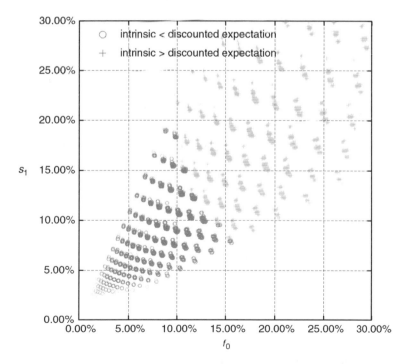

Figure 12.10 The exercise domain in the f_i–s_{i+1} projection of the evolved yield curve at $t_i = 2$

strategy in the Monte Carlo simulation:

$$E_i(f(t_i)) = \left(f_i(t_i) - \left[p_{i1} \cdot \frac{s_{i+1}(0)}{s_{i+1}(t_i) + p_{i2}} + p_{i3} \right] \right) \cdot \left\{ \begin{array}{l} +1 \text{ for payer's swaptions} \\ -1 \text{ for receiver's swaptions} \end{array} \right\}. \tag{12.38}$$

This function is hyperbolic in s_{i+1} and depends on three coefficients, the initial (i.e. at the calendar time of evaluation or inception of the derivative contract) value of $f_i(0)$ and $s_{i+1}(0)$, and their respective evolved values as given by the simulation procedure. Since we have to make an exercise decision at each exercise opportunity time t_i, we allow for a new set of exercise function coefficients for each such time slice. For non-standard Bermudan swaptions that have payments in between exercise dates, we use the shortest swap rate from t_i to the next exercise time instead of f_i. The parametric exercise decision given an evolved yield curve is then simply to exercise if $E_i > 0$.

At the very last exercise opportunity at time t_{n-1} we have exact knowledge if exercise is optimal, namely when the residual swap is in-the-money. This easily integrates into the parametric description given by equation (12.38) by setting $p_{(n-1)1}$ and $p_{(n-1)2}$ to zero and $p_{(n-1)3}$ to the strike:

$$\begin{aligned} p_{(n-1)1} &= 0, \\ p_{(n-1)2} &= 0, \\ p_{(n-1)3} &= K. \end{aligned} \tag{12.39}$$

12.8 THE ALGORITHM

The Monte Carlo method for the pricing of Bermudan swaptions can now be described. First, a *training set* $\mathbb{P}^{\text{training}}$ of N_{training} evolutions of the yield curve into the future out to the last exercise time t_{n-1} is precalculated and stored:

$$\mathbb{P}^{\text{training}} = \{ f_{jk} \} \quad j = 1, \dots, N_{\text{training}}, \ k = 0, \dots, n-1. \tag{12.40}$$

Also, for each evolution of the yield curve, the residual intrinsic value I_{jk} in the chosen numéraire as seen at time t_k is precalculated and stored.

Then, a set of $n-1$ optimisations is carried out, one for each exercise opportunity t_i apart from the last one[8] in order to determine the best values to use for the coefficients p_{ij}. Naturally, the optimisations are done in reverse order, starting with the penultimate exercise time t_{n-2}. Prior to each optimisation, we assign a path value v_j, $j = 1, \dots, N_{\text{training}}$ to each evolution path in the training set $\mathbb{P}^{\text{training}}$ which represents the value of the Bermudan swaption on this path if no exercise occurs up until and including t_i. This path value vector v is initialised to be zero in all its elements before we enter the following loop, which counts down in the time index variable i from $n-2$ to 0.

1. For each path $f_{j(\cdot)}$ in $\mathbb{P}^{\text{training}}$, **if** $(E_{i+1}(f_{ji}) > 0)$ **and** $(I_{j(i+1)} > 0)$, reassign $v_j := I_{j(i+1)}$, **else** leave v_j unchanged.

---

[8]On the very last exercise opportunity, the optimal exercise parameters are given by equation (12.39) whence no optimisation is required.

2. Optimise the average of the exercise decision-dependent value

$$U_i(\boldsymbol{p}_i) = \frac{1}{N_{\text{training}}} \sum_{j=1}^{N_{\text{training}}} \left\{ \begin{array}{ll} I_{ji} & \textbf{if} \quad (E_i(\boldsymbol{f}_{ji} ; \boldsymbol{p}_i) > 0) \\ v_j & \textbf{else} \end{array} \right\} \qquad (12.41)$$

over the three parameters p_{i1}, p_{i2} and p_{i3}. Specifically, one can use the Broyden–Fletcher–Goldfarb–Shanno multi-dimensional variable metric method for this optimisation [PTVF92].

3. It is worth noting at this point that, since *absolutely all values are precalculated and stored*, the function to be optimised given by equation (12.41) requires merely N_{training} evaluations of the exercise decision function $E_i(\boldsymbol{f}_{ji} ; \boldsymbol{p}_i)$ and the same number of additions and is thus *linear in the number of training paths and independent of the dimensionality or maturity of the problem*.

4. Decrement i by 1 and **if** $(i \geqslant 0)$ continue with step 1.

The final value $U_0(\boldsymbol{p}_0)$ then gives an estimate of the value of the Bermudan swaption with a slight upward bias. Therefore, we finally rerun the simulation with a new set of N_{sampling} yield curve evolutions using the established exercise strategy parametrisation given by the set of n exercise decision functions E_i. Typically, I find $N_{\text{sampling}} \simeq 2N_{\text{training}}$ to be well sufficient, especially when the driving number generator method was a low-discrepancy sequence.

12.9 NUMERICAL RESULTS

In order to highlight the outcome of the training procedure described in the previous section, the parametrised exercise boundary as resulting[9] from $N_{\text{training}} = 32\,768$, $N_{\text{training}} = 131\,072$ and $N_{\text{training}} = 1,048,576$ is superimposed on the exercise decisions given by the non-recombining tree (already shown in Figure 12.10) in Figure 12.11. The resulting prices were 5.062% for $N_{\text{training}} = 32, 768$ (total run time 5.1 s[10]), 5.066% for $N_{\text{training}} = 131\,072$ (26.5 s) and 5.069% for $N_{\text{training}} = 1\,048\,576$ (211 s). The most accurate price estimate I could obtain from the non-recombining tree is 5.084% ± 0.015%, which demonstrates the remarkable accuracy of this new Monte Carlo method. This example also highlights that the Monte Carlo approximation for the *true* price (defined by the absolutely optimal exercise strategy), in the vicinity of the optimal exercise strategy, depends only weakly on slight changes in the boundary. After all, if we view the price approximation as a function of the location of a given exercise boundary, then the *real* Bermudan option price is the one resulting from an optimisation over all possible exercise boundary locations. As it happens, with the value of a function at its maximum, the first derivative with respect to its argument must be zero at the extremum, and thus the price approximation depends only weakly (i.e. as of second order) on minor changes in the exercise boundary location near the optimal point.

---

[9] All reported results are from calculations with a high-dimensional Sobol' sequence. Using this sequence generator, European option prices are typically highly stable and accurate with 1024 paths, in most cases even 512 paths would have sufficed for the same accuracy. The Bermudan swaption prices are typically sufficiently accurate and robustly stable with around 16,384 training paths (and twice that for the final evaluation), but in order to make the diagrams appear even smoother somewhat larger numbers of paths were used.

[10] Run times are given for a Pentium II at 300 MHz with the number of sampling points always being double the number of training points.

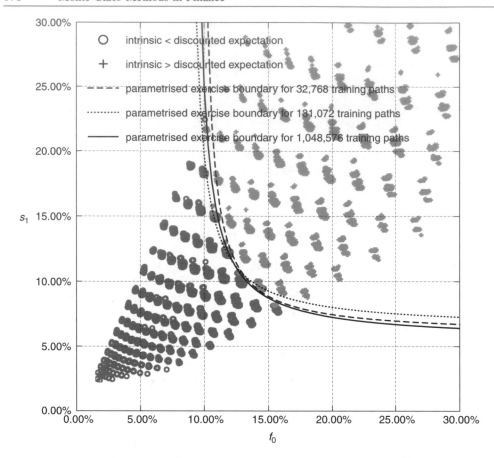

Figure 12.11 The exercise domain in the f_i–s_{i+1} projection of the evolved yield curve at $t_i = 2$, together with the parametrised exercise boundary resulting from training with different sizes of the training set

Now, the results for a 6-non-call-2 semi-annual payer's Bermudan swaption for a typical Sterling yield curve and volatility environment are presented. This means the yield curve was slightly downward sloping, and the implied swaption volatilities increased from 19.53% for the first one up to 22.46% for the last one (which is a caplet). The forward rates were again assumed to have piecewise constant instantaneous volatility, but calibration in this case was done such that the entailed European swaptions' prices are independent of the number of factors used. The option was again at-the-money[11] with a strike of 6.63%. In Figure 12.12, a diagram of the Bermudan swaption price calculated using the presented Monte Carlo method in comparison to the values obtained from a non-recombining tree model is shown. For reference, the prices obtained from both models for the most expensive European are also included. Since the non-recombining tree model must by construction converge to the same value as the Monte Carlo model for European contracts, including both European prices gives a good indication for the residual error of

---

[11] In all my tests, at the money Bermudan swaptions are always the most difficult ones to price using a Monte Carlo method since they contain the most relative optionality.

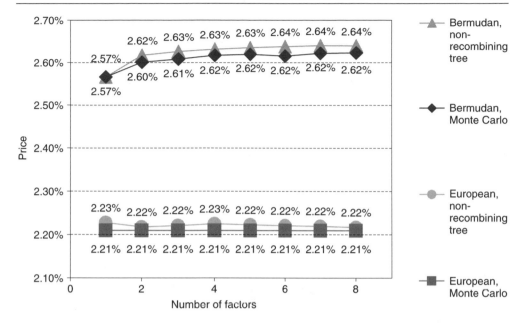

Figure 12.12 Bermudan swaption prices from the Monte Carlo model in comparison to those obtained from a non-recombining tree model for a 6-non-call-2 semi-annual payer's swaption

the non-recombining tree model. As can be seen, the Monte Carlo model returns prices that are within the error margin of the non-recombining tree model. The upwards trend of the prices with increasing numbers of factors is very typical for calibration to European swaptions when no attempt is made to keep the prices of caps constant at the same time. The non-recombining tree calculation time required to obtain sufficient accuracy for the curves in Figure 12.12 to look reasonably smooth was approximately 8 h on a Pentium II at 300 MHz parallelised over two CPUs using multi-threading, whilst the total calculation time for the Monte Carlo results was 92 s (without multi-threading).

Next, in Figures 12.13 and 12.14, examples are shown for longer dated contracts, namely a 15-non-call-5 annual Bermudan payer's and receiver's swaption with a flat yield curve at 10% and calibration to European swaption implied volatilities taken from the GBP market. Forward rate volatilities were again modelled as piecewise constant in time. In this case, prices from the non-recombining tree were only calculated up to two factors. The points shown for the non-recombining trees indicate by how much the price varies if the number of steps is increased slightly, thus giving an indication for the error margin from the tree. Again, the Monte Carlo model is very accurately in agreement with the non-recombining tree.

In Figure 12.15 the results are shown for the same 15-non-call-5 annual payer's swaption, only this time the yield curve was assumed to be steeply upwards sloping from initially 2.5% up to 9% for the last FRA. Finally, in Figure 12.16, the results for a 20-non-call-10 semi-annual payer's swaption are shown. Here, I used a slightly upwards sloping yield curve taken from the USD market, and market-typical European swaption implied volatilities beginning at 14.56% for the longest swaption and ending at 22.50% for the last one. In this case, the forward rates were modelled to follow a slightly humped

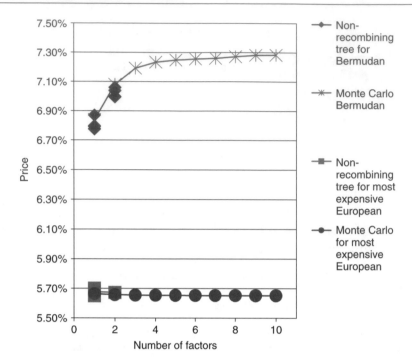

Figure 12.13   15-non-call-5 annual payer's swaption

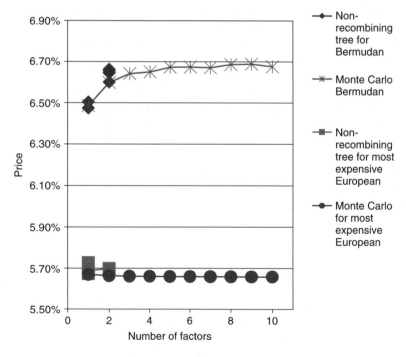

Figure 12.14   15-non-call-5 annual receiver's swaption

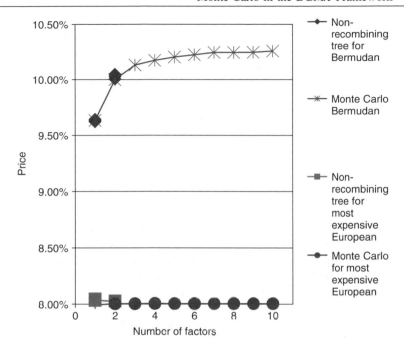

Figure 12.15   15-non-call-5 annual payer's swaption for steeply upwards sloping yield curve

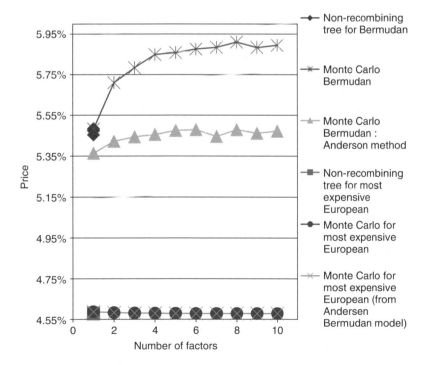

Figure 12.16   20-non-call-10 semi-annual payer's swaption in comparison to Andersen's method I [And00]

instantaneous volatility curve, as is believed by practitioners to be the most realistic representation of econometric observations [Reb99]. Also, the results as obtained from the model (method I) published by Andersen [And00] were added for comparison. For this contract, due to the sheer number of payment and exercise times, only single factor calculations were completed with the non-recombining tree model.

12.10   SUMMARY

In this chapter, a number of separate issues relating to the pricing of Bermudan swaptions in the BGM/J framework have been addressed. The state dependence of the drift coefficients poses a problem for Monte Carlo simulations whenever we wish to avoid using a small-step Euler scheme. The proposed *predictor–corrector log-Euler BGM/J* Monte Carlo scheme is very stable and allows us to use single steps over any time horizon that may be encountered in the pricing of Bermudan swaptions. Then, a new Monte Carlo method tailormade specifically for the pricing of Bermudan swaptions was presented. The main idea behind the new approach is to exploit the heuristics obtained from a different but numerically not widely applicable method, namely a non-recombining multi-factor tree. This knowledge is then used to devise a suitable parametric exercise decision function in fewer dimensions than the state space is embedded in. Also, the importance of a careful selection of the coordinate system used for the projection of the exercise boundary was demonstrated. This approach was compared to the method suggested by Andersen [And00], which relied solely on a financial intuition of what variables should be most indicative. The new method was tested with a large number of yield curve and volatility scenarios, and in *all* of them proved to be remarkably accurate. A small selection of the test results are presented in this document. I have also given examples of the calculation time involved on a computer which, at the time of writing, can be considered to be at least a factor of five slower than what is readily available to practitioners on a trading floor. The remarkable speed, stability and accuracy of the developed model are partly due to the use of high-dimensional Sobol' numbers, but also due to the careful design of the optimisation algorithm and the detailed attention to precalculation and storage of all involved quantities wherever possible.

In general, it cannot be expected that the technique of projecting the exercise domain onto just two dimensions will result in a single simple curve delineating the exercise boundary. Examples of this are American max options where the higher of two asset values minus a strike level determines the intrinsic value [BG97a]. Still, out of all the mathematical problems one may conceivably subject to a Monte Carlo simulation evaluation, the very nature of financial derivatives makes them appear comparatively benign. In other words, I believe that for most exercise strategy-dependent derivatives contracts invented thus far, a suitable projection of the exercise domain can be found to make the boundary amenable to a description by only one or a few reasonably simple functions in two variables. Whenever this is possible, a multi-dimensional optimisation over a small set of free parameters using a training set of paths can be carried out, resulting in a highly accurate price estimate. I therefore believe that the presented approach of using a non-recombining tree (which is very flexible with respect to payoff specifications but very limited with respect to deal maturity and the number of involved time slices) to devise a bespoke Monte Carlo exercise strategy parametrisation for a specific product can be applied to a wide class of American or Bermudan-style derivatives.

Non-recombining Trees

13.1 INTRODUCTION

Traditionally, implementations of option pricing models tended to use some form of lattice method. In most cases, this meant an explicit finite differencing approach was chosen. In fact, many of the early quantitative analysts would describe this as 'having been brought up on *trees*'. This tendency towards the use of tree methods is also reflected in the option pricing literature. Cox, Ross and Rubinstein [CRR79] described the option pricing procedure on a binomial tree in 1979. Some of the breakthrough publications in derivatives modelling were first formulated as an algorithm for a tree node construction matching a market given set of security prices and Black implied volatilities. These include the Ho–Lee model whose continuous counterpart is that of an Ornstein–Uhlenbeck process [HL86, Jam96], the lognormal interest rate model by Black, Derman and Toy [BDT90] and the deterministic but spot-dependent instantaneous volatility model by Derman, Kani and Zou [DKZ96]. The great advantages of recombining tree methods are their comparative ease of implementation, equally easy applicability to the calculation of Greeks, and fast performance.

Alas, we cannot always use recombining tree methods. This is typically so when the stochastic process chosen to model the evolution of the underlying quantities is strongly state-dependent. The state dependence of the drift term of forward rates in the Brace–Gatarek–Musiela/Jamshidian framework is one such case. This makes it a prime application of Monte Carlo methods. However, when we wish to price options of American style, we really need to compare the expected payoff as seen from any one node with the intrinsic value. This means, the only method that can in principle give an unbiased result is a non-recombining tree. Whilst there are many publications on recombining tree methods and how to construct them for optimal performance, very little is in the literature on the construction of non-recombining trees. What's more, the few descriptions of the construction of non-recombining tree methods and analysis of their performance [JW00, MW99, Rad98a, Rad98b] focus on no more than three factors. In this chapter, I present a generic method to construct a non-recombining tree for any given number of factors and provide the algebraic equations needed to calculate the coefficients that determine the branches.

Before we start the explanation of a generic method to construct a non-recombining tree with the minimal number of branches out of each node required, let us briefly compare non-recombining tree methods with Monte Carlo techniques. The two approaches share several features. For both of them, an evaluation is always done along a specific evolution path such that they could both allow for a non-Markovian stochastic process (within the limits of the time-discretisation). The two most crucial quantities that determine the evolution over one time step are in both cases the expectation conditions (i.e. drift terms or martingale conditions) and the covariance matrix of all the state variables, and it is those that tell us how we have to construct the paths. Both techniques are traditionally perceived to be very slow, and rightly the non-recombining trees are considered so slow as not to be a viable method in front office systems although, as we will see, to some extent they can be useful for benchmarking purposes. For both methods, paying particular attention to implementation details can make tremendous differences to the performance, i.e. calculation time required. Both approaches are designed to generate a representative sample set of all possible evolutions. It is for those similarities that I include a chapter on non-recombining tree methods in this book. The main differences between non-recombining tree methods and Monte Carlo techniques entail the following points. Non-recombining tree methods, by their very nature, are a recursive representation of the option pricing problem and thus suggest and easily support a recursive implementation. The very same feature allows for easy integration of free boundary conditions, i.e. early exercise decisions as we have them for Bermudan or American options. Non-recombining trees are susceptible to pathological problems where they may fail systematically because of the very selective path construction method. Finally, the convergence behaviour of non-recombining trees depends very strongly on the dimensionality of the problem, i.e. the number of driving factors. Despite their differences, from a constructional point of view, the similarities are remarkable. In common with Monte Carlo methods, using simple techniques, it is possible to implement them such that they perform orders of magnitude better than is frequently thought.

The remainder of this chapter is organised as follows. First, I briefly summarise the setting of the BGM/J model and discuss its factorisation in section 13.2, and also explain how the evolution of forward rates can be modelled in a non-recombining tree method. Next, we discuss in more detail some of the aspects of the high-dimensional geometry of the branching scheme in section 13.3. Following this, I elaborate a few points on the efficient implementation of the algorithm. The main results on the performance and applicability of the method are then presented in section 13.5. Next, we explain possible improvements that can be done to match the variance as it would result from a continuous description in section 13.6. Furthermore, I discuss a different technique to account for the state-dependent drift of the underlying forward rates in section 13.7, such that all martingale conditions are met exactly. Following that, we demonstrate how the clustering effect that can be observed for flat volatility structures is broken up by the use of a time-varying term structure of instantaneous volatility in section 13.8. For those of us who like a visual demonstration of how things work, I give a simple example in section 13.9. Finally, a summary of this chapter is given.

13.2   EVOLVING THE FORWARD RATES

Let us reiterate some of the basic setup of the BGM/J Libor market model which was already explained in section 12.2. The state of the yield curve is represented by a set of n spanning forward rates f_i which evolve lognormally according to the stochastic differential equation

$$\frac{\mathrm{d}f_i}{f_i} = \mu_i(f, t)\,\mathrm{d}t + \sigma_i(t)\,\mathrm{d}\widetilde{W}_i. \tag{13.1}$$

As in section 12.2, we construct from this starting point a (possibly m-factor truncated) covariance matrix $C(t, t + \Delta t)$ for the time step $t \to t + \Delta t$ and its pseudo-square root A, taking into account our correlation function of choice as in equations (12.1) to (12.7). Clearly, equation (12.8) means that the drifts are state-dependent and thus indirectly stochastic. For the purpose of derivatives pricing, we need to sample the space of all possible evolutions of the yield curve into the future. If we approximate the drift coefficients μ_i as constant over a small time step Δt, we can represent the evolved forward rates by

$$f_i(t + \Delta t) = f_i \cdot e^{\bar{\mu}_i(t, t+\Delta t)\Delta t - \frac{1}{2}c_{ii} + \sum_{j=1}^{m} a_{ij} z_j} \tag{13.2}$$

with z_j being independent normal variates. The coefficients a_{ij} are the elements of the (possibly m-factor truncated) pseudo-square root A of the covariance matrix C' which contains the integrals over the small time step Δt:

$$c'_{ij} = \int_{t'=t}^{t+\Delta t} \sigma_i(t')\sigma_j(t')\varrho_{ij}\, dt'. \tag{13.3}$$

To summarise, the steps that have to be carried out for the construction of Δt-evolved forward rates as in equation (13.2) are as follows.

1. Populate the marginal covariance matrix $C'(t, t + \Delta t)$ using equation (13.3).
2. Decompose (e.g. using the Cholesky method or by spectral decomposition) such that

$$A' \cdot A'^{\top} = C'. \tag{13.4}$$

3. Form the m-factor truncated coefficient matrix A in analogy to equation (12.7), i.e. using

$$a_{ij} = a'_{ij} \sqrt{\frac{c'_{ii}}{\sum_{k=1}^{m} a'^2_{ik}}}. \tag{13.5}$$

4. Build the m-factor approximation covariance matrix C:

$$C = A \cdot A^{\top} \tag{13.6}$$

which will in general, for $m < n$, not be identical to C' but by construction we preserve the diagonal elements $c_{ii} = c'_{ii}$.

Given the above definitions, we can now specify $\bar{\mu}_i$ in equation (13.2):

$$\bar{\mu}_i(t, t + \Delta t)\Delta t = \begin{cases} -\sum_{k=i+1}^{N-1} \dfrac{f_k(t)\tau_k}{1 + f_k(t)\tau_k} c_{ik}(t, t + \Delta t) & \text{for } i < N - 1, \\[2mm] 0 & \text{for } i = N - 1, \\[2mm] \sum_{k=N}^{i} \dfrac{f_k(t)\tau_k}{1 + f_k(t)\tau_k} c_{ik}(t, t + \Delta t) & \text{for } i \geqslant N. \end{cases} \tag{13.7}$$

In a Monte Carlo framework, we would now construct Δt-forward yield curves by drawing many independent m-dimensional normal variate vectors z and applying them to equation (13.2). In order to build a tree for the pricing of derivatives that require the comparison between expectation and intrinsic value such as Bermudan swaptions, we now wish to use the minimal number of such vectors necessary. In order to see how to construct variate vector sets $\{z\}$ for any given m, it is conducive to state clearly the requirements on the elements of the matrix $S \in \mathbb{R}^{m' \times m}$ whose rows comprise the vectors z to be used for each realisation of the evolved yield curve as given by equation (13.2). Assuming that we wish to assign equal probability to each of the m' realisations, we thus have[1]:

$$\sum_{i=1}^{m'} s_{ij} = 0 \quad \text{(mean)} \tag{13.8}$$

$$\frac{1}{m'} \sum_{i=1}^{m'} s_{ij} s_{ik} = \delta_{jk} \quad \text{(covariance)} \tag{13.9}$$

$$\sum_{j=1}^{m} s_{ij} s_{kj} = \begin{cases} m & \text{for } i = k \\ -1 & \text{for } i \neq k \end{cases} \quad \text{(equal probability).} \tag{13.10}$$

The smallest m' for which it is possible to construct S satisfying the above equation is $m + 1$. In other words, for an m-factor tree model, we need a minimum of $m + 1$ branches out of each node. For any discrete set $\{z\}$ satisfying the above conditions (13.8) to (13.10), it can be shown that the Δt-step evolution equation (13.2) produces a set of evolved forward rates that is accurate up to order $\mathcal{O}\left((\sigma\sqrt{\Delta t})^3\right)$ (inclusive) both in the expected value and in variance.

In the case of a one-factor model, we can simply use the set $\{z\} = \{+1, -1\}$ and thus construct a non-recombining binomial tree. In this case, we can change equation (13.2) to

$$f_i(t + \Delta t) = f_i \cdot e^{\bar{\mu}_i(t,t+\Delta t)\Delta t - \frac{1}{2}c_{ii} + \frac{1}{12}c_{ii}^2 - \frac{1}{45}c_{ii}^3 + \frac{17}{2520}c_{ii}^4 + \sum_{j=1}^{m} a_{ij} z_j} \tag{13.11}$$

which corrects the expected value up to order $\mathcal{O}\left((\sigma\sqrt{\Delta t})^9\right)$ (inclusive) and reduce the coefficient in front of the order $\mathcal{O}\left((\sigma\sqrt{\Delta t})^4\right)$ for the variance from $-5/6$ to $-2/3$. For a trinomial setup with $\{z\} = \left\{+\sqrt{\frac{3}{2}}, 0, -\sqrt{\frac{3}{2}}\right\}$, the terms that correct the expectation up to $\mathcal{O}\left((\sigma\sqrt{\Delta t})^9\right)$ (inclusive) are given by

$$f_i(t + \Delta t) = f_i \cdot e^{\bar{\mu}_i(t,t+\Delta t)\Delta t - \frac{1}{2}c_{ii} + \frac{1}{16}c_{ii}^2 - \frac{13}{960}c_{ii}^3 + \frac{123}{35840}c_{ii}^4 + \sum_{j=1}^{m} a_{ij} z_j} . \tag{13.12}$$

Note that the coefficients of the corrective terms are smaller in the trinomial case, which is as one would expect from the fact that no corrections are required in the limit of infinitely many branches out of each node (provided that, at least asymptotically, we match more moments as we add more branches). In practice, though, there is very little difference in the convergence behaviour when replacing equation (13.2) with equation (13.11) for a binomial scheme or (13.12) in the trinomial case. This indicates that other factors such as the coarse sampling of the payoff horizon dominate the convergence behaviour.

The elements of the matrix S defined by equations (13.8) to (13.10) describe the Cartesian coordinates of a perfect simplex in m dimensions. Equation (13.10) can best be

---

[1]This set of equations is not strictly independent. Stating all of them, however, aids the clarification of the simplex concept.

understood by the geometrical interpretation that in order to define equally probable tree branches, all the angles in the simplex must be equal (which makes it a perfect simplex). Note that we have made no statements about the alignment of this simplex in our coordinate system yet.

13.3   OPTIMAL SIMPLEX ALIGNMENT

Given a Cartesian coordinate system, we can write the coordinates of the corner points defining a perfect simplex in m dimensions as

$$
s_{ij}^{(m)} = \begin{cases} -\sqrt{\frac{m+1}{(j+1)j}} & \text{for} \quad j \geqslant i, \\ \sqrt{\frac{(m+1)j}{j+1}} & \text{for} \quad j = i-1, \\ 0 & \text{for} \quad j < i-1. \end{cases}
\tag{13.13}
$$

Examples:

$$
S^{(1)} = \begin{pmatrix} -1 \\ 1 \end{pmatrix}
\tag{13.14}
$$

$$
S^{(2)} = \begin{pmatrix} -\sqrt{\frac{3}{2}} & -\sqrt{\frac{1}{2}} \\ \sqrt{\frac{3}{2}} & -\sqrt{\frac{1}{2}} \\ 0 & \sqrt{2} \end{pmatrix}
\tag{13.15}
$$

$$
S^{(3)} = \begin{pmatrix} -\sqrt{2} & -\sqrt{\frac{2}{3}} & -\sqrt{\frac{1}{3}} \\ \sqrt{2} & -\sqrt{\frac{2}{3}} & -\sqrt{\frac{1}{3}} \\ 0 & \sqrt{\frac{8}{3}} & -\sqrt{\frac{1}{3}} \\ 0 & 0 & \sqrt{3} \end{pmatrix}
\tag{13.16}
$$

$$
S^{(4)} = \begin{pmatrix} -\sqrt{\frac{5}{2}} & -\sqrt{\frac{5}{6}} & -\sqrt{\frac{5}{12}} & -\sqrt{\frac{1}{4}} \\ \sqrt{\frac{5}{2}} & -\sqrt{\frac{5}{6}} & -\sqrt{\frac{5}{12}} & -\sqrt{\frac{1}{4}} \\ 0 & \sqrt{\frac{10}{3}} & -\sqrt{\frac{5}{12}} & -\sqrt{\frac{1}{4}} \\ 0 & 0 & \sqrt{\frac{15}{4}} & -\sqrt{\frac{1}{4}} \\ 0 & 0 & 0 & \sqrt{4} \end{pmatrix}.
\tag{13.17}
$$

Using the definition of S, we can now specify a branch coefficient matrix B as

$$
B = A \cdot S^{\top}.
\tag{13.18}
$$

The tree construction algorithm is thus as follows. At each node with its associated yield curve given by the set of n forward rates $\{f_i(t)\}$, construct a set of $n(m+1)$ forward rates to represent all possible evolutions over a time interval Δt according to

$$f_{ik}(t + \Delta t) = f_i(t) \cdot e^{\bar{\mu}_i(t)\Delta t - \frac{1}{2}c_{ii}(t) + b_{ik}(t)} \quad i = 1, \ldots, n, \quad k = 1, \ldots, m + 1.$$
(13.19)

There may be situations when we would like to have more than $m + 1$ branches. An example is the pricing of a path-dependent derivative on a single FRA. In this case, we only need one factor, i.e. $m = 1$, and thus only two branches out of each node, but we might want to construct a non-recombining trinomial tree because of the inherently higher convergence rate and stability in comparison to the binomial tree. Examples are not only standard payoff derivatives like a caplet but also barrier options, trigger derivatives, etc. This can be achieved very easily in the above framework by using only the first m columns of the matrix describing a perfect simplex in $(N_{\text{branches}} - 1)$ dimensions instead of S in equation (13.18), i.e.

$$S^{(m, N_{\text{branches}})} = S^{(N_{\text{branches}} - 1)} \cdot \begin{pmatrix} \mathbf{1}_m \\ \mathbf{0}_{(N_{\text{branches}} - 1 - m) \times m} \end{pmatrix}$$
(13.20)

with

$$\mathbf{1}_m \in \mathbb{R}^{m \times m}$$

being the m-dimensional identity matrix, and

$$\mathbf{0}_{(N_{\text{branches}} - 1 - m) \times m} \in \mathbb{R}^{(N_{\text{branches}} - 1 - m) \times m}$$

being a matrix whose elements are all zero.

In general, there are no limitations to how many branches one may use out of each node. In fact, many recombining tree-like methods or PDE solvers use effectively[2] more than three nodes for improved convergence. Examples include fast convolution methods such as the ones using Fourier [CM99] or Laplace transformations [FMW98], but also the willow tree method [Cur96]. However, using the simplex coordinates as given by equation (13.13) will quickly result in redundant, i.e. identical branch coefficients. For instance, if we were to choose a four-branch construction for a single factor model, we would probably want the four branches to end in four different realisations of the evolved forward rate. As we can see in equation (13.16), however, two of the branch coefficients in the first column are identical, namely 0. In fact, if we look at the branch coefficients of the first modes in the higher dimensional simplices, i.e. the entries in the first columns of the $S^{(\cdot)}$ matrices, we realise that there are never more than three different values. In geometrical terms, this is a consequence of our particular choice of alignment of the simplex as specified by equation (13.13). In order to obtain the maximum benefit out of the additional effort in using more branches, we may want them to spread as much and as evenly as possible. In each column, we may wish to have the entries to be symmetrically distributed around zero, to whatever extent this can be achieved. It turns out, for any m-dimensional perfect simplex, that it is possible to find a rotation $R^{(m)}$ of the simplex $S \xrightarrow{R^{(m)}} S'$ such that

$$s'^{(m)}_{ij} = -s'^{(m)}_{m+2-ij} \quad \text{for } m \text{ even and } j = 1, \ldots, m/2,$$

$$s'^{(m)}_{ij} = -s'^{(m)}_{m+2-ij} \quad \text{for } m \text{ odd and } j = 1, \ldots, (m + 1)/2.$$
(13.21)

---

[2]In a general sense, even implicit finite differencing methods can be seen as a technique to use many nodes at a future time slice to infer the values at an earlier time slice.

Figure 13.1 The placement of (z_1, z_2) nodes with (bottom) and without (top) the use of the *alternating simplex direction* method. In this example, three branches emanate out of each node in each step to account for two stochastic factors. In the top row, the three new nodes that are centred around each of the previous nodes always form an upwards pointing triangle. In the bottom row, the triangle formed by the three new nodes (shown as crosses) in step 1 (leftmost diagram) points upwards. In the second step, the three new nodes around each cross form a downwards pointing triangle. Next, the triangles formed by the new nodes (hollow squares) around the previous nodes all point upwards. Finally, in the rightmost figure of the bottom row, each triangle formed by filled squares around a hollow square can be seen to point downwards, again. Note the effectively increased symmetry when the simplex direction is alternated in each step

An appropriate rotation for the m-dimensional simplex can be found by specifying a rotation matrix

$$R^{(m)} = \prod_{\substack{k=1 \\ l=k+1}}^{\substack{l=m \\ k=m-1}} R_{kl}^{(m)}(\theta_{kl}) \tag{13.22}$$

with $R_{kl}^{(m)}(\theta_{kl}) \in \mathbb{R}^{m \times m}$ being the rotation matrix in the (k, l) plane by an angle θ_{kl}, i.e. $R_{kl}^{(m)}(\theta_{kl})$ is equal to the m-dimensional identity matrix apart from the elements $r_{kk}^{(m)} = r_{ll}^{(m)} = \cos \theta_{kl}$ and $r_{kl}^{(m)} = -r_{lk}^{(m)} = \sin \theta_{kl}$. The rotated simplex is then given by

$$S' = S \cdot R^{(m)}. \tag{13.23}$$

Allowing all of the $m(m - 1)/2$ angles to vary, a simple iterative fitting procedure then very quickly finds a suitable rotation to minimise the χ^2-error in the conditions given by equation (13.21). To give a specific example, one alignment of the simplex for $m = 4$ that satisfies equation (13.21) is given by

$$S^{(4)} = \begin{pmatrix} -1.5811 & -0.91287 & -0.6455 & -0.5 \\ 1.5811 & -0.91287 & -0.6455 & -0.5 \\ 0 & 1.8257 & -0.6455 & -0.5 \\ 0 & 0 & 1.9365 & -0.5 \\ 0 & 0 & 0 & 2 \end{pmatrix} \xrightarrow{R^{(m)}} S'^{(4)} = \begin{pmatrix} -1.1306 & -1.1053 & 0 & 1.22474 \\ 1.1053 & -1.1306 & 0.91287 & -0.8165 \\ 0 & 0 & -1.8257 & -0.8165 \\ -1.1053 & 1.1306 & 0.91287 & -0.8165 \\ 1.1306 & 1.1053 & 0 & 1.22474 \end{pmatrix}.$$
$$\tag{13.24}$$

Once we have identified a suitable alignment of the simplex, there is yet another easy method to improve the convergence behaviour of the non-recombining multinomial tree method. This technique is called *alternating simplex direction* and entails simply switching the signs of all the simplex coordinates in every step. How this improves convergence by increasing the overall symmetry of the procedure can be seen if we visualise the points generated by subsequent branching in the (z_1, z_2) plane for a two-factor, three-branch model. This is shown in Figure 13.1. Since we are merely adding up the coordinates of subsequent steps, the branching evolution appears to recombine. The moment we actually use the state-dependent drift terms in a forward rate-based yield curve model as in equation (13.19), this will no longer be the case. However, as we will find justified later, it is not unreasonable to expect that the added near-symmetry, in general, improves convergence.

13.4   IMPLEMENTATION

It is worth noting that neither the variance coefficients c_{ii} nor the branch evolution coefficients b_{ik} in equation (13.19) depend on the current yield curve given by the $f_i(t)$. Therefore, they can be precalculated for all time steps. The only thing that needs to be calculated immediately prior to looping through all of the branches is the current set of drift terms $\{\bar{\mu}_i\}$. These, in turn, are the same for all branches out of each node. Taking all of the above considerations into account, we see that the non-recombining tree calculation can be implemented extremely efficiently using a recursive method, since none of the

```
double BushyNFactorFraBGMTree::Recurse(unsigned long h){
  if (h==NSteps)
    return Intrinsic(h); // Termination of the recursion.
  unsigned long i,k;
  for (i=0;i<NRates;i++){ //      Calculate the drift for all rates and store them.
    mu_dT[i] = 0.;
    for (k=NumeraireIndex;k<=i;k++)
      mu_dT[i] += C[h][i][k] * EvolvedFra[h][k] * Tau[k] / ( 1. + EvolvedFra[h][k] * Tau[k] );
    for (k=i+1;k<NumeraireIndex;k++)
      mu_dT[i] -= C[h][i][k] * EvolvedFra[h][k] * Tau[k] / ( 1. + EvolvedFra[h][k] * Tau[k] );
  }
  double tmp=0;
  for (k=0;k<NBranches;k++){ // Loop over all branches.
    for (i=0;i<NRates;i++){
      EvolvedFra[h+1][i] = EvolvedFra[h][i] * exp( mu_dT[i] + LogShiftOfBranch[h][k][i] );
    }
    tmp += Recurse(h+1); // Sum up the results from all of the branches.
  }
  // Average, unless the intrinsic value is higher.
  return CheckForEarlyExercise(h,tmp/NBranches);
}
```

Code Example 13.1   The recursive implementation of the non-recombining tree

evolved yield curves need to be reused after all branches out of any one node have been evaluated. The only storage we need to allocate is a full set of $\{\bar{\mu}_i\}$ for each time step, a full yield curve specifying FRA set $\{f_i\}$ for each time step, and of course the c_{ii} and b_{ik} for each time step. In the code snippet shown in Code Example 13.1, the array element `LogShiftOfBranch[h] [k] [i]` contains $-\frac{1}{2}c_{ii} + b_{ik}$ for the time step from t_h to t_{h+1}, the array element `C[h] [i] [k]` holds the associated covariance matrix entry c_{ik} for the time step, and all the other variable names should be self-explanatory. After the initial setting up, a call to the function `BushyNFactorFraBGMTree::Recurse(0)` returns with the expected value as given by the payoff specified in the function `Bushy-NFactorFraBGMTree::Intrinsic()`, taking into account possible early exercises. The return value of the `BushyNFactorFraBGMTree::Recurse(0)` call still has to be discounted by multiplying with the present value of the zero-coupon bond chosen as numéraire.

13.5   CONVERGENCE PERFORMANCE

In order to give the reader a feeling for the effectiveness of the methods suggested in the previous sections, I carried out a set of numerical calculations for a four-year payer's option on a two-year semi-annual European swaption. I used the yield curve and caplet implied volatilities for GBP interest rates as tabulated in Table 13.1, and assumed an instantaneous volatility of the individual forward rates as in[3]

$$\sigma_i(t) = [a + b(t_i - t)]\,\mathrm{e}^{-c(t_i-t)} + d \tag{13.25}$$

with $a = -2\%$, $b = 0.5$, $c = 1$ and $d = 10\%$, which is consistent with the given caplet implied volatilities. The correlation between forward rates f_i and f_j as given by ϱ_{ij} in

---

[3]Cf. [Reb99], eqn (11.4).

Table 13.1 The yield curve for GBP interest rates and the caplet implied volatilities used in the examples

i	t_i	Discount factor	f_i	$\hat{\sigma}_i = \sqrt{\int_{t'=0}^{t_i} \sigma_i(t')^2 \, dt'/t_i}$
0	4	0.762757096	6.652%	21.43%
1	4.5	0.739640975	6.251%	20.67%
2	5	0.717225412	6.044%	19.98%
3	5.5	0.696187117	6.044%	19.35%
4	6	0.675765937		

equations (12.2) and (13.3) was assumed to be

$$\varrho_{ij} = e^{-\beta|t_i - t_j|} \tag{13.26}$$

with $\beta = 0.1$. The strike for the swaption was set at 7.50%. Since the forward swap rate results in 6.15% for this particular yield curve, the option under consideration is out-of-the-money. I also calculated the results for the equivalent Bermudan contract, i.e. a 6-non-call-4 semi-annual Bermudan swaption. In Figure 13.2, I show how the non-recombining tree model converges as a function of the number of steps to maturity for the pricing of European swaptions and, more interestingly, in Figure 13.3 the convergence behaviour for Bermudan swaptions is shown. Note how the ASD method improves convergence most for two or three factors, and how the optimal alignment technique ensures convergence consistently for as little as five steps for three or more factors, especially when used in conjunction with the ASD method.

13.6 VARIANCE MATCHING

Given an enumeration $t_1, \ldots, t_{N_{\text{steps}}}$ of the discrete points in time over which the tree algorithm is constructed, and defining γ_{hi} to represent all drift and Itô terms over the time step $t_h \to t_{h+1}$, i.e. $\gamma_{hi} := e^{\bar{\mu}_i(t_h)(t_{h+1}-t_h) - \frac{1}{2}c_{ii}(t_h)}$, we can rewrite equation (13.19) as

$$f_{(h+1)ik} = f_{hi} \, \gamma_{hi} \, e^{b_{hik}}. \tag{13.27}$$

Let us now recall that the coefficients b_{hik} were constructed such that their discrete average over all emerging branches is zero and their discrete covariances equal the elements of the given covariance matrix of the logarithms of the forward rates over the specified time step. Alas, matching the discrete covariances of logarithms means that the covariances of the forward rates themselves are not exactly matched due to the convexity of the exponential function, as is known from Jensen's inequality. However, the variance of any random variate x with a continuous lognormal distribution such as

$$x = \xi e^{\omega z} \quad \text{with } z \sim \mathcal{N}(0, 1) \tag{13.28}$$

can be calculated as

$$V[x] = \xi^2 e^{\omega^2}(e^{\omega^2} - 1). \tag{13.29}$$

In other words, if we wish to construct the tree such that the variances of the forward rates themselves have the correct value, as would result from the continuous description,

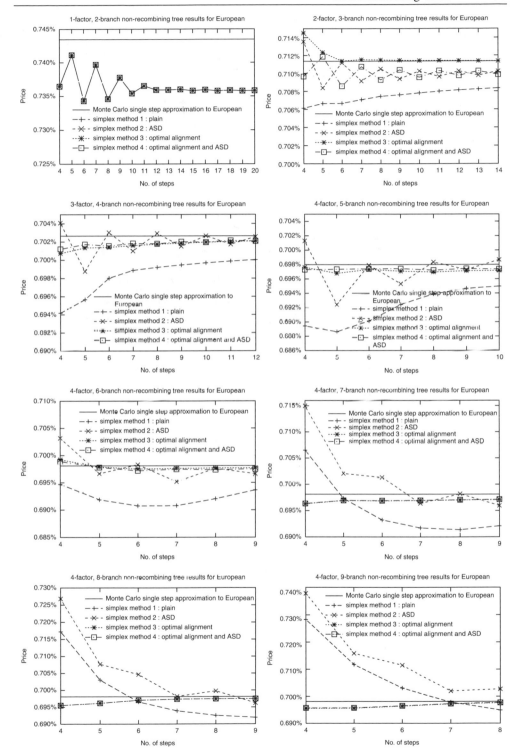

Figure 13.2   The convergence behaviour of the non-recombining tree for European swaptions

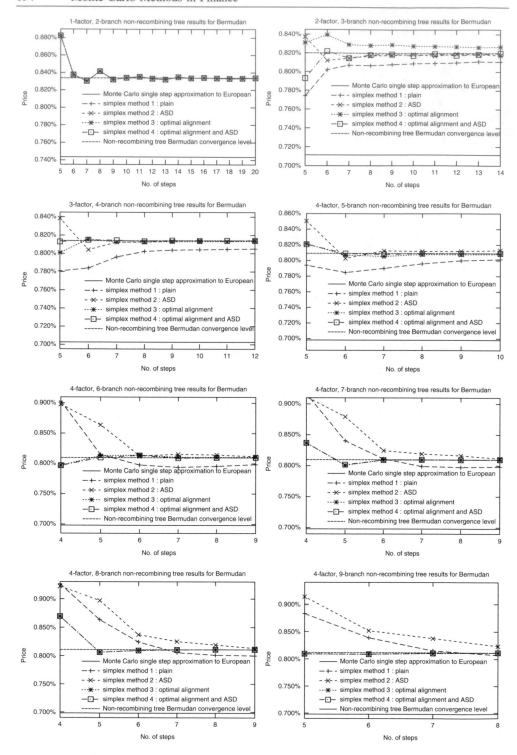

Figure 13.3   The convergence behaviour of the non-recombining tree for Bermudan swaptions

we can introduce a volatility scale parameter p_{hi} to be used in the branch construction as in

$$f_{(h+1)ik} = f_{hi}\,\gamma_{hi}\,e^{p_{hi}b_{hik}} \tag{13.30}$$

such that

$$\frac{1}{N_{\text{branches}}}\left[\sum_{k=1}^{N_{\text{branches}}} e^{2p_{hi}b_{hik}} - \frac{1}{N_{\text{branches}}}\left(\sum_{k=1}^{N_{\text{branches}}} e^{p_{hi}b_{hik}}\right)^2\right] - e^{c_{hii}}\left(e^{c_{hii}} - 1\right) = 0. \tag{13.31}$$

In order to meet this non-linear condition for p_{hi}, define $\phi_{hi}(p_{hi})$ as the left-hand side of equation (13.31). Given the initial guess of $p_{hi}^{(0)} = 1$ and the partial derivative

$$\frac{\partial\phi_{hi}(p_{hi})}{\partial p_{hi}} = \frac{1}{N_{\text{branches}}}\left[\sum_{k=1}^{N_{\text{branches}}} 2b_{hik}e^{2p_{hi}b_{hik}} - \frac{2}{N_{\text{branches}}}\left(\sum_{k=1}^{N_{\text{branches}}} e^{p_{hi}b_{hik}}\right)\left(\sum_{k=1}^{N_{\text{branches}}} b_{hik}e^{p_{hi}b_{hik}}\right)\right] \tag{13.32}$$

a Newton iteration converges to the solutions of $\phi_{hi}(p_{hi}) = 0$ very fast indeed. The non-linear root solving has to be done for each forward rate and for each time step separately. This can be done during the start-up period of the tree algorithm, though, and in my tests took no measurable computing time whatsoever[4].

The above procedure does indeed result in an exact match of the variances as given by the continuous description. I would like to remark at this point that this may not be generally desirable, though. To see this, let us consider a call option of a quantity with a standard normal distribution, and let us ignore discounting effects. For a strike of zero, the value of the option is

$$\int_0^\infty s\,\frac{e^{-\frac{1}{2}s^2}}{\sqrt{2\pi}}\,ds = \frac{1}{\sqrt{2\pi}}. \tag{13.33}$$

A single step binomial tree discretisation of this distribution that matches both the expectation and the variance of the continuous counterpart exactly is the set $\{+1, -1\}$ of equiprobable values for s. Clearly, the latter results in an option of 0.5 while the continuous description gives us a value around 0.3989. We therefore expect that products with some kind of convexity in the payoff profile will be slightly overvalued by the discretised tree when continuous variances are matched. Therefore, comparing the values as they result from the variance matched tree construction (13.30) and the original scheme (13.19) could provide some comfort about the possible mispricing due to the approximate volatility representation in the discretised scheme. In general, we would only expect the variance matched construction to provide faster convergence for directly volatility-related products such as variance or volatility swaps.

13.7   EXACT MARTINGALE CONDITIONING

In the recursion procedure of calculating all yield curve branches emanating out of one yield curve node, we always need to calculate the discrete time step drift approximation for each forward rate. As we know from section 13.2, the stepwise constant drift

---

[4]The granularity of the computation time measuring function was approximately $\frac{1}{100}$ s.

approximation (13.7) guarantees the martingale conditions that the expected value of any asset divided by the chosen numéraire asset equals its initial value only in the limit of small time steps. Choosing the numéraire to be the longest involved zero-coupon bond, i.e. $N := n$ such that the payment time of the chosen zero-coupon bond numéraire asset is the payment time of the last forward rate that is to be modelled, it is possible to meet the martingale conditions in each step exactly without any computational overhead. This can be seen as follows. For $N = n$, the martingale conditions are that for any time step $t_h \rightarrow t_{h+1}$ we have

$$E\left[f_{(h+1)i} \prod_{j=i+1}^{N-1} \left(1 + \tau_j f_{(h+1)j}\right) \right] = f_{hi} \prod_{j=i+1}^{N-1} \left(1 + \tau_j f_{hj}\right). \qquad (13.34)$$

Following equations (13.19) and (13.30), I denote the realisation of forward rate f_i on the k-th branch at time t_{h+1}, i.e. the k-th possible evolution of f_i in the time step $t_h \rightarrow t_{h+1}$ as f_{hik} and factorise it according to

$$f_{(h+1)ik} = \gamma_{hi} e^{p_{hi} b_{hik}} f_{hi}. \qquad (13.35)$$

Hereby, f_{hi} is the realisation of f_i at time t_h, i.e. at the current node. By virtue of equation (13.34), we can calculate the expectation correcting factors γ_{hi} recursively starting with the last forward rate at $i = n - 1$:

$$\gamma_{hi} = \frac{N_{\text{branches}} \prod\limits_{j=i+1}^{N-1} \left(1 + \tau_j f_{hj}\right)}{\sum\limits_{k=1}^{N_{\text{branches}}} e^{p_{hi} b_{hik}} \prod\limits_{j=i+1}^{N-1} \left(1 + \tau_j f_{hj} \gamma_{hj} e^{p_{hj} b_{hjk}}\right)}. \qquad (13.36)$$

Note that whilst we have γ_{hi} on the left hand side, the right hand side only involves γ_{hj} for $j > i$. Clearly, it makes sense to precalculate the branching coefficients $\eta_{hjk} := e^{p_{hj} b_{hjk}}$ and store them[5]. The above described algorithm now exactly meets all martingale conditions. A side-effect of this procedure is that it obviates the evaluation of any exp ( ) function calls in the recursion procedure. For simple products, it can easily be about half the actual computing time that is spent in the evaluation of this particular function[6]. As the above expectation correction (13.36) calculation does not require significantly many more floating point operations than the drift approximation (13.7), it is thus not surprising that the procedure presented in this section not only makes all calculations, even those with very few steps, meet the martingale conditions *exactly*, but also provides a speed-up by factors ranging from 1.7 to 2.8 for the tests that I conducted, depending on product type, maturity, length of the modelled yield curve, etc.

13.8   CLUSTERING

For most major interest rate markets, as a consequence of the prevailing rates and volatilities, the drift terms in equation (12.8) are comparatively small. This means that any one

---

[5]For calculations without variance matching, the scaling coefficients p_{hj} are, of course, all identically 1.

[6]My benchmark tests on an i686 architecture indicate that the time taken for a single evaluation of exp ( ) is in the range of 100 to 200 floating point multiplications. Even though, as discussed in section 14.6, for newer processor models this speed ratio is less, substantial speed-ups can still be achieved if a single multiplication can be carried out instead of an evaluation of exp ( ).

interest rate undergoing first an upwards and then a downwards move in two subsequent steps through the tree appears to almost recombine at its initial level. Choosing any two forward rates on the yield curve for a two-dimensional projection on a given time slice, this produces the effect of *clustering*. This phenomenon is widely known and various methods to avoid it have been discussed in publications. McCarthy and Webber [MW99] and Radhakrishnan [Rad98a] discuss the question of the clustering of nodes and suggest methods to overcome it, such as varying the step size, for instance in a linearly increasing or decreasing fashion, or changing both the length of some of the branches and their associated probabilities. For realistic applications, however, one tends to use a noticeably time-varying term structure of volatility which effectively changes the width of the branches over different time steps sufficiently to remove most of the harmful effect of clustering, and therefore I don't consider this issue of major importance. Still, since an actual demonstration is often more convincing than an off-hand reasoning, I display in this section how much the clustering effect is automatically suppressed simply by the choice of an appropriate term structure of volatility.

An example of the clustering effect is given in Figure 13.4. Each point in the figure represents an evolved yield curve two years into the future. The 12-month Libor rate resetting at year 2 is along the abscissa, whilst the 12-month Libor rate resetting at year 3 is given by the ordinate. In total, four annual forward rates were included in the modelling of the yield curve for a 6-non-call-2 annual Bermudan swaption. Using four factors and six steps until $t = 2$, there were five branches out of each node in the tree and a total of $5^6 = 15\,625$ evolved yield curves in that time slice. The initial yield curve was set at

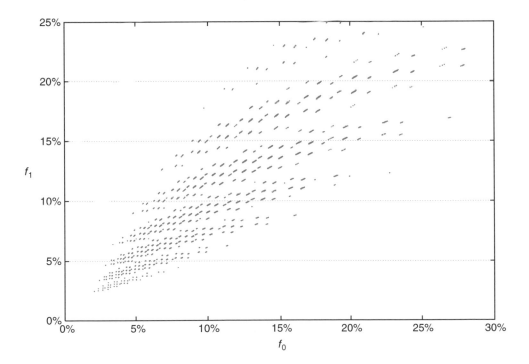

Figure 13.4   The clustering effect for flat volatilities

$f_i = 10\%$ for all i, and the instantaneous volatility was assumed to be 30% flat for all forward rates. As can be seen, there are only a comparatively small number of significantly different (f_0, f_1) pairs that are realised in the non-recombining tree. For the sake of brevity, I don't show any of the other projections, but the reader may rest assured that the effect is just as pronounced for the remaining forward rates on the modelled yield curve.

However, if we use a more market-realistic shape for the term structure of volatility, such as

$$\sigma_i(t) = k_i \left([a + b(t_i - t)] e^{-c(t_i - t)} + d \right) \tag{13.37}$$

with $a = -10\%$, $b = 1$, $c = 1.5$, $d = 10\%$ and:

i	k_i
0	1.179013859
1	1.319725423
2	1.458673516
3	1.57970272

(the k_i ensure that all caplets still have the same implied volatility of 30% as before), we obtain a very different diagram for the f_0–f_1 projection at $t = 2$ as can be seen in Figure 13.5. Therefore, for realistic applications, I don't envisage the clustering phenomenon to be an issue of foremost importance.

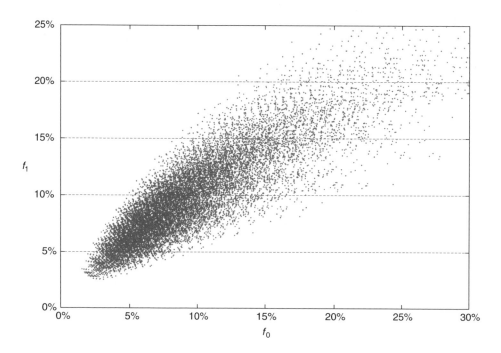

Figure 13.5   The clustering effect disappears for non-flat volatilities

13.9   A SIMPLE EXAMPLE

Starting from a flat yield curve of annual forward rates that are all equal to 6.18365% (which corresponds to a constant continuously compounded interest rate of 6%), and given that we assume the covariance matrix of the forward rates to be determined by equations (13.3), (13.25) and (13.26), I will now evolve the yield curve according to $a = -2\%$, $b = 0.125$, $c = 1$, $d = 20\%$ and $\beta = 0.1$. In Figure 13.6, the evolution of the interest rates between year 2 from now and year 10 from now is shown, as they evolve by two one-year steps into the future, whereby a five-branch non-recombining evolution was carried out in each step using the simplex described by equation (13.24). In Figure 13.7,

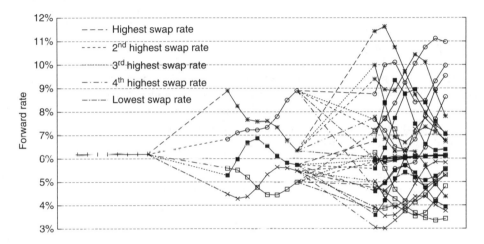

Figure 13.6 The evolution of a flat yield curve over two one-year steps in a four-factor model. In this case, out of each forward yield curve, there are five evolved yield curves indicated by the connecting branches. The branches are labelled by the order of the associated (forward) swap rate over the full yield curve to which the evolution out of the respective yield curve leads.

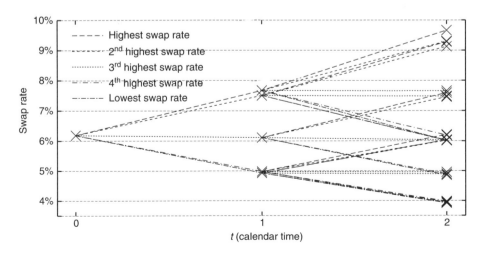

Figure 13.7 The swap rates associated with the yield curves in Figure 13.6.

I then show the associated swap rates resulting from each of the yield curves consisting of eight annual forward rates.

13.10   SUMMARY

I have demonstrated how comparatively simple geometrical considerations can aid the construction of the branches of a non-recombining multi-factor tree model. The results show that particularly when several factors are desirable, the use of the ASD method in conjunction with optimal simplex alignment provides substantial benefits. In this case, the model easily converges with five fewer steps than are needed in a plain branch construction approach. Since the computing time grows exponentially at least proportionally to $(N_{\text{factors}} + 1)^{N_{\text{steps}}}$, this means a speed-up of, for instance, a factor of 3125 when four factors are required, five branches are used, and five fewer steps are needed due to the use of optimal alignment + ASD.

In addition to the detailed explanations of a constructive algorithm for multi-factor non-recombining trees, we also showed how the effective variance implied by the tree model can be adjusted to meet that of the analytical continuous description. Furthermore, I presented a method that guarantees the martingale conditions to be met exactly by construction. A side-effect, or an added bonus, as it were, of the latter technique is an additional computation time-saving of around 50%.

It should be mentioned that the methods described in this chapter do not resolve the problem of the geometric explosion of the computational effort required for the pricing of contracts involving many exercise decisions and cashflows. However, using the techniques outlined above, one can calculate the values of moderately short exercise strategy-dependent contracts such as 6-non-call-2 semi-annual Bermudan swaptions using many factors and achieve a comfortable level of accuracy. In fact, using multi-threading programming techniques to which the non-recombining tree algorithm is particularly amenable, I have been able to carry out overnight runs of up to 10 steps for 10 factors on average computing hardware (dual PII at 300 MHz). This means one can now produce benchmark results against which other numerical approximations, such as exercise strategy parametrised Monte Carlo methods (see Chapter 12), can be compared. It is mainly for this purpose that the methods presented here have been developed, and for this purpose only I envisage them to be useful.

Miscellanea

Finally, there are a few additional thoughts that don't fit into any of the other chapters, and thus I present them here.

14.1 INTERPOLATION OF THE TERM STRUCTURE OF IMPLIED VOLATILITY

When we value an exotic derivative contract, we will hardly ever have market information about implied volatility for all of the relevant time horizons. As a consequence, we have to use an interpolation rule to construct paths for a Monte Carlo simulation. When practitioners require a Black-Scholes implied volatility at a point in time that is in between two maturities for which there are traded options, they frequently use linear interpolation in implied volatility over maturity. As long as all of the ordinate entries in the interpolation table are positive, this will lead to positive implied volatilities at the intermediate time horizons and thus plain vanilla option prices can be calculated. However, this alone is not sufficient to ensure that Monte Carlo paths can be constructed. In figure 14.1, I show two given term structures of volatility, together with linear interpolation in between the given points, and the monthly forward variance implied by the respective term structures and interpolation rule. Just to remind ourselves: the forward variance given by the implied volatilities $\hat{\sigma}_1$ associated with maturity T_1, and $\hat{\sigma}_2$ associated with maturity T_2, is

$$v(T_1, T_2) = \hat{\sigma}_2^2 T_2 - \hat{\sigma}_1^2 T_1. \tag{14.1}$$

The implied volatilities used to construct the linear interpolations are tabulated in table 14.1. As you can readily verify, the forward variance inbetween each of the original data points is positive and thus there should, in principle, be no problem with the construction of Monte Carlo paths. However, if you look closely at the monthly forward variance of curve #2 over the last three months of year 3 in figure 14.1, you may notice that the forward variance dips below zero and thus we'd need imaginary forward volatility! Of course, you may attribute this problem to the particularly steep (albeit not unrealistic) term structure of implied volatility. In practice, though, we sometimes need to deal with such steep term structures of implied volatility, and therefore we have to be able to handle them.

The cause of the problem lies with the choice of the interpolation method. Whilst being conceptually simple and easy to use, linear interpolation in implied volatility can, sadly, give rise to periods of negative forward variance even though the original data points are perfectly self-consistent. The problem will not occur if instead of interpolating directly in implied volatility, we tabulate the *cumulative variance* $v(0, T)$ as a function of T and choose a monotonicity preserving interpolation method. The simplest such interpolation method is, of course, linear interpolation, but other methods such as monotonicity preserving cubic interpolation [Kva00] can also be implemented easily. Figures 14.2 and 14.3 are examples for this. As you can see, both of these interpolation methods avoid the problem of negative forward variance. Linear interpolation in cumulative variance,

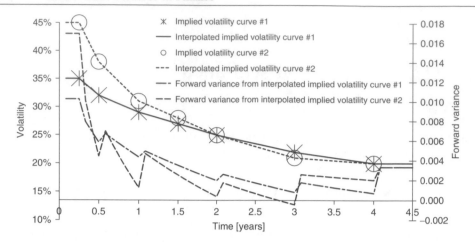

Figure 14.1 Two term structures of implied volatility and their monthly forward variance determined by the use of linear interpolation in implied volatility.

Table 14.1 The implied volatilities used for the interpolation in figure 14.1.

T	curve #1	curve #2
0.25	35%	45%
0.5	32%	38%
1	29%	31%
1.5	27%	28%
2	25%	25%
3	22%	21%
4	20%	20%

as one would expect, results in piecewise constant interpolation in instantaneous forward variance, and thus in piecewise constant interpolation in instantaneous volatility. It may be arguable if this is the ideal choice of interpolation since the sudden very abrupt changes in instantaneous volatility, whilst being as risk-neutral as any other choice, may appear rather arbitrary indeed. Monotone cubic interpolation in cumulative variance, in contrast, leads to a continuous instantaneous volatility curve, albeit at the price of some (possibly equally questionable) undulations. However, on balance, as can be seen in figure 14.4, monotone cubic interpolation in variance might deliver the best compromise between smooth forward volatility and the requirement of non-negative forward variance.

14.2   WATCH YOUR CPU USAGE

A Monte Carlo method comes to life the moment we run it on a computer. At that point, once we have devised our techniques to the best of our knowledge of the underlying maths and numerical analysis, we feel that our job is done and now the machine has to do all the work. However, it can be useful to keep an eye on the box, to see how it is doing. In other words, it may be a good idea to have some kind of information about the resources required by any one Monte Carlo simulation. Whilst keeping an eye on the

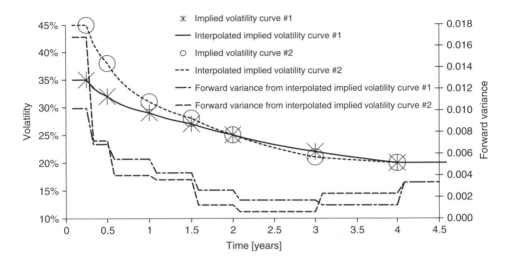

Figure 14.2 The same two term structures of implied volatility as in figure 14.1 and their monthly forward variance as resulting from linear interpolation in variance.

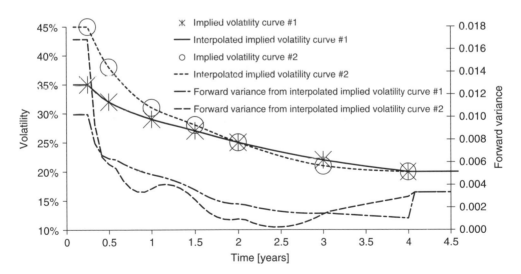

Figure 14.3 The same two term structures of implied volatility as in figure 14.1 and their monthly forward variance as resulting from monotone cubic interpolation in variance.

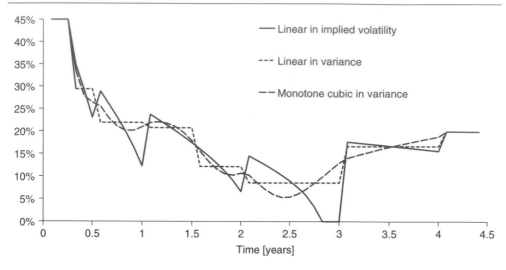

Figure 14.4 Forward volatilities for curve #2 for different interpolation types. Note that the forward volatility between 2.75 and 3 is not defined for linear interpolation in implied volatility.

memory usage in order to avoid bottlenecks caused by unnecessary swapping of memory pages at run time is only due diligence, more importantly, make sure that along with the result(s) of *every* Monte Carlo simulation you run you also get an estimate of the CPU time required for the calculation. Not only will this be a very good early warning system to indicate something went wrong after you made some changes you thought should not affect the performance, it can sometimes also show that there is a fundamental flaw with the executable code, *which may not even be your fault*. At some point in the past, for instance, it was necessary to explicitly provide a particular compile time flag to tell the Sun compiler to change the way it handled the numerical evaluation of expressions like e^{-1000}. Clearly, for the purpose of our financial Monte Carlo simulation, this number can just be rounded down to zero. By default, however, the Sun compiler produced code such that the floating point unit would at this point cause a hardware interrupt which in turn invoked an operating system handling mechanism. As a consequence, for parameter settings such that certain conditions would have an extremely low probability, the code would appear to run several times slower, even though it was carrying out the same number of arithmetical operations. Once we had identified the problem, it was easy to fix: the Sun compiler manual gave us information on how to avoid this problem. This kind of situation can give rise to tremendous amounts of frustration if you jumped through several hoops to make your Monte Carlo method converge several times faster, only to find that an equal amount of speed-up can result from a more fortuitous choice of compile time flags.

The above example is not specific to Sun compilers. Similar situations can arise on almost all hardware with various different compilers. With the newer processor models and newer, adapted, compiler versions, it is well worth experimenting a little with the compile time flags to find out what makes your code run fastest. Also, if you manage to run some kind of profiling analysis on your Monte Carlo engine and identify where most of the time is spent, remember the good old C `register` keyword. Identify the iterator or addition variables that are being used most inside the innermost loop and stick register in front of them, and compare the run time. It is not unheard of that in lucky circumstances this may lead to an up to 20% performance improvement, or at least a few percent, and just for as much work as experimenting with the register keyword for an hour. At this level of finetuning, there is no reason why the compiler's optimisation stage should be able to guess correctly which variables to provide with the most optimisation boost, simply because the compiler cannot know how many times you will be going around that innermost loop.

14.3   NUMERICAL OVERFLOW AND UNDERFLOW

For most financial modelling problems, there are combinations of parameters that can lead to numerical over- or underflow. Your best case scenario (which is bad enough) is that at this point the final result of the whole calculation is completely invalidated and you just get NaN, i.e. the IEEE floating point value indicating 'not a number'. Worse, though, is the situation when instead the computation does return with an apparently meaningful answer, only that it is very wrong, and usually very wrong indeed. It is because of these nasty little accidents that I recommend always ensuring that over- and underflow are handled correctly in your numerical routines, and mathematical functions handle extreme cases graciously. An example of this is our insisting in Chapters 7 and 9 that pseudo- and low-discrepancy number generators based on the unit interval from 0 to 1 should always ensure that they do not actually return the number 0 or 1, just to make sure that any routine using those numbers, such as the inverse cumulative normal distribution, never incurs those extreme events which would have to be mapped to $+\infty$ or $-\infty$.

This kind of numerical over- and underflow can happen in many situations, though. Most implementations for the second modified Bessel function $I_\nu(x)$, for instance, don't handle the case of large ν very well. They either end up iterating far too long, return NaN or even a seriously wrong number. This situation can be avoided by choosing a suitable threshold at which to switch over to one of the highly accurate asymptotic expansions [AS84].

14.4   A SINGLE NUMBER OR A CONVERGENCE DIAGRAM?

For many applications where the practitioner has to resort to a Monte Carlo technique, one ideally wishes to obtain a single number as *the answer*. There are many situations where, due to the embedding of the calculation engine, one can only afford to return a single number from a calculating subroutine due to application programming interface restrictions, automation of daily reports, etc. However, in most applications, and here I speak from experience, it is possible to have a slight paradigm shift with respect to the concept of 'the numerical solution to a mathematical problem'. Reality is that every single calculation comes with an inevitable inaccuracy, and in most cases we have at best some idea about the order of magnitude of the error. This is particularly true for Monte Carlo methods, ironically especially for those that utilise high performance variance reduction techniques such as low-discrepancy numbers. In my professional life it has therefore proved to be invaluable to *never just return a single number from a Monte Carlo calculation, even if accompanied by an estimate of the standard error.* When we use Excel as our user interface, it requires very little additional effort to return an entire convergence diagram in an array back into the spreadsheet, rather than just a single number. The human eye, or in other words the experience and intuition of the practitioner, can judge surprisingly well from the convergence diagram whether a Monte Carlo simulation has converged, especially for methods that appear to converge mainly from one side as low-discrepancy numbers very often do. It is, alas, wishful thinking to hope for a certain number of samples to always be sufficient for a specific type of problem given certain convergence enhancement techniques and, unfortunately, many practitioners still think this way. Very often this is realised and the Monte Carlo number is accompanied by a standard error estimate. That's fair enough for methods whose convergence enhancement is reflected in the standard error measure. The most powerful ones that are independent of problem-specific enhancements, though, are low-discrepancy numbers, and for those the standard error is typically hugely overestimating the residual error in the calculation. Since no better reliable error estimates are available for those methods, and also because the standard error only gives a probability measure of the error, it has always proved invaluable to see the convergence behaviour.

Implementation of a convergence diagram is straightforward for most Monte Carlo techniques. Instead of iterating over all of the samples to be drawn and averaging, then eventually only returning a single quotient, we calculate a running estimate at certain sampling intervals and return an array of the running estimates next to the number of samples to the calling application. In Excel or other spreadsheet programs such as Applix, the user then has the choice of either displaying and graphing the convergence diagram, or just using a single element of the return array. For standalone main( ) programs, the situation is even better. One can easily design the program such that it prints running estimates at certain intervals, and direct this output to a file. Using standard Unix and GNU utilities[1] and the gnuplot plotting program, one can even monitor live on-screen how the simulation progresses with the aid of a little shell program such as the Plot script in Code Example 14.1. To use it is quite simple: once you have started your calculation as in main --myargumentlist > outputfile &, you simply monitor it with Plot outputfile. If the data you wish to have graphed is not in column 1 and 2 but, say, in 5 and 3, you start it up like Plot -5:3 outputfile. It is, of course, possible to extend this for the display of surfaces from a live updated file and you can find a corresponding Splot script on the accompanying CD.

14.5   EMBEDDED PATH CREATION

Assuming you have a number generator class which at the time of instantiation of an object of this class accepts a covariance matrix such that the vector variates subsequently produced by the new object satisfy the given covariances, you can have the construction of paths done for you with great ease. The path construction is then done by whatever covariance matrix splitting method is used inside your vector generator class. Typically,

---

[1]The GNU family of utilities is available for many operating systems. All major Linux distributions come with it, they are available for all Unix-like systems, and for NT there is the CygWin [Cyg] set of utilities which is readily installed on an internetworked computer, although the Excel interface is certainly preferable on the Windows platform.

```
#!/bin/bash
x=1
y=2
case ''$1'' in
 -*) a=${1#-}; x=${a%%:*}; a=${a#*:}; y=${a%%:*}; shift;
esac
{
 echo ''set parametric ; set xlabel '$x' ; set ylabel '$y'''
 echo -en ''plot ''
 {
  for i; do
    echo -n '''$i' u $x:$y,''
  done
  echo
 } | sed 's/,$//'
 echo
 while : ; do
  echo 'replot'
  sleep 1
 done
} | gnuplot -geometry 900x600
```

Code Example 14.1 The Plot script for the live monitoring of a file which is the output destination of a running Monte Carlo calculation

this will be the spectral pseudo-square root method outlined in section 6.2, and consequently the path construction will implicitly be carried out using the spectral method which is optimal for low-discrepancy numbers as explained in section 10.8.2.

14.6 HOW SLOW IS exp()?

The most frequently used non-trivial mathematical operation in most financial Monte Carlo simulations is almost certainly the evaluation of the exponential function. Of course, it is always advisable to precalculate as many formulae or parts of them as we can in order to avoid their re-evaluation inside the heavily iterated inner loops of our simulation code. However, there are almost always some evaluations of the exp() function required inside the fast loops where performance matters most. The first timing experiments that I ever carried out on Pentium processors with very tightly wound Monte Carlo loops did indeed reveal that about 90% of the total run time of any Monte Carlo simulation for derivatives pricing was spent in the evaluation of exp(). Gladly, though, the calculation of the exponential function can nowadays be carried out not only faster by virtue of the increase in raw CPU clock speed, but also due to the way in which it can be computed. When the most sophisticated commodity processor[2] available was the Pentium chip, it still seemed well worth while to implement a purpose-built replacement for the system given call to exp(). The replacement could be made much faster by the use of large lookup tables and linear interpolation, whilst sacrificing no noticeable accuracy. However, as of the Pentium Pro processor, the optimised version of exp() makes use of the set of raw floating point unit (formerly known as the maths co-processor) instructions given

---

[2]In this discussion, I focus on Intel and similar ×86 processors.

Table 14.2   The instructions used on a Pentium Pro and higher for the evaluation of exp()

fldl2e	load the base-2 logarithm of e into the main calculation register
fmul qword ptr[x]	multiply the calculation register by the variable x
f2xm1	calculate $2^{(r)}-1$ where r is the current content of the calculation register and store the result in the calculation register; r must be in the range $-1,\ldots,1$
frndin	round a double to an int; needed because f2xm1 requires an argument in the range $-1,\ldots,1$
fld1	push the value 1.0 onto the calculation register stack
faddp	add the value previously pushed onto the stack to the value beneath on the stack
fscale	multiply the result by a power of two which was scaled out earlier because f2xm1 requires an argument in the range $-1,\ldots,1$

in Table 14.2. It makes use of the following basic equality:

$$e^x = \left[2^{(x\cdot\log_2 e)} - 1\right] + 1. \tag{14.2}$$

The instructions used in this optimised decomposition cannot be expected to be executed by the CPU in a single clock cycle. In fact most take more than a single cycle. The most CPU-intensive instruction among them is probably f2xm1, which can take several tens of CPU cycles, even on Pentium II processors. However, along with the ever increasing sophistication of the newer CPU models, not only does their raw clock rate increase, but they also require fewer cycles for the more complex floating point unit instructions such as f2xm1. Since the introduction of the Pentium III model, even the fastest implementation of a lookup table-based exp() replacement no longer provides any speed-up when compared with the optimised system given code for this function[3]. The total CPU time spent in the evaluation of the exponential function does indeed only comprise a few percent of an average option pricing simulation. What's more, at the time of writing, the Pentium IV model is being introduced to the marketplace. Whilst I have no timing information for this new type available yet, I am confident that in the future the exp() function will no longer be the cause of any execution bottlenecks and the Monte Carlo method will become ever more acceptable in the world of financial modelling.

Despite all the improvements in the newer processor models, it remains a matter of expedience to avoid unnecessary calculations inside the innermost loops of any Monte Carlo simulation. Even if one day the ratio of the average execution times of a floating point multiplication and an evaluation of exp() drops to a small number, maybe even three or two, by replacing the computation of the exponential function by a single multiplication, if precalculation is somehow possible, your Monte Carlo simulation could run two to three times faster if this evaluation is the main bottleneck. *Never let the continuous progress of CPU speeds and processing power be an excuse for ill-thought-out algorithm design.*

---

[3]My thanks go to Carl Seymour for providing the disassembly of the optimised exp() function on Pentium Pro (and higher) processors, and for having carried out the comparative tests with respect to the run time required.

14.7   PARALLEL COMPUTING AND MULTI-THREADING

Most financial institutions' large-scale middle- and back-office computing servers have been equipped with multi-processor technology for quite some time now, and more and more desktop computers nowadays also feature multiple central processor units, especially in the trading environment of investment banks. Sadly, in particular the desktop's multiple CPU power remains largely unused for most applications. With respect to financial calculations, this is to some extent due to the fact that many numerical methods are very difficult to adapt to parallel computing techniques. Monte Carlo (and non-recombining tree) methods, however, are particularly well amenable to parallelisation. Conceptually it clearly makes sense to start a set of *subprocesses* or *threads* to evaluate independently a subset of all individual function evaluations that constitute the Monte Carlo estimator

$$\hat{v}_N := \frac{1}{N} \sum_{i=1}^{N} f(x_i). \tag{14.3}$$

Of course, we must ensure that there are no duplicates among the vector draws x_i taken by the various subprocesses if we wish to avoid the possibility of a biased result. For pseudo-random numbers, one might think that this can be done by initialising a new number generation engine with a different seed for each subprocess. This simplistic approach is a fallacy, though. If we initialise each pseudo-random generator with a different seed, we have absolutely no knowledge about which part of the overall cycle of the number generator we end up using. A worst case scenario could be that one of the subprocesses uses almost the same sequence as another one, only with a little offset just to cause a severe bias of the Monte Carlo estimator. We therefore need to shift each of the subprocess number generators to an offset such that we are certain not to suffer any risk of overlap in the number sequence.

In contrast to pseudo-random number generators, the Sobol' sequence (and other low-discrepancy methods) is wonderfully easy to shift to an offset n of iterations by calculating the Gray code of the shift n (which is $G(n) = n \oplus_2 [n/2]$) as given in equation (8.22) and using it as the generating integer $\gamma(n) := G(n)$ in the (re-)initialisation equation (8.20) of the internal integer variables of the Sobol' sequence. This means that the shift of the Sobol' sequence generator can be done in practically no time at all, very much unlike pseudo-random number generators for which we have to loop through a total of $n \cdot d$ one-dimensional draws (with d representing the dimensionality of the vector sequence) in order to achieve an offset of n vector draws from the beginning of the sequence.

The first decision that has to be made when we multi-thread a Monte Carlo simulation is what parallelisation paradigm we are going to use. Personally, I recommend keeping it as simple as possible (KISS, right?), and going for the straightforward master–slave method. This means, our Monte Carlo evaluation engine is given a parameter m of the number of threads to use. If this number is zero, it will ignore any parallelisation issues and just carry out the simulation of N evaluations itself. For $m > 0$, it will set up an array of the number of iterations that each of the slaves has to do, and an array of shifts in the sequence of the selected number generation method. Denote the shift for the jth thread as s_j, and the number of iterations to be evaluated by this thread as n_j, with $\sum_{k=1}^{j} n_k = s_j$ and $\sum_{j=1}^{m} n_j = N$. An example of how to set up these numbers is given in

```
vector <unsigned long> IterationsToBeSkipped (NumberOfThreads),
    NumberOfIterations(NumberOfThreads);
unsigned long j, n = 0;
for(j=0; j<NumberOfThreads; ++j) {
    NumberOfIterations[j] = TotalNumberOfIterations / ( NumberOfThreads - j );
    IterationsToBeSkipped[j] = n;
    n += NumberOfIterations[j];
    TotalNumberOfIterations -= NumberOfIterations[j];
}
```

Code Example 14.2   Setting up the shift and number of iterations for each subprocess

Code Example 14.2. Given are `unsigned long NumberOfThreads` (which is the number of threads m) and `TotalNumberOfIterations` (the total number of iterations N). The code sample will then set up $n_j =$ `NumberOfIterations[ j ]` and $s_j =$ `IterationsToBeSkipped[ j ]`.

The Monte Carlo estimator is then effectively decomposed into

$$\hat{v}_N := \frac{1}{N} \sum_{j=1}^{m} \sum_{i=1}^{n_j} f(x_{s_j+i}). \tag{14.4}$$

An open question is still how many subprocesses we wish to employ. For systems that have many processors and are being shared by many applications, this is a rather difficult decision and requires a judgement call. For computers that are dedicated to this Monte Carlo simulation, we would ideally wish to use as many subprocesses as there are CPUs on the machine. For most operating systems, it is possible to enquire about this at run time. For instance, the Linux operating system provides a globally readable file `/proc/cpuinfo` whose output can be parsed for the lines beginning with '`processor        :`'. The CPUs are enumerated from 0, so we can simply take the last of those lines and add 1 to the integer following the colon. For Windows NT, we can enquire about the number of processors on the machine using the function `NumberOfCPUs` given in Code Example 14.3.

```
#include <windows.h>
unsigned long NumberOfCPUs(void) {
    SYSTEM_INFO sysInfo;
    GetSystemInfo(&sysInfo);
    return static_cast<unsigned long>(sysInfo.dwNumberOfProcessors);
}
```

Code Example 14.3   Enquiry about the number of CPUs under Windows NT

Finally, I would like to comment on the resource multiplication requirements for multi-threaded Monte Carlo simulations. Clearly, each slave needs to have a clone of the master's number generation object since all number generation methods use internal state variables that must not be shared by the slaves. It is paramount for all multi-threaded applications that no functions possibly involved in a multi-threaded task contain any `static` variables for obvious reasons. The simultaneous attempt of more than one thread to write to the same memory space will invariably lead to a hardware exception which may be intercepted by the application but will certainly invalidate the simulation's result. Unlike simultaneous writing, the attempt to simultaneously read from the same memory is perfectly tolerable by conventional symmetric multi-processing (SMP) hardware. This means that, at least in theory, all of the slave processes may be allowed to read-access variables and parameters stored in the master process's memory space. Doing so, alas, can lead to rather unexpected bottlenecks that are not easy to explain. I personally suffered from this misconception when I once implemented a multi-threaded Monte Carlo engine such that each of the slaves would carry out the copy construction of all the global objects they needed for their private write-access themselves. Since a lot of complex data had to be copied, creating a single copy of all the required objects took a noticeable fraction of a second. Asking the master process to copy all of the objects for each of the slaves prior to invoking them thus took the number of threads times that fraction of a second. Thinking that read-access leads to no problems, I designed the multi-threaded algorithm such that each thread took its own copies in parallel, in order to reduce the overhead in the copying stage. Little did I know. Suddenly, taking two complete copies of all required objects in parallel on two CPUs not only took the time it takes to copy one, but *almost 10 times as long*, thus producing an additional overhead of several seconds where I had thought I would end up with a faster start-up period. The best explanation I could come up with is that, whilst being a perfectly valid thing to do, the simultaneous read-access to the same memory area by both CPUs leads to a hardware contention that causes the SMP architecture to serialise those access requests, and execute them in turn, involving hardware interrupt handling, hardware wait locks on individual CPUs, and probably a whole load of other unpleasant hardware actions. The moral of this story is: *the master process ought to create a whole set of copies of all variables and objects required for the simulation both for write- and read-access for each individual slave process, before starting the slave processes.* Note this does not mean that two threads cannot simultaneously execute the same function at the same time: this is handled by the operating system since each CPU has a local copy of the program code loaded into its level-1 cache before executing it. Automatic variables in a function are also not subject to these considerations since they are created on the individual CPU's local stack. In other words, if you only invoke static member functions of a class, there is no need to create and copy an object of this class. However, even the call of a virtual function that does not use an object's member variables can lead to a hardware contention. After all, a virtual function call is resolved by looking up a pointer-to-a-function variable in the object's `vtable` which is effectively the same as accessing a member variable at assembler level. So, have the master copy everything before invoking the slaves to do all the hard work: *it's only fair.*

Bibliography

[AA00]   L. Andersen and J. Andreasen. Volatility skews and extensions of the Libor market model. *Applied Mathematical Finance*, 7(1), 2000.

[ABG97]   P. Acworth, M. Broadie and P. Glassermann. A comparison of some Monte Carlo and quasi Monte Carlo techniques for option pricing. In [NHLZ97], pp. 1–18.

[Ack00]   P. J. Acklam. An algorithm for computing the inverse normal cumulative distribution function. University of Oslo, Statistics Division, June 2000. http://www.math.uio.no/~jacklam/notes/invnorm.

[Alb72]   A. Albert. *Regression and the Moore–Penrose Pseudo-Inverse*. Academic Press, 1972.

[Ale98a]   C. Alexander. *Risk Management and Analysis. Volume 1: Measuring and Modeling Financial Risk*. John Wiley and Sons, 1998.

[Ale98b]   C. Alexander. *Risk Management and Analysis. Volume 2: New Markets and Products*. John Wiley and Sons, 1998.

[Amd67]   G. M. Amdahl. Validity of the single processor approach to achieving large scale computing capabilities. In *AFIPS Conference Proceedings*, Reston, VA, 1967, pp. 483–485.

[AMH78]   M. M. Ali, N. N. Mikhail and M. S. Haq. A class of bivariate distributions including the bivariate logistic. *Journal of Multivariate Analysis*, 8: 405–412, 1978.

[And00]   L. Andersen. A simple approach to the pricing of Bermudan swaptions in the multifactor LIBOR market model. *The Journal of Computational Finance*, 3(2): 5–32, Winter 1999/2000.

[AS79]   I. A. Antonov and V. M. Saleev. An economic method of computing lp-sequences. *USSR Computational Mathematics and Mathematical Physics*, 19(1): 252–256, 1979.

[AS84]   M. Abramowitz and I. A. Stegun. *Pocketbook of Mathematical Functions*. Harri Deutsch, 1984.

[AW88]   L. Afflerbach and K. Wenzel. Normal random numbers lying on spirals and clubs. *Statistische Hefte*, 29: 237–244, 1988.

[BBG97]   P. Boyle, M. Broadie and P. Glassermann. Monte Carlo methods for security pricing. *Journal of Economic Dynamics and Control*, 21(8/9): 1267–1322, 1997.

[BDT90]   F. Black, E. Derman and W. Toy. A one-factor model of interest rates and its appllication to Treasury bond options. *Financial Analysts Journal*, Jan/Feb: pages 33–39, 1990.

[Bec80]   S. Beckers. The constant elasticity of variance model and its implications for option pricing. *The Journal of Finance*, XXXV(3): 661–673, June 1980.

[BF88]   P. Bratley and B. L. Fox. Algorithm 659: implementing Sobol's quasirandom sequence generator. *ACM Transactions of Mathematical Software*, 14: 88–100, 1988.

[BFN94]   P. Bratley, B. L. Fox and H. Niederreiter. Algorithm 738: programs to generate Niederreiter's low-discrepancy sequences. *ACM Transactions of Mathematical Software*, 20(4): 494–495, December 1994.

[BFS83]   P. Bratley, B. L. Fox and E. L. Schrage. *A Guide to Simulation*. Springer, 1983.

[BG96]   M. Broadie and P. Glassermann. Estimating security price derivatives using simulation. *Management Science*, 42(2): 269–285, 1996.

[BG97a]   M. Broadie and P. Glassermann. Monte Carlo methods for pricing high-dimensional American options: an overview. *Net Exposure: The Electronic Journal of Financial Risk*, 1(3): 15–37, 1997.

[BG97b]   M. Broadie and P. Glassermann. Variance reduction techniques. In *Global Derivatives 97*, 1997.

[BG98]   M. Broadie and P. Glasserman. Monte Carlo methods in option pricing and risk management. In [Ale98a], pp. 173–208.

[BGK99]   M. Broadie, P. Glassermann and S. Kou. Connecting discrete and continuous path-dependent options. *Finance and Stochastics*, 3: 55–82, 1999.

[BGM97]   A. Brace, D. Gatarek and M. Musiela. The market model of interest rate dynamics. *Mathematical Finance*, 7: 127–155, 1997.

[BK91]   F. Black and P. Karasinski. Bond and option pricing when short rates are lognormal. *Financial Analysts Journal*, Jul/Aug: pp. 52–59, 1991.

[BM58]   G. E. P. Box and M. E. Muller. A note on the generation of random normal deviates. *Annals of Mathematical Statistics*, 29: 610–611, 1958.

[BM87]   R. M. Bookstaber and J. B. McDonald. A general distribution for describing security price returns. *Journal of Business*, 60(3): 401–424, July 1987.

[BMW92]   J. W. Barrett, G. Moore and P. Wilmott. Inelegant efficiency. *RISK Magazine*, 5(9): 82–84, 1992.

[Boy77]   P. Boyle. Options: a Monte Carlo approach. *Journal of Financial Economics*, 4: 323–338, May 1977.

[Bro48]   B. Brown. *Some Tests of the Randomness of a Million Digits*. Technical Report RAOP-44. The RAND Corporation, Santa Monica, CA, 19 October 1948.

[Bro51]   G. Brown. History of RAND's random digits—summary. In [Mon51], pp. 31–32.

[BS96]   A. N. Borodin and P. Salminen. *Handbook of Brownian Motion — Facts and Formulae*. Birkhäuser, 1996.

[CDM90]   J. D. Cummins, G. Dionne and J. B. McDonald. Application of the GB2 family of distributions in modeling insurance loss processes. *Insurance: Mathematics and Economics*, 9: 257–272, 1990.

[Chi00]   L. N. Childs. *A Concrete Introduction to Higher Algebra*. Springer, 2nd edn, 2000.

[CHS81]   S. Cambanis, S. Huang and G. Simons. On the theory of elliptically contoured distributions. *Journal of Multivariate Analysis*, 11: 368–385, 1981.

[CIR85]   J. C. Cox, J. E. Ingersoll and S. A. Ross. A theory of the term structure of interest rates. *Econometrica*, 53: 385–408, 1985.

[CM99]   P. Carr and D. B. Madan. Option valuation using the fast Fourier transform. *The Journal of Computational Finance*, 2(4): 61–73, 1999.

[Cod69]   W. J. Cody. Rational Chebyshev approximations for the error function. *Mathematics of Computation*: 631–638, 1969.

[Cox75]   J. C. Cox. Notes on option pricing I: constant elasticity of variance diffusions. Working paper, Stanford University, 1975.

[CRR79]   J. C. Cox, S. A. Ross and M. Rubinstein. Option pricing: a simplified approach. *Journal of Financial Economics*, 7: 229–263, September 1979.

[Cur94]   M. Curran. Strata gems. *RISK Magazine*, March 1994.

[Cur96]   M. Curran. Willow power. Technical report, Quantin' Leap working paper, 1996. http://www.quantinleap.com.

[Cur98]   M. Curran. Greeks in Monte Carlo. In [Dup98].

[Cyg]   Cygnus. GNU utilities for Windows. http://www.cygwin.com.

[Dev86]   L. Devroye. *Non-Uniform Random Variate Generation*. Springer, 1986.

[DKZ96]   E. Derman, I. Kani and J. Zou. The local volatility surface: unlocking the information in option prices. *Financial Analysts Journal*, Jul/Aug: 25–36, 1996.

[Dup98]   B. Dupire (ed.) *Monte Carlo: Methodologies and Applications for Pricing and Risk Management*. Risk Publications, 1998.

[ELM01]   P. Embrechts, F. Lindskog and A. McNeil. Modelling dependence with copulas and applications to risk management. Working paper, Department of Mathematics, ETH Zürich, Switzerland, 2001. http://www.risklab.ch/ftp/papers/DependenceWithCopulas.pdf.

[EM82]   D. C. Emmanuel and J. D. MacBeth. Further results on the constant elasticity of variance call option pricing model. *Journal of Financial and Quantitative Analysis*: 533–554, 1982.

[Fey48]   R. Feynman. Space–time approach to non-relativistic quantum mechanics. *Reviews of Modern Physics*, 20: 367–387, 1948.

[FFvR00] K. Fang, H. Fang and D. von Rosen. A family of bivariate distributions with non-elliptical contours. *Communications in Statistics—Theory and Methods*: 1885–1898, 2000.

[FLL+99] E. Fournié, J. M. Lasry, J. Lebuchoux, P. L. Lions and N. Touzi. Applications of Malliavin calculus to Monte Carlo methods in finance. *Finance and Stochastics*, 3(4): 391–412, 1999.

[FLLL01] E. Fournié, J. M. Lasry, J. Lebuchoux and P. L. Lions. Applications of Malliavin calculus to Monte Carlo methods in finance II. *Finance and Stochastics*, 5(2): 201–236, 2001.

[FMKL88] M. Freimer, G. S. Mudholkar, G. Kollia and C. T. Lin. A study of the generalized Tukey lambda family. *Communications in Statistics—Theory and Methods*, 17: 3547–3567, 1988. A web applet showing the distribution for different parameters can be found at http://www.ens.gu.edu.au/robertk/gld/.

[FMM77]   G. E. Forsythe, M. A. Malcolm and C. B. Moler. *Computer Methods for Mathematical Computations*. Prentice-Hall, 1977.

[FMW98]   M. C. Fu, D. B. Madan and T. Wang. Pricing continuous Asian options: a comparison of Monte Carlo and Laplace transform inversion methods. *The Journal of Computational Finance*, 2(2): 49–74, 1998.

[For51]   G. E. Forsythe. Generation and testing of random digits at the National Bureau of Standards, Los Angeles. In [Mon51], pp. 34–35.

[FV97]   E. W. Frees and E. A. Valdez. Understanding relationships using copulas. In *32nd Actuarial Research Conference*, Calgary, Alberta, Canada, 6–8 August 1997. School of Business, University of Wisconsin, Madison, WI. http://www.soa.org/library/naaj/1997-09/naaj9801_1.pdf.

[Gan92]   W. Gander. *Computermathematik*. Birkhäuser, 1992.

[GG00a]   W. Gander and W. Gautschi. Adaptive Gauss–Lobatto quadrature, 2000. http://www.inf.ethz.ch/personal/gander/adaptlob.m.

[GG00b]   W. Gander and W. Gautschi. Adaptive quadrature—revisited. *BIT*, 40(1): 84–101, March 2000. CS technical report: ftp://ftp.inf.ethz.ch/pub/publications/tech-reports/3xx/306.ps.gz.

[GH83]   J. Guckenheimer and P. Holmes. *Nonlinear Oscillations, Dynamical Systems, and Bifurcations of Vector Fields*. Volume 42 of *Applied Mathematical Sciences*. Springer, 1983.

[GK65]   G. H. Golub and W. Kahan. Calculating the singular values and pseudo-inverse of a matrix. *SIAM Journal of Numerical Analysis, Series B*, 2: pages 205–224, 1965.

[GR00]   C. Genest and L. Rivest. On the multivariate probability integral transformation. Technical report, Département de mathématiques et de statistique, Université Laval, Québec, Canada July 2000. http://www.mat.ulaval.ca/pages/genest/k.pdf.

[Gus88]   J. L. Gustafson. Re-evaluating Amdahl's Law. *Communications of the ACM*, 31(5): 532–533, May 1988.

[GZ99]   P. Glassermann and X. Zhao. Fast greeks by simulation in forward Libor models. *The Journal of Computational Finance*, 3(1): 5–39, Fall 1999.

[Ham51]   P. C. Hammer. The mid-square method of generating digits. In [Mon51], p. 33.

[Har90]   J. M. Harrison. *Brownian Motion and Stochastic Flow Systems*. Wiley/Krieger, 1985/1990.

[Hau97]   E. G. Haug. *The Complete Guide to Option Pricing Formulas*. McGraw-Hill, October 1997.

[Hes93]   S. L. Heston. A closed-form solution for options with stochastic volatility with applications to bond and currency options. *The Review of Financial Studies*, 6: 327–343, 1993.

[HJJ01]   C. Hunter, P. Jäckel and M. Joshi. Getting the drift. *RISK Magazine*, July 2001. http://www.rebonato.com/MarketModelPredictorCorrector.pdf.

[HJM92a]   D. Heath, R. Jarrow and A. Morton. Bond pricing and the term structure of interest rates. *Econometrica*, 61(1): 77–105, 1992.

[HJM92b]   D. Heath, R. Jarrow and A. Morton. Bond pricing and the term structure of interest rates: a new methodology. *Econometrica*, 60(1): 77–105, 1992.

[HL86]   T. S. Y. Ho and S.-B. Lee. Term structure movements and pricing interest rate contingent claims. *Journal of Finance*, 41, December 1986.

[HL98]   P. Hellekalek and G. Larcher (eds). *Random and Quasi-Random Point Sets*, Volume 138 of *Lecture Notes in Statistics*. Springer, 1998.

[HP81]   J. M. Harrison and S. Pliska. Martingales and stochastic integrals in the theory of continuous trading. *Stochastic Processes and their Applications*, 11: 215–260, 1981.

[Hug96]   L. Hughston (ed.). *Vasicek and Beyond*. RISK Publications, 1996.

[Hul97]   J. Hull. *Options, Futures, and Other Derivatives*. Prentice-Hall, 1989, 1993, 1997.

[HW90]   J. Hull and A. White. Pricing interest rate derivative securities. *Review of Financial Studies*, 3(4): 573–592, 1990.

[Hym83]   J. M. Hyman. Accurate monotonicity preserving cubic interpolation. *SIAM Journal on Scientific and Statistical Computing*, 4(4): 645–653, 1983.

[Jäc97]   P. Jäckel. Maple V routine for the calculation of a static table of primitive polynomials modulo 2, 1997. http://www.nr.com/contrib/.

[Jam96]   F. Jamshidian. Pricing of contingent claims in the one-factor term structure model. In [Hug96], pp. 111–127.

[Jam97]   F. Jamshidian. Libor and swap market models and measures. *Finance and Stochastics*, 1: 293–330, 1997.

[JKB94]   N. L. Johnson, S. Kotz and N. Balakrishnan. *Continuous Univariate Distributions*. Volumes I and II. John Wiley and Sons, 1994.

[Joh49]   N. L. Johnson. Systems of frequency curves generated by methods of translation. *Biometrika*, 36: 14–76, 1949. A fitting algorithm for Johnson distributions can be found in ALGORITHM AS 99 APPL. STATIST. (1976) VOL.25, P.180, http://lib.stat.cmu.edu/apstat/99.

[JP99]   X. Ju and N. Pearson. Using value-at-risk to control risk taking: how wrong can you be? *Journal of Risk*, 1(2): 5–36, Winter 1999.

[JR00]   P. Jäckel and R. Rebonato.   Linking Caplet and Swaption Volatilities in a BGM/J Framework: Approximate Solutions. Technical report, 2000. http://www.rebonato.com/capletswaption.pdf.

[JW00]   J. James and N. Webber. *Interest Rate Modelling*. Financial Engineering Series. John Wiley and Sons, May 2000.

[Kac51]   M. Kac. On some connections between probability theory and differential and integral equations. In *Proceedings of the 2nd Berkeley Symposium on Mathematics Statistics & Probability*, pp. 189–215, 1951.

[Kau01]   R. Kaufmann. Copulas as an integrated risk management tool. In *Risk 2001 Europe Conference*, 10–11 April, Paris. RiskLab, Department of Mathematics, ETH Zürich, Switzerland, 2001.

[KDM96]   Z. E. Karian, E. J. Dudewicz and P. McDonald. The extended generalized lambda distribution system for fitting distributions to data: history, completion of theory, tables, applications, the 'final word' on moment fits. *Communications in Statistics—Simulation and Computation*, 25: 611–642, 1996.

[Knu81]   D. Knuth. *The Art of Computer Programming: Seminumerical Algorithms*. Volume 2. Addison-Wesley, 1969, 1981.

[KP99]   P. E. Kloeden and E. Platen. *Numerical Solution of Stochastic Differential Equations*. Springer, 1992, 1995, 1999.

[KS]   S. Kucherenko and I. M. Sobol'.   BRODA: British–Russian Offshore Development Agency. http://www.broda.co.uk.

[KS91]   I. Karatzas and S. E. Shreve. *Brownian Motion and Stochastic Calculus*. Springer, 1991.

[Kva00]   B. Kvasov. *Methods of Shape-Preserving Spline Approximation*. World Scientific Publishing, 2000.

[L'E88]   P. L'Ecuyer. Efficient and portable combined random number generators. *Communications of the ACM*, 31: 742–749, 774, 1988.

[LGM69]   P. A. W. Lewis, A. S. Goodman and J. M. Miller. A pseudorandom number generator for the System/360. *IBM System Journal*, 8: 136–146, 1969.

[LMS01]   F. Lindskog, A. McNeil and U. Schmock. Kendall's tau for elliptical distributions. Working paper, RiskLab, Department of Mathematics, ETH Zürich, Switzerland, 2001.

[LS98]   F. A. Longstaff and E. S. Schwartz. Valuing American options by simulation: a simple least squares approach. Working paper, The Anderson School, UCLA, 1998.

[LY00a]   C. F. Lo and P. H. Yuen.   Constant elasticity of variance option pricing model with time-dependent parameters. *International Journal of Theoretical and Applied Finance*, 3(4): 661–674, 2000. http://www.phy.cuhk.edu.hk/~cflo/papers/CEV_IJTAF.pdf.

[LY00b]   C. F. Lo and P. H. Yuen. Option risk measurement with time-dependent parameters. *International Journal of Theoretical and Applied Finance*, 3(3): 581–589, 2000. http://www.phy.cuhk.edu.hk/~cflo/papers/optionrisk_IJTAF.pdf.

[Mac96]   A. MacLead. ACM Algorithm 757. *ACM Transactions of Mathematical Software*, 22(3): 288–301, 1996. http://www.netlib.org/toms/757.

[Mac97]   D. J. C. MacKay.   Introduction to Monte Carlo methods.   Technical report, Department of Physics, Cambridge University, 1997. ftp://wol.ra.phy.cam.ac.uk/pub/mackay/erice.ps.gz or http://l3www.cern.ch/homepages/susinnog/finance/Articles4/erice.ps.gz.

[Mar78]   W. Margrabe. The value of an option to exchange one asset for another. *Journal of Finance*, 33: 177–186, 1978.

[May76]   R. M. May. Simple mathematical models with very complicated dynamics. *Nature*, 26: 459–467, 1976.

[MCC98]   D. B. Madan, P. Carr and E. C. Chang. The Variance Gamma process and option pricing. Working paper, University of Maryland, College Park, MD, June 1998.

[Mer90]   R. C. Merton. *Continuous-Time Finance*. Blackwell Publishers Ltd., 1990.

[MM91]   D. B. Madan and F. Milne. Option pricing with Variance Gamma martingale components. *Mathematical Finance*, 1(4): 39–55, 1991.

[MN97]   M. Matsumoto and T. Nishimura. Mersenne twister: a 623-dimensionally equidistributed uniform pseudorandom number generator, 1997. http://www.math.keio.ac.jp/~matumoto/emt.html.

[MN98]   M. Matsumoto and T. Nishimura. Mersenne twister: a 623-dimensionally equidistributed uniform pseudorandom number generator. *ACM Transactions on Modeling and Computer Simulation*, 8(1): 3–30, January 1998.

[Mon51]   Monte Carlo method. U.S. Department of Commerce, National Bureau of Standards, Applied Mathematics Series 12, June 1951. A 42-page booklet on number generation methods and applications of the Monte Carlo method.

[Mor95]   B. Moro. The Full Monte. *Risk Magazine*, 8(2): 57–58, February 1995.

[MR97]   M. Musiela and M. Rutkowski. Continuous-time term structure models: forward measure approach. *Finance and Stochastics*, 1: 261–292, 1997.

[MS90]   D. B. Madan and E. Seneta. The Variance Gamma model for share market returns. *Journal of Business*, 63(4): 511–524, 1990.
[MSS97]   K. R. Miltersen, K. Sandmann and D. Sondermann. Closed-form solutions for term structure derivatives with lognormal interest rates. *Journal of Finance*, 52: 409–430, 1997.
[MU49]   N. Metropolis and S. Ulam. The Monte Carlo method. *Journal of the American Statistical Association*, 44(247): 335–341, September 1949.
[MW99]   L. A. McCarthy and N. J. Webber. An icosahedral lattice method for three-factor models. Working paper, University of Warwick, 1999. http://www.warwick.ac.uk.
[MWCM98]   D. J. Medeiros, E. F. Watson, J. S. Carson and M. S. Manivannan (eds). *Proceedings of the 1998 Winter Simulation Conference*, 1998.
[MZM94]   G. Marsaglia, A. Zaman and J. Marsaglia. Rapid evaluation of the inverse of the normal distribution function. *Statistics and Probability Letters*: 259–266, 1994.
[Nat94]   S. Natenberg. *Option Volatility & Pricing: Advanced Trading Strategies and Techniques*. Probus, July 1994.
[Nea73]   H. R. Neave. On using the Box–Muller transformation with multiplicative congruential pseudo-random number generators. *Applied Statistics*, 22: 92–97, 1973.
[NHLZ97]   H. Niederreiter, P. Hellekalek, G. Larcher and P. Zinterhof (eds). *Monte Carlo and Quasi-Monte Carlo Methods*. Volume 127 of Lecture Notes in Statistics. Springer, 1997.
[Nie88]   H. Niederreiter. Low-discrepancy and low-dispersion sequences. *Journal of Number Theory*, 30: 51–70, 1988.
[Nie92]   H. Niederreiter. *Random Number Generation and Quasi-Monte Carlo Methods*. SIAM, 1992.
[Nie96]   H. Niederreiter. Low-discrepancy sequences and global function fields with many rational places. *Finite Fields and their Applications*, 2: 241–273, 1996.
[Øks98]   B. Øksendal. *Stochastic Differential Equations*. Springer, 5th edn, 1998.
[Owe98]   A. B. Owen. Monte Carlo extension of quasi-Monte Carlo. In [MWCM98]. http://www.informs-cs.org/wsc98papers/076.PDF.
[Pic88]   C. A. Pickover. A note on chaos and Halley's method. *Communications of the ACM*, 31(11): 1326–1329, November 1988.
[PM88]   S. K. Park and K. W. Miller. Random number generators: good ones are hard to find. *Communications of the ACM*, 31(10): 1192–1201, October 1988.
[PT95]   S. H. Paskov and J. F. Traub. Faster valuation of financial derivatives. *Journal of Portfolio Management*, 22(1): 113–120, 1995. There are also several Columbia University technical reports on the subject.
[PTVF92]   W. H. Press, S. A. Teukolsky, W. T. Vetterling and B. P. Flannery. *Numerical Recipes in C*. Cambridge University Press, 1992.
[Rad98a]   A. R. Radhakrishnan. An empirical study of the convergence properties of the non-recombining HJM forward rate tree in pricing interest rate derivatives. Working paper, Department of Finance, Stern School of Business, New York University, New York, 1998. http://www.stern.nyu.edu/~aradhakr
[Rad98b]   A. R. Radhakrishnan. Does correlation matter in pricing caps and swaptions? Working paper, Department of Finance, Stern School of Business, New York University, New York, 1998. http://www.stern.nyu.edu/~aradhakr.
[RDTM79]   J. S. Ramberg, E. J. Dudewicz, P. R. Tadikamalla and E. F. Mykytka. A probability distribution and its uses in fitting data. *Technometrics*, 21(2), May 1979.
[Reb98]   R. Rebonato. *Interest Rate Option Models*. John Wiley and Sons, 1998.
[Reb99]   R. Rebonato. *Volatility and Correlation*. John Wiley and Sons, 1999.
[Rip87]   B. D. Ripley. *Stochastic Simulation*. John Wiley and Sons, 1987.
[RJ00]   R. Rebonato and P. Jäckel. The most general methodology to create a valid correlation matrix for risk management and option pricing purposes. *The Journal of Risk*, 2(2), Winter 1999/2000. http://www.rebonato.com/correlationmatrix.pdf.
[RS74]   J. S. Ramberg and B. W. Schmeiser. An approximate method for generating asymmetric random variables. *Communications of the ACM*, 17: 78–82, 1974.
[Rub83]   M. Rubinstein. Displaced diffusion option pricing. *Journal of Finance*, 38: 213–217, March 1983.
[Sch89]   M. Schroder. Computing the constant elasticity of variance option pricing formula. *Journal of Finance*, 44(1): 211–219, 1989.
[Shr98]   S. E. Shreve. Stochastic calculus lecture notes, 1998. http://www.math.cmu.edu/users/shreve.
[Sob67]   I. M. Sobol'. On the distribution of points in a cube and the approximate evaluation of integrals. *USSR Computational Mathematics and Mathematical Physics*, 7: 86–112, 1967.
[Sob76]   I. M. Sobol'. Uniformly distributed sequences with additional uniform properties. *USSR Computational Mathematics and Mathematical Physics*, 16(5): 236–242, 1976.
[Sob94]   I. M. Sobol'. *A Primer for the Monte Carlo Method*. CRC Press, 1994.
[ST95]   T. R. Scavo and J. B. Thoo. On the geometry of Halley's method. *American Mathematics Monthly*, 102: 417–426, 1995.

[Tez95]   S. Tezuka. *Uniform Random Numbers: Theory and Practice*. Kluwer Academic, 1995.

[UvN47]   S. M. Ulam and J. von Neumann. On combinations of stochastic and deterministic processes. *Bulletin of the American Mathematical Society*, 53(11): 1120, November 1947. Preliminary report from the summer meeting in New Haven.

[Vas77]   O. A. Vasicek. An equilibrium characterisation of the term structure. *Journal of Financial Economics*, 5: 177–188, 1977.

[vN51]   J. von Neumann. Various techniques used in connection with random digits. In [Mon51], pp. 36–38.

[Wat62]   E. J. Watson. Primitive polynomials (mod 2). *Mathematics of Computation*, 16(79): 368–369, July 1962.

[Whe80]   R. E. Wheeler. Quantile estimators of Johnson curve parameters. *Biometrika*, 67: 725–728, 1980.

[Wil98]   P. Wilmott. *Derivatives*. John Wiley and Sons, 1998.

[Wil00]   P. Wilmott. *Quantitative Finance*. John Wiley and Sons, 2000.

Index

Ali–Mikhail–Haq copula, 57
alternating simplex direction, 172, 189
antithetic sampling, 111
Archimedean copulae, 51
asymmetric lambda distribution, 17
attractive invariant set, 68

Bermudan swaption, 159, 163
    Monte Carlo algorithm for the pricing of,
        176
Bernoulli, 10
Bessel, 27
beta, 12
BGM/J market model, 159
binomial, 11
Box–Muller, 105
BRODA, 88
Brownian bridge, 38, 124
Brownian motion, 23
bushy tree, *see* non-recombining tree, 183

calibration of BGM/J to European swaptions,
    163
Cantor set, 70
Cauchy distribution, 14
central limit theorem, 18
chaos, 68
χ^2 distribution, 13
Clayton copula, 52
clustering of non-recombining tree, 196
concordance, 44
congruential generation, 72
congruential generator, 72
constant elasticity of variance, 28
continuous mapping theorem, 19
continuously monitored, 1
control variates, 113
convergence
    almost surely, 18,
    strong, 31

convergence diagram, 205
copula, 45
    Ali–Mikhail–Haq, 57
    Archimedean, 51
    Clayton, 52
    Frank, 52
    Gaussian, 46
    Gumbel, 51
    t-, 49
correlation and co-movement, 41
correlation matrix decomposition
    hypersphere, 60
    lower triangular form, 62
    spectral, 61
covariance, 6
CPU time, 201
cost of transcendental and trigonometric func-
        tion evaluations, 207
cumulative, 5
    normal probability function, 10
    probability function, 5
curse of dimensionality, 8

decomposition
    hypersphere, 60
    lower triangular form, 62
    spectral, 61
Delta, 139
dichotomic, 10
Dirac density, 5
discordance, 44
discrepancy, 78
    expected L_2-norm discrepancy of truly
        random numbers, 97
    explicit formula for the L_2-norm
        discrepancy, 96
discrete-time dynamical system, 68
discretely monitored, 1
dispersion matrix, 26, 169
displaced diffusion, 29

distribution
  Bernoulli, 10
  beta, 12
  binomial, 11
  Cauchy, 14
  χ^2, 13
  conversion of, 99
  density of, 5
  dichotomic, 10
  exponential, 11
  gamma, 12
  generalised beta 2, 15
  generalised lambda, 17
  generalised Pareto, 16
  geometric, 11
  Gumbel, 16
  lognormal, 14
  normal, 9
  Pareto, 15
  Poisson, 11
  Student's t, 13
  uniform, 9
  Weibull, 16
domain $\mathcal{D}(X)$ of the random experiment, 5
draw, 5
drift, 26
driving matrix, 26

effective dimensionality, 120
  reduction of, 124
embedded path generation, see path
    generation, 206
equiprobable, 9
equivalent swaption volatility, 167
error estimation, 20
error function, 10
Euler scheme, 32
exact expectation matching of non-recombining
    tree, see exact martingale conditioning
    of non-recombining tree, 196
exact martingale conditioning of
    non-recombining tree, 196
exercise boundary
  heuristics of, 171
  Monte Carlo algorithm based on
    parametrisation of, 176
  parametrisation of, 160, 174
exp ( ), 207
expected value, 6
exponential, 12

factorisation of the BGM/J model, 161
Feynman–Kac theorem, 21
finite differencing for Greeks calculation, 140
forward rates
  evolution of under the BGM/J model, 161,
    184

Frank copula, 52
Frechet, 16

Gamma, 139
Gaussian copula, 46
  two exponential variates under, 48
  two uniform variates under, 46
generalised
  beta 2 distribution, 15
  function, 5
  lambda distribution, 17
  Pareto distribution, 16
GGL generator, 74
Gray code, 83, 84
Greeks, 139
Gumbel, 16
  copula, 51

Hölder's inequality, 7
Haar functions, 131
Halton numbers, 79
hedge-and-forget, 139
hypersphere decomposition, 60

iid see independent identically distributed, 18
importance sampling, 115
  for Greeks calculations, 143
  methods, 104
independent, 42
independent identically distributed, 18
infinitesimal perturbation analysis, 144
intermittency, 72
invariant measure, 71
inverse cumulative probability, 99
Itô's lemma, 24

Jensen's inequality, 6
Johnson I distribution, 30

Kendall's tau, 44
  for Gaussian copula, 46

Latin hypercube sampling, 119
likelihood, 5
likelihood ratio
  for Rho, 156
  for sensitivity with respect to dividend
    yield, 157
  for Vega, 149
  for Greeks calculation, 145
linear congruential generator, 73
linear correlation, 42
logistic map, 68
lognormal, 14
Lorentz distribution, 14
low-discrepancy numbers, 77
  empirical discrepancies, 91

Halton, 79
Niederreiter, 88
pairwise projections, 88
Sobol', 80
lower triangular form decomposition, 62

Malliavin calculus, 146
marginal distribution, 42
Markovian, 27
  Wiener process embedding dimension, 26
measures for co-dependence, 42
Mersenne twister, 74
mid-square method, 72
Milstein scheme, 33
Minkowski's inequality, 7
mirrored paths, *see* antithetic sampling, 111
moment matching (variance reduction
    techniques), 116
moment of a distribution, 6
Monte Carlo
  estimator, 8
  integration, 7
  maximisation, 7
  simulation, 7
  superior to lattice methods for higher
      dimensionalities, 8
Moore–Penrose pseudo-inverse, 21
multi-threading, 209
multi-dimensional integration, 8

near-periodicity, 70
nearly lognormal, 15
Neave effect, 106
Niederreiter numbers, 88
non-linearity, 68
non-recombining tree, 183
  clustering of, 196
  convergence of, 191
  exact expectation matching of, 196
  practical example, 199
  recursive implementation of, 188
  variance matching of, 192
non-uniform variates, 99
normal variates, 9
normalised sampler density Monte Carlo
    estimator, 101
number generators
  ideal choice of, 75
  low-discrepancy, 77
  pseudo-random, 67
numerical over- and underflow, 205

optimal simplex alignment, 172, 187
Ornstein–Uhlenbeck process, 26

parallelisation, 209
Pareto distribution, 15

path construction, 120
  Brownian bridge, 124
  incremental, 120
  spectral, 122
path generation
  embedded, 206
path recycling, 113
pathwise differentiation for Greeks
    calculation, 144
Pearson's r, 43
Plot script, 206
Poisson distribution, 11
predictor–corrector, 35, 169
primitive polynomials modulo two, 81
probability density function, 5
pseudo-inverse, 21
pseudo-random, 67
pseudo-square root, 59, 61
  truncated, 61

Ran0, 68
Ran1–3, 74
random experiment, 5
random number generator
  ideal choice of, 75
randomness, 67
RANDU, 73
rank correlations, 45
recursive implementation of non-recombining
    tree, 190
reducible, 27
rejection sampling, 104
Rho, 112, 147, 156
running estimate, 205

sampler density
  Monte Carlo estimator, 101
technique, 101
Schauder functions, 131
shape correction, 167
singular values, 22
  decomposition, 22
Sobol' numbers, 80
  construction of, 82
  initialisation, 85, 86
Sobol' sequence
  commercial software, 88
Spearman's rho, 43
spectral decomposition, 61
Splot script, 206
standard deviation, 6, 9
standard error, 20
  error estimate of, 21
standard normal variate, 9
strange attractor, 68, 71
stratified sampling, 114

strong convergence, 31
strong law, 18
Student's *t* distribution, 13
subprocesses, 209
swaption volatility, 167

t-copula, 49
threads, 209
training set, 177
transformations of SDEs, 33
truly random numbers, 67

uniform distribution, 9

variability explained, 124
variance explained, *see* variability
    explained, 124
variance matching for a non-recombining
    tree, 192
variance reduction, 111
variate, 5
    recycling, 112, 113
Vega, 112, 147, 149

weak convergence, 31
Weibull, 16
Wiener process, 23